Walsh

James Joyce a

James Joyce and sexuality

RICHARD BROWN

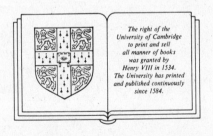

The right of the
University of Cambridge
to print and sell
all manner of books
was granted by
Henry VIII in 1534.
The University has printed
and published continuously
since 1584.

CAMBRIDGE UNIVERSITY PRESS

Cambridge
New York   New Rochelle
Melbourne   Sydney

Published by the Press Syndicate of the University of Cambridge
The Pitt Building, Trumpington Street, Cambridge CB2 1RP
32 East 57th Street, New York, NY 10022, USA
10 Stamford Road, Oakleigh, Melbourne 3166, Australia

First published 1985
First paperback edition 1988

Printed in Great Britain at
the University Press, Cambridge

Library of Congress catalogue card number: 84-14287

British Library Cataloguing in Publication Data
Brown, Richard, 1954–
James Joyce and sexuality.
1. Joyce, James, 1882–1941 – Criticism and
interpretation
I. Title
823'.912   PR6019.09Z/

ISBN 0 521 24811 6 hard covers
ISBN 0 521 36852 9 paperback

CE

He is from the Royal University, I thought, and he thinks that everything has been settled by Thomas Aquinas, so we need not trouble about it. I have met so many like him. He would probably review my book in the newspapers if I sent it there. But the next moment he spoke of a friend of mine who after a wild life had turned Catholic on his death bed. He said that he hoped his conversion was not sincere. He did not like to think that he had been untrue to himself at the end. No, I had not understood him yet.

(W.B. Yeats from Richard Ellmann, *The Identity of Yeats*, Oxford University Press, 1954.)

Acknowledgements

For their assistance in the preparation of this book I am indebted to the staffs of The British Library, The Bibliothèque Nationale in Paris, The Bodleian Library, Cambridge University Library, The University of London Senate House Library, and of the Joyce collections at The State University of New York at Buffalo and Cornell University (who also gave permission to quote from manuscript materials in their possession). I am indebted to The University of London Central Research Fund for a grant to visit Paris, to David Monro of Monro Pennefather and Co. and to Richard Ellmann for responding to queries, and to Jane Lidderdale and Peter du Sautoy for helpful discussions about Joyce. This book was first written as a Ph.D. thesis at University College London and I am especially grateful to Michael Mason who supervised my research, to Professor Karl Miller and to Geoffrey Soar of the Joyce Centre at University College Library for their help, interest and support. Patrick Parrinder, Charles Peake, Colin MacCabe, Fritz Senn and Ulrich Schneider of the University of Erlangen all read earlier versions of the book and made valuable suggestions. Pieter Bekker, my co-editor on *The James Joyce Broadsheet*, has been a constant Joycean companion. I have to thank Terence Moore and Margaret Sharman at Cambridge University Press, Fiona for typing, and Ian for help with some points of law.

Most of all I am grateful to my wife Jane, without whose untiring support this work would not have been possible.

Contents

Abbreviations

Abbreviated references in the text and notes are to the following editions of Joyce's works. Initials are followed by a page number (for *Finnegans Wake* page and line).

CM	*Chamber Music*. London: Cape, 1927.
CW	*The Critical Writings of James Joyce*. Ed. Ellsworth Mason and Richard Ellmann. London: Faber, 1959.
D	*Dubliners*. Ed. Robert Scholes. London: Cape, 1967.
E	*Exiles*. London: Cape, 1952.
FW	*Finnegans Wake*. London: Faber, 1939.
GJ	*Giacomo Joyce*. Ed. Richard Ellmann. London: Faber, 1968.
LI	*The Letters of James Joyce*. Vol. I. Ed. Stuart Gilbert. London, Faber, 1957.
LII/III	*The Letters of James Joyce*. Vols. II and III. Ed. Richard Ellmann. London: Faber, 1966.
P	*A Portrait of the Artist as a Young Man*. Ed. Chester Anderson. London: Cape, 1968.
SH	*Stephen Hero*. Ed. Theodore Spencer. London: Cape, 1956.
SL	*Selected Letters of James Joyce*. Ed. Richard Ellmann. London: Faber, 1975.
U	*Ulysses*. London: Bodley Head, 1960.

Introduction

At one time it was hardly doubted that sexual matters in Joyce's fiction should be the object of critical attention. Many of the early reviewers based their reaction to Joyce on this aspect of his work, though they did not by any means approve of it and they rarely had a clear distinction in their minds between Joyce's treatment of sexuality and what they considered to be his exaggerated interest in all the workings of the body. The review of *Ulysses* from *The Sporting Times* of 1922 is the best known of these early reactions with its philistine condemnation of Joyce's 'literature of the latrine' and his 'stupid glorification of mere filth'.[1] Many of the more reflective reviewers also felt the need to discuss what they saw as a rather indiscriminate kind of realism. To many of them, including Shaw, Virginia Woolf, Arnold Bennett, Wells and Rebecca West, his work seemed to dwell on subjects that were unliterary or else literary only in a way which they found it difficult to approve.[2]

Joyce's defenders must also have recognized this quality of his work but, rather than attempt to argue that the treatment of sexuality was of the utmost importance to Joyce's creativity and at the heart of what his fiction might be trying to investigate, they chose to change the focus of the debate to questions of literary form and to analogies with past literary greatness. Stuart Gilbert claimed that readers had taken an interest in sexual matters 'disproportionate, as it appears to me, to their real importance'. He offered the familiar but rather insubstantial defence that 'these passages are, in fact, cathartic and calculated to allay rather than to excite the sexual instincts'.[3] What Gilbert said on the subject is, perhaps, not so interesting as the evident desire he had to say as little as possible and to turn his attention, just as T.S. Eliot had done in his famous '*Ulysses*, Order and Myth' essay of 1923, away from subject-matter and towards what seemed to be comparatively unexceptionable correspondences between *Ulysses* and *The Odyssey*.[4]

It was a significant part of contemporary aesthetic discuss-ions, of Eliot's thoughts about the role of 'tradition', that such an emphasis on literary correspondences should have devel-oped. But we may remember that both Eliot's essay, and the first edition of Gilbert's book, were produced in highly unusual circumstances, whilst *Ulysses* itself was legally unavailable in England and America. It was arguably a prudent as well as a critically sensitive course to attend to legitimizing literary con-nections rather than to potentially subversive or offensive char-acteristics of the book. There is almost an anticipation of the argument of the defending lawyers at the 1933 trial which made *Ulysses* available to a wider public, stressing that Joyce was an 'austere Olympian' and that issues like sex were 'relegated to a position of relative unimportance' in his work.[5]

The treatment of sexuality in Joyce's work was obscured and it has never been fully investigated, though there is such a strong *prima facie* case for such an investigation, though it offers a means of dealing with Joyce's whole oeuvre from *Chamber Music* to *Finnegans Wake* in the same frame of refer-ence and though the vast body of secondary work on Joyce might lead one to suppose that every aspect of his work has been investigated in full.

Whilst the initial reluctance to give too much attention to these matters may be in part explained as a prudent defensive strategy, their continued neglect is more attributable to peren-nial characteristics of Joycean criticism. William Schutte, in his book on *Joyce and Shakespeare*, made a highly cogent attack on the 'bad start' made by critics of Joyce's work, and things have not necessarily improved. Wayne Booth is among the most telling critics of a situation where readers of Joyce seem to find mutually exclusive ideas and attitudes in his work. Joyce criti-cism has suffered from isolation, developing a partly autono-mous language and field of reference dominated by certain almost talismanic 'Joycean' terms like 'epiphany' and 'exile' and relying on its best-known product, Richard Ellmann's monu-mental biography, to the extent that it has seemed easier to account for items in Joyce's texts through an investigation of their similarity to events in his life, than to ask questions about the relevance of such items to contemporary issues and to a contemporary reading public.[6]

The stress on the more eccentric parts of Joyce's personality and attitudes, the hurried accumulation of detailed explicatory glosses and the attention to Joyce's developments in literary form that have characterized the criticism, have reinforced the impression that Joyce was a recluse from contemporary historical and intellectual pressures. The broad issues have been left out of account, and it is only recently that a study like Dominic Manganiello's *Joyce's Politics* has begun to piece together the implication of Joyce's fictions in the ideas of their time.[7]

Such attempts as there have been to discuss Joycean sexuality have been partial and inconclusive. Book-length studies, like Mark Shechner's *Joyce in Nighttown*, have attempted pseudo-psychoanalytic investigations or, like Margaret Solomon's *Eternal Geomater: The Sexual Universe of 'Finnegans Wake'*, have identified the prominence of sexuality in Joyce's texts without relating the ideas to a contemporary context.[8]

Feminists, who might have been expected to produce some critique of Joyce, have been, until quite recently, silent. Even a well-known feminist like Marilyn French wrote a book on Joyce which (though referring to the 'sexual theme' of *Ulysses* and suggesting that Joyce's approach to sexuality 'was primarily one of exposure') suggested that other questions were more important.[9]

Molly Bloom used to be discussed either as an affirming life-force and symbolic Gea-Tellus figure or else as wanton and immoral, but the debate about her soon became more a matter of discerning the 'facts' about her famously uncertain list of 25 lovers in 'Ithaca' than an interest in the contentious presentation of sexuality.[10] Leopold Bloom aroused some concern because of his lack of self-assertiveness. This, and his so-called perversions, presented a considerable problem for critics who wished to work out the morality of *Ulysses* and to use Bloom as their hero. Clive Hart effectively closed this issue several years ago when he announced that Bloom was neither hero nor villain and that '*Ulysses* contains no active moral paradigm, . . . it depicts a morally static universe in which moral development is neither possible nor necessary, nor even perhaps desirable'.[11]

This is a familiar position in Joyce criticism and no doubt it was at one time necessary to stress that *Ulysses* was not straightforward in its intentions nor didactic in a conventional way.

But a book as universally significant as *Ulysses* can never be abandoned to the idea that it is 'static' in its morality. If by morality we mean a system of values, or outlook on the world, then it is hard to see how even Joyce's oeuvre, with its characteristically modern reticence, may be entirely free from morality. Joyce's portrayal of sexuality has its place in the array of possible contemporary positions alongside the discussion of modern morality in Ibsen and Shaw, the portrayal of a tension between middle-class customs and disruptive sexual passions in the novels of E.M. Forster or Ford Madox Ford, the enthusiastic investigation of erotic self-fulfilment in D.H. Lawrence, and alongside the detached ironic depiction of the hollow sexual modernity of 'Bright Young People' in Evelyn Waugh's *Vile Bodies* or in the seduction scene of Eliot's 'The Waste Land'.

The years in the first part of this century when Joyce was writing are recognized as a time of much questioning of conceptions about sexuality and as a time of considerable visible change in the institution of marriage, in legal control over the position of women in society and in attitudes to sexual perversity. They are most familiarly represented as years of transition from 'Victorian' sexual repression and ignorance to 'modern' enlightenment and toleration, though Michel Foucault has argued that this distinction may be an illusion of our modern perspective and that it would be more appropriate to speak of an enormous growth in both discussion and control of sexuality since the seventeenth century.[12] Leaving aside, for the moment, the questions of intellectual history raised by Foucault's critique, Joyce's fiction, I argue, would have less stature, less of a sense of centrality to the intellectual life of our century, less 'modernity' in our estimation, did it not respond to this felt importance of sexuality and sexual change. Some interest in sexuality is clearly present throughout the fiction yet no characteristic Joycean attitude has been identified, or still less been accepted in the way that aspects of the attitudes of Ibsen, Shaw and Lawrence have been taken up by subsequent generations. It would hardly be appropriate for such a thing to happen. Joyce was not this kind of author and the interest for a reader consists not so much in the application of a Joycean scheme of morality as in gradually sensing the implication of his fiction in such a context. We need a means of establishing the relevant context of contemporary ideas, perhaps even a way of discussing Joyce that is partly independent of the dominant practices of Joyce criticism, whose tendency has been to play down exactly these issues which we wish to confront. To this end, the knowledge we have of Joyce's reading provides a real opportunity for investigation. The information derives from a number of sources. In the first place there is the discussion of books in his letters. During his residence in Trieste and Rome between 1904 and 1907, for instance, when he was separated from his brother Stanislaus, he kept in touch by reading the *Daily Mail* notices of new books, and he discussed his reading at some length. In later years he offered Harriet Shaw Weaver suggestions for reading that might help her in tackling passages from his 'Work in Progress'. We know the books that Joyce reviewed in the first decade or so of the century for the Dublin *Daily Express* and for the Trieste paper *Il Piccolo della Sera*. The reviews survive to give us an indication of the attitudes he took.[13] These reviews and the lectures Joyce gave at the Università Popolare in Trieste on Blake and Defoe have been little discussed by Joyce critics, yet they constitute an important body of ideas on literature and contemporary issues which can play their part in refining our attitudes to the major work.

Equally useful are the records of Joyce's personal libraries. These begin with brief records of books Joyce had in Dublin, listed by C.P. Curran and by Slocum and Cahoon in their Joyce bibliography.[14] For the Trieste years (1905–15 and 1919–20) a much larger collection of books has survived and has been catalogued by Richard Ellmann in *The Consciousness of Joyce*. The collection consists of books Joyce left with Stanislaus in Trieste when he departed for Paris in 1920. It includes books bought in Trieste before 1915 which are most relevant to his completion of *A Portrait of the Artist as a Young Man*; books which, on the evidence of date and booksellers' marks, Joyce bought in Zurich where he lived during the First World War; and books which he bought during his last stay in Trieste from October 1919 to June 1920, some of which suggest the 'Nausicaa' and 'Oxen of the Sun' episodes of *Ulysses* on which he was working at the time.[15] Ellmann added to these books several other titles from a partial inventory which Joyce made of his library around 1920 and from the surviving bill of a Trieste bookseller dating from 1913–14. We may also add titles listed on two other book bills sent by shops in London and Leipzig from 1920. This Trieste collection represents some 45 per cent of the books that Joyce owned during these years.[16]

A third collection of Joyce's books has been available for many years in the Buffalo Joyce collection in New York State and has been catalogued by Thomas E. Connolly.[17] The collection represents books that Joyce left in his Paris flat on his hurried departure to Zurich at the beginning of the Second World War. It contains less than 800 items, including some presentation and association items, which contrasts strongly with the 'ten cases of books and manuscripts', and 'three sacks of newspapers'[18] mentioned to Harriet Shaw Weaver in 1923, or the room 'full of books and old newspapers' which Arthur Power remembered.[19] As James Atherton long ago remarked, they can only represent a part of his working library, and yet it is remarkable that, despite the supposed eccentricity, diffusion or sheer encyclopaedism of Joyce's reading at this time,[20] titles, including *The Arabian Nights*, Chaucer, FitzGerald's *Rubaiyat*, Hauptmann, *The Iliad* and *Odyssey*, Ibsen plays, Keats, Rabelais, Scott and Synge, recur from collection to collection and provide a common core.

The collections are not complete but they can give us a coherent sense of Joyce's reading and of the intellectual context in which he wrote. We may note (though Joyce took pains to include unfamiliar languages in *Finnegans Wake* and the Joyce family often spoke Triestine Italian at home) that English clearly predominates in his reading. The surviving book bills from H. Glover of London and Simmel & Co. of Leipzig show that Joyce was prepared to go to some lengths to get books in English and the occurrence of some 49 Tauchnitz reprints in the Trieste list (Tauchnitz reprints were the most easily available English books 'for residents and travellers on the continent of Europe'[21]) helps give a sense of the collection.

The libraries can be used to provide a reliable indication of what kinds of information and what kinds of intellectual stance interested Joyce. We must, of course, be wary of introducing into a study of his reading a frame of reference which will pre-judge its usefulness. One Joyce critic, discussing 'the influence of Joyce's reading', says that 'Joyce seems to have been impressed mainly, both as impersonal artist and supreme egotist, by analogies to his own life and to the books he himself was planning'.[22] Such an approach does not allow the extent to which Joyce must have been conditioned by his reading, or, at any rate, bound up in the same kinds of dilemmas. Sometimes the need to annotate has reduced the world of Joyce's reading to a mere collection of reference books. Even in Richard Ellmann's introduction to Joyce's library we can see the problem. 'Most of the subjects that come up in *Ulysses* are documented here,' he writes. 'Writing about masturbation he had a book entitled *Onanisme seul et à deux*. Magrini's *Manuale di Musica* was helpful for the 'Sirens' episode. His interest in micturition led him to obtain a book on *Uric Acid*.' Ellmann seems to imply that these books were no more than neutral packages of information in their respective fields but, as I shall show, a rediscovered sense of the debates in which such books participated can be of the utmost importance for our understanding of what motivated Joyce.[23]

The final source of information on Joyce's reading and on the attitudes he adopted in relation to contentious issues is the works themselves and they are the point to which all other information must be referred and by which its usefulness may be judged. Joyce's works are a rich source of information since they are full of quotation, allusion and reference, as works like Weldon Thornton's *Allusions in 'Ulysses'*[24] and Gifford and Seidman's *Notes for Joyce*[25] have made clear. It would be short-sighted to extend our understanding of the intellectual context of Joyce's fictions from inventories of his reading without noticing the part that such inventories play in the fictions themselves: inventories like Bloom's bookshelf spelled out in 'Ithaca' (*U* 832–3); Mr Duffy's fondness for Wordsworth, the *Maynooth Catechism*, Hauptmann and Nietzsche in 'A Painful Case'; the childhood bookishness of 'An Encounter' (*D* 18), 'Araby' (*D* 29), and the early chapters of *A Portrait of the Artist as a Young Man* and even the list of titles for ALP's 'mamafesta' in *Finnegans Wake*.

Books crowd into Joyce's writings on many levels. In *Stephen Hero*, Stephen's father, his teachers and his schoolfellows are defined by the literary critical views they hold, such as Mr Daedalus' notion that '*A Doll's House* would be a triviality in the manner of *Little Lord Fauntleroy*' or that *Ghosts* 'would probably be some uninteresting story about a haunted house' (*SH* 93). In *A Portrait*, the action builds to a climax that may be said to be a climax of literary theory and, as well as the books quoted or alluded to in the course of narrative and dialogue, passages of hell-fire sermon, or of the language of childhood take over or colour the narrative for long periods. In *Ulysses*, bookish themes and techniques are still further developed. Parts of the day's activities take place in a newspaper office, at a bookstand by the River Liffey and in literary-critical discussion at the National Library. Stephen's achievement of the day may also be said to be in literary criticism: this time it is a theory of Shakespeare he constructs. Bloom's own daily activity, the canvassing for news-paper advertisements, though not conventionally 'literary', is from an economic and practical point of view an occupation which supports more serious writing in the most direct and substantial way. The tendency towards parody seen in *Dubliners* and *A Portrait* is fully developed in *Ulysses*, where the first part of 'Nausicaa' famously exploits the language of popular romance, and in 'Cyclops' passages of evident parody punctuate a narrative which in its self-centred aggressive manner is itself a parody of a certain way of seeing the world.

Comments and references in Joyce's letters, his literary criti-cal writings and the knowledge we have of his personal libra-ries, may provide reliable sources for the intellectual historian, but the works themselves are a more treacherous source since their allusions, references or parodic dependencies are intro-duced for aesthetic purposes. Here we need not only the wariness of the historian in avoiding misconceptions about the material under our gaze but also the sensitivity of the critic to the variety of means by which such material may be introduced into a work and the variety of purposes which it might serve. The dangers of using such material to produce a contextual reading of Joyce are many but there are corresponding rewards, since it is by charting the use of, and attitude to, other books in Joyce's works that we stand to learn most about his literary achievement.

The importance of quotation, allusiveness and parody has often been felt by Joyce critics. Ulrich Schneider in an account of allusiveness in *Ulysses*[26] reached similar conclusions to those of James Atherton in his better-known study, *The Books at the Wake*.[27] Both felt that allusions have larger 'structural' import-ance in the works, which extends beyond the local importance of the allusive trifle. Criticism of Joyce has seized on the issue of correspondence, charting, as I have said, the connections between *Ulysses* and *The Odyssey*, between *A Portrait* and the Daedalus story in Ovid, between Joyce's works and a host of Biblical, liturgical and classic literary texts, as the familiar titles of critical books testify: *Joyce and Ibsen, Joyce and Aquinas, Joyce and Shakespeare, Joyce and the Bible, Joyce and Dante* and, more ingeniously, *Joyce between Freud and Jung* or *Byron and Joyce through Homer*.

To distinguish between the local and the 'structural' allusion or to chart mythic correspondence as a way of finding significance in Joyce is to reinforce the understanding provided by Eliot of a 'continuous parallel between contemporaneity and antiquity', whose purpose is an 'ordering' or 'controlling' one. But that is only one aspect of what is becoming more widely understood as one of the most significant aspects of a literary work: its relation to other works. The problem is one that has always been recognized in relation to modernist works. Edmund Wilson talks of Eliot and Pound as having 'founded a school of poetry which depends upon literary quotation and reference to an unprecedented degree'.[28] It was the energetically and heterogeneously allusive and parodic characteristics of Pound that led Ivor Winters to condemn him as 'a barbarian on the loose in a museum'.[29] Eliot's 'The Waste Land' is, of course, a poem which comes with its own notes, which, if they are often inadequate to explain the poem's meaning, at least identify it as a poem in which allusions and quotations are substantial parts.

Some of the most ambitious of recent literary theoreticians have taken the relationship between literary texts as their theme, including Harold Bloom whose theory of poetry invokes the notion that poetry is a 'misprision' or intentional misreading of earlier work, and Roland Barthes, who sees literary meaning as a bottomless play of 'intertextual' connections in which the reader's own knowledge and background as well as that of the author plays its part.[30] The narrative theorist Gérard Genette has most recently produced an account of literary fictions as '*palimpsestes*', as modes of rewriting earlier themes or texts for a variety of aesthetic purposes.[31] Critics of the novel have become so intensely aware of allusiveness that Hugh Kenner, in his recent study of *Ulysses*, found it necessary to include Mulligan's opening quotation from the Latin mass not just in one but in six sets of quotation marks.[32]

It is, of course, not only modernist works that rely on allusion. Eliot in his two controversial essays on Milton, we might remember, compared Milton to Joyce's 'Work in Progress' in certain respects.[33] But it is in relation to modernist works that allusiveness becomes an especially significant issue. In modernist works to an unprecedented degree there is a semantic and aesthetic dependence on earlier texts. This can easily be demonstrated in Joyce by a glance at the titles of the works which in the case of *Ulysses, Finnegans Wake* and *Stephen Hero* make a deliberate gesture not just to the work that they name but to earlier works: *The Odyssey* and the ballads 'Finnegan's Wake' and 'Turpin Hero'. The titles of *A Portrait of the Artist* and *Chamber Music* similarly advert to the familiar genre titles of other works of art. The significance and the appeal of these titles derives from this doubleness of reference and it is an appeal which Joyce exploits throughout his writings. We need to look no further than the opening of *A Portrait*, whose 'once upon a time ...' is a typically bold dependence on the most familiar of narrative openings, one further taken up in *Finnegans Wake*, where the memory both of that phrase and of *A Portrait* come into play at the start of the 'Mookse and the Gripes' story in 'Eins within a space ...' (*FW* 152.18) or later in 'once upon a drunk and a fairly good drunk it was ...' (*FW* 453.20).

If semantics and aesthetics in Joyce's work are importantly bound up with this allusive dependence on earlier writing, it is the purpose of this study to show how Joyce's polemicism, the attitudes adopted by his fiction, may also express themselves by these means. It is not for explicit statements that we look in Joyce's fiction but, it seems to me, a more or less consistent outlook can be divined by attending to the contentious significance of a parody, or by following the trace of a contentious issue in an allusion.

In what follows I shall argue for a renewed sense of the importance of subject-matter in Joyce's fiction. His works seem importantly connected to attitudes to marriage, to the scientific interest in sexuality, to non-reproductive priorities in sex and to women, that we characterize as modern. The need to write about such subjects was a strong determining force in his fiction and writing about sexuality represented for him a kind of modernity that is present in relatively neglected works like

Chamber Music, Giacomo Joyce and *Exiles*, just as it is in *A Portrait, Ulysses* or *Finnegans Wake*. It is a modernity that was as important to Joyce's own stated concept of literature as was formal experimentation. There are two aspects of this study. One tries to place Joyce's work in the context of ideas in which he participated. The other tries to show that it was by attitudes to and aesthetic exploitations of other works, more than by explicit comment, that Joyce's attitudes were expressed.

Michel Foucault not only challenges our sense of the shape of the intellectual history of sexuality; he also encourages us to attend to a new sense of the relationship between spoken and written attitudes and social and political constraints. For him conventional social history is not so important as is trying to identify the ways in which sexuality is 'put into discourse'.[34] In some ways, Joyce's imaginative reaction to the question of sexuality, the reticence whereby his fiction pursues inexplicit means of parody, allusion and quotation, is analogous. One of the effects of his method is to highlight precisely those attitudes to which sexual modernity is normally opposed, to draw attention to that which we might expect to find concealed. The situation is, as a recent student of Joyce's language reports, a paradoxical one where we may find 'a sort of inverse ratio, wherein what is least important is expressed in the greatest number of words'.[35]

It is possible to discern the attitudes that Joyce's fiction takes on important contemporary issues, and to see his fiction arising out of certain aspects of literary realism as well as in reaction to them. In treating Joyce in relation to his attitudes on sexual subjects, we can investigate these possibilities; and in concentrating on Joyce's qualities of allusiveness and parody we can make sense of these issues in such a way that the exigencies of his stylistic modernity can also be felt.

1   Love and marriage

Modern love

During the nineteenth century few questions were so high on
the agenda for discussion and reform as questions of marriage.
In Dickens's *Hard Times*, for instance, a novel whose dedication
to Carlyle and whose northern industrial setting might lead us
to expect some call for reform in the conditions of the labouring
poor, Dickens provides, in the eleventh chapter, a call for
reform in the marriage law.[1] As some recent critics have felt,
this may tell us something about the indirection of Dickens's
analysis of industrial society but it also gives us some indication
of the felt importance of the marriage issue at the time.[2]

In 1857, three years after the publication of Dickens's novel,
the law was forced to change and judicial divorce was made
possible in England for the first time. The 1857 Act was not,
however, an anticipation of modern sexual attitudes in every
way. It did not so much legitimize sexual pleasure as make a
wife's adultery an actionable offence. In one way the act merely
extended to a wider public a right that had already been
available by act of parliament but in another way it serves as a
convenient indication of a decisive shift that took place in
attitudes to sexual questions.

The form of marriage that had dominated up to that point
was a Christian one, established for the Catholic world by the
Council of Trent in 1563 and in its English version by the
equally venerable *Book of Common Prayer*. It was an institution
whose great precepts of monogamy and indissolubility were
based, not on biological or sociological conceptions of the
sexual needs of the married partners but on a metaphysical
notion. The relationship, as the Church of England service puts
it, is one which we should see as 'signifying unto us the mystical
union that is betwixt Christ and his Church'.

Introducing judicial divorce, the 1857 Act made a significant intrusion into the authority of this metaphysical notion, reflected the growing dissatisfaction of the age with the account of the natural world offered by Christian tradition, and anticipated the growing influence of medical, psychological and sociological accounts of sexuality that are characteristic of our modern approach. The hold of the traditional view was not easily shaken off. A controversy could still be caused as late as 1918 by a book like Marie Stopes's *Married Love*, whose challenge was to treat marriage in terms of happiness, especially the sexual happiness, of the partners.[3] Indeed it was not until 1937 in England that concepts of 'mutual consent' were even discussed as alternatives to the principle of indissolubility in marriage law.[4] The shift from traditional to modern conceptions of marriage seems now, however, largely to be complete and popular debates about sexuality centre on different issues.

For Joyce, brought up a Catholic at the end of the nineteenth century in Ireland, the issue was very much a live one and it is striking that Joyce, at those times in his life when he made the clearest declarations of personal and artistic self-definition, allied himself to contemporary rational rejections of marriage. The most obvious gesture was his departure from Ireland with Nora on 8 October 1904 to live together in a free-love-style unmarried union for the next 27 years. Joyce's rejection of marital conventionality has been taken for granted by most critics and passed over, so that much more attention has been given to the symbolic overtones of his 'exile', to its role in the construction of a mythologized artistic personality. The immediate issue of sexual politics was nevertheless an important one.

Before setting up the irregular union, Joyce's sexual life was by no means conventional. Perhaps the ideal marriage, in terms of social and economic security as well as sexual conformity, would have been with one of the daughters of the Sheehy household, whose social gatherings are recorded in the 'Epiphanies' and *Stephen Hero*. Joyce was, though, something of an outsider to that circle both for his outrageous views and, perhaps, for his less than secure economic expectations. Rather than enter a socially competitive marriage market he (as his fictionalized self-portraits and accounts by his brother and by Oliver St John Gogarty confirm) frequented Dublin prostitutes. The deromanticized, unmistakably sexual nature of such encounters apparently answered more closely his youthful sexual desires and his growing understanding of sex.

For Stephen Dedalus in *A Portrait* such activities are not undertaken lightly – without an awareness of the extent to which they are sinful in the eyes of the Church.[5] Joyce too must have been highly conscious of the guilt of his actions but rather than succumb to it he pursued his youthful desire to live blatantly in contradiction to Church morality, to live in sin. He seems to have been anxious to avoid falling into the familiar pattern of youthful profligacy followed by easy repentance and conformism. Gogarty's marriage, of which he heard in 1906, prompted him to an outburst of rage against the lapse into conformity that it seemed to represent.[6]

Some record of Joyce's motivations in his elopement with Nora survives in the letters he wrote to her from the first uncertain postcard dated 15 June 1904 to their departure from Ireland that autumn. He is anxious to present himself to her as an opponent of Church and family, and will not (like Robert in *Exiles*) indulge in the conventionalism of calling his feelings towards her love.[7] When their elopement plan is accomplished he continues to justify to Stanislaus his 'attempt to live a more civilized life than my contemporaries'[8] and his 'intention of living in conformity with my moral nature'.[9]

Joyce refers to Nora in their first year together as his 'companion'.[10] It is a term that had some currency for advanced sexual unions, sometimes used by Joyce in a lightly satirical spirit against his feminist friend Francis Sheehy-Skeffington, but used also in *Chamber Music* in poem XXI, whose original title was 'To Nora': 'That high unconsortable one / His love is his companion.'[11]

Joyce sometimes allowed the legal status of their relationship to take a low profile. He was prepared as early as October 1904 'to sign all papers as for married people'[12] and despite the revelation by Richard Ellmann of certain 'adulterous' encounters,[13] their relationship turned out to be as consistently monogamous as any marriage of which we have such detailed private knowledge. But Joyce's commitment to the principles of their unmarried union remained constant for many years. The moments of uncertainty, like that recorded in a letter to Stanislaus before the birth of Giorgio in 1905, when Joyce feared that 'this present absurd life is no longer possible for either of us'[14] and that Nora might end up in the Serpentine like Harriet Shelley, were short-lived, and Joyce was able to reassert the advanced notion that 'Paternity is a legal fiction' and to maintain his resistance to 'the atrocities of the average husband'.[15]

In his relationship with Nora, Joyce followed, in an accelerated form, the larger intellectual movement of his time, rejecting the theological in favour of a rational conception of the sexual relationship. The Church system failed, in his view, in that it did not recognize his full biological humanity, as he wrote to Lady Gregory: 'there is no heresy or no philosophy which is so abhorrent to my church as a human being'. But what was a human being? Joyce's letter goes on to give some indication of what is meant. 'Accordingly', he continues, 'I am going to Paris. I intend to study medicine at the University of Paris ... '[16] Evidently it was not so much a career that he hoped to gain from his studies as a knowledge of himself from medicine that it was impossible for him to acquire from theology. Though his study of medicine was short (Ellmann plays down Joyce's interest in the subject and emphasizes the literary contacts that he hoped to make in Paris) it was an important part of his self-image to which he referred in later years. He included this trip, for instance, in the account of his life that he sent to *The Egoist* in 1916 to help with their publicizing of his work.[17]

Perhaps Joyce's interest in a medical career, frustrated in reality, was fired by the progressive, freethinking bourgeois doctors who figure in the Ibsenite drama that he admired, doctors like Stockmann in *An Enemy of the People*, like Wangel in *The Lady from the Sea* (who is no doubt more able to understand his wife's mysterious cravings because of his medical training), like Rank in *A Doll's House* (whose rationalism is a contributing liberalizing force for Nora Helmer) and like Loth in Hauptmann's *Before Sunrise* that Joyce translated at this time. Doctors in these plays seem to be associated with progressive humanistic awareness, a disregard of mere conventionality and an implicit recognition of sexuality. Alfred Loth is almost a caricature of the Stockmann type of doctor whose materialistic mental training leads him to an understanding of which the blind (in this case drunken and corrupt) people around him are not capable.

Joyce's celebrated faith in himself, which he proclaimed and

Yeats noted in these years, might itself be interpreted not just as self-publicizing and high spirits. His feelings are, in a way, a confirmation of this movement from Christianity to a kind of humanism, from faith in God to faith in 'the impulses of my nature'.[18] The letters to Nora bear out this shift in ideas. 'My mind rejects the whole present social order and Christianity,' he writes,[19] and elsewhere adds, 'How I hate God and death! How I like Nora!'[20]

There is an abrupt transition here but one that has its own highly revealing logic. Joyce, in rejecting marriage and in forming his relationship with Nora, was echoing the larger shift from divine to humanistic authority. In his diary Joyce's brother Stanislaus noted the shift from Catholicism to sexual liberalism thus: 'He has ceased to believe in Catholicism for many years. It is of little use to say that a man rejects Catholicism but because he wants to lead the life of a libertine. This is not the last word that can be said.'[21] Stanislaus may have found it 'of little use', but Joyce evidently did reject Christianity, to some extent, 'to lead the life of a libertine'. It was the beastly and most of all the sexual part of his humanity that Joyce felt the Church most excluded and it was highly appropriate for him, in trying to found a new concept of his humanity, to base it upon that rejected but insistent part. In the precise formulation of the 'Ithaca' episode of *Ulysses* Joyce made it clear that Stephen and Bloom share this habit of mind:

Both indurated by early domestic training and an inherited tenacity of heterodox resistance professed their disbelief in many orthodox religious, national, social and ethical doctrines. Both admitted the alternately stimulating and obtunding influence of heterosexual magnetism.   (*U* 777)

They disbelieve in religion but believe in sex.

Victorian dissatisfactions with marriage, reflected in the new law, were just as prominently aired in fiction. The tension between emotional individualism and a patriarchal marriage system is, in Ian Watt's well-known account, an important element in the evolution of the novel itself.[22] Tony Tanner, in his *Adultery in the Novel*, reminds us that 'many of those nineteenth-century novels that have been characterized as "great" – and in varying ways to varying degrees are felt to contain the furthest reaching explorations into their age – center on adultery'.[23]

Joyce, like so many of the great European novelists of the nineteenth century, relies upon the affective power of adulterous situations for many of his most central scenes and most powerful emotional effects, to an extent that was rarely recognized when so much criticism sought for deeper significances concealed in his language and when recent attention has focussed so strongly on his experimentations with narrative style and technique.

The end of the story 'The Dead' has been rightly celebrated as a uniquely evocative piece of prose writing. It has been described as a moment of sudden and deep realization for Gabriel Conroy, as a moment of 'epiphany', as if the mere repetition of that Joycean term were sufficient explanation without enquiring into what exactly Gabriel's recognition is a recognition of. The resonating associations of mortality and the fragility of human ideals, the strong symbolic suggestiveness of the snowfall and Gabriel's mysterious feeling that his world is dissolving and that he is approaching 'the region of the dead' are all highly important, but we should not forget that all are built on a sudden recognition that Gabriel has about his marriage. Gretta's emotional life, he realizes, does not conform to the pattern that he might have expected, the 'grace and mystery in her attitude' that he perceives are not, as he first hopes, the result of her wifely feelings for him (no more than the 'spot of joy' in the glance of Browning's 'Last Duchess' is aroused by her husband) but rather of her feelings for another man.

Gabriel is an aggrieved husband but his jealousy is short-lived. Gretta's feelings are perceived by him not as criminal but as legitimate and rather touching and are presented as such to the reader. Romantic love, in the familiar novelistic manner, is shown to be at odds with the institution of marriage but it is not a heroic confrontation in which the tide of passion triumphs. Our sympathies are engaged with the wronged husband and his brave and poignant recognition of the independence of his wife's affections and the incongruity between the mental conception of their relationship and its reality.

This is a rather more subtle critique of marriage than Joyce's unequivocal gesture of elopement but is a critique nonetheless. The treatment of Gabriel and Gretta was one which Joyce evidently found to his liking and he returned to it in *Exiles*, a play whose thematic interests are all the more prominent because here Joyce's stylistic experiments were at their least evident. That theme is adultery and once more the centre of attention is the situation of the husband. The situation is more urgent in *Exiles* than in 'The Dead' because here the adulterous moment is not a distant memory but a present threat. Throughout the play we are tantalized by the possibility of a sexual contact between Robert and Bertha and share Richard Rowan's torment. But his torment is as far from that of the murderous Othello or the aggrieved comic cuckolds of later seventeenth-century drama as it is from the forgotten husband of the conventional romance. It differs also, though more subtly, from what is arguably the most important fiction of the husband's situation that was available to Joyce, in *Madame Bovary*. In *Exiles* the situation has moved on from Flaubert inasmuch as sexual fidelity has been intellectualized into an investigation of the philosophic possibility of ever knowing another person's desires or motivations, much as it is in contemporary novels like Ford's *Good Soldier* or the climax of Joseph Conrad's *Victory*.[24] It differs inasmuch as Robert's thoughts and feelings are presented as more worthy of our interest than the romantic feelings of the transgressing couple, or (in the case of Emma Bovary) their romantic vanities. As Joyce said in his notes to the play (describing Flaubert, in fact, though more pertinently accounting for this feature of his own play) 'the centre of sympathy appears to have been aesthetically shifted from the lover or fancyman to the husband or cuckold' (*E* 165). Richard Rowan's situation is not one of ignorance, compromise, comedy and victimization but one where high principles and a degree of heroism may be attained. It is Bertha and Robert who, by behaving like adulterous deceivers, may lapse into conventionality and Robert, with his spraying of perfume around the love-nest at the start of Act 2,[25] is in danger of appearing ridiculous. There may be an element of Charles Bovary in Gabriel's feelings at the end of 'The Dead', for Bovary loses his jealousy in 'the immensity of his sorrow'.[26] There is, on the other hand, very little of him in Rowan. No one could say that he was 'good-natured to excess and, on the whole, rather despicable' as Rodolphe does of Bovary when he is forgiven at the end of Flaubert's book. Neither would one say of Rowan that he 'was not the sort of man to go very deeply into things', for it is Rowan's remorseless investigation, confession and discussion of the issues that gives *Exiles* so much of its character.[27]

In *Ulysses* Joyce returns to the drama of the adulterous situation once more and, though it is apparent that the sequence of eighteen Odyssean episodes provides the structure or pattern for Joyce's experiments with narrative style, it is the marital situation that provides the centre of much of the book's narrative content and provides the basis of its surest affective appeal.

The situation is a close reworking of that in *Exiles* and at the end of 'The Dead'. Once more the adulterous moment is not narrated in full (it is suspected, feared and imagined by Bloom and remembered by Molly but never narrated explicitly to the reader) and yet it is arguably the most important element in the characters' actions and consciousnesses. The decentering of the adulterous passions that began in the presentation of the romantic but rather unidimensional Michael Furey in 'The Dead' and continued in the almost comic stereotype of the seducer in Robert Hand's approach to Bertha in *Exiles* is developed in *Ulysses*, for Boylan is a stereotypical 'gay Lothario' who engages our sympathies hardly at all. Once more the central character is the cuckolded husband and far from the adopting of a jealous or revenging attitude Bloom's achievement of tolerance and emotional equilibrium constitutes the climax of the book's activities.

Critics may argue that it is impossible to determine Joyce's sympathies. But is it really so hard? Bloom frequently seems debased by his recognition of and near complicity in Molly's adultery – a dark possibility brought home most vividly in 'Circe', where he dreams up an especially potent Boylan to make love to Molly while he looks on (*U* 670–1). Bloom is a 'wittol' or conniving cuckold but not the despised stereotype that he might have been, and in Molly's malapropism for 'cornuto' – 'coronado' (*U* 924) we have a hint that he, like Richard Rowan and Gabriel Conroy, triumphs through his lack of jealous possessiveness. '*Et exaltabuntur cornua iusti*' ('and the horns of the just shall be exalted') exclaims Stephen in

'Circe' in an elaboration of his theory that Shakespeare was deceived by Anne Hathaway (*U* 672). Whereas in 'The Dead' and *Exiles* there is only one central adulterous moment, the situation in *Ulysses* broadens the adulterous possibilities and embodies in events and memories the situation anticipated or dimly foreshadowed at the end of *Exiles* where, in refusing to accept Bertha in 'the darkness of belief' but desiring her 'in restless living wounding doubt' (*E* 162), Richard suggests that from no marital situation can the possibility of adultery ever be excluded.

In *Ulysses* Molly is not just adulterous on 16 June 1904. Bloom, throughout the day, draws on his memories of their past life, especially on the events of the years 1887 to 1894 which the experienced reader begins to piece together from their scattered recurrence in the novel.[28] There are Bloom's memories of the 'first night when I saw her at Mat Dillon's in Terenure' in 1887, when Bloom 'sailed inside' John Henry Menton for Molly's affections.[29] There are memories of their early married life when Molly, breastfeeding Milly, is half-seen by the pale-faced student Penrose,[30] and is walked home from singing practice by the tenor Bartell d'Arcy.[31] Whilst living in Lombard Street West in 1893 Molly seems to enjoy the old-fashioned gentlemanly attentions of her accompanist Professor Goodwin[32] and at the Lord Mayor's Dinner in Glencree, and on her journey home from it, she arouses the interest of both the leech-like Lenehan and the Lord Mayor himself.[33]

These past events are structured echoes of the present situation and that situation is not merely one in which Molly, by virtue of some special laxity of her morals, is the only adulterous party. Bloom too is involved in extramarital relationships which closely parallel those of his wife. Whilst Molly receives an adulterous letter from Boylan in 'Calypso', in the very next episode Bloom is shown walking to the Post Office in Westland Row, where he picks up his letter from Martha Clifford. Though at one point he denies all interest in the 'other chap's wife' (*U* 483), Bloom has a past which verges on the adulterous, most prominently in his association with Josie Powell, Molly's one-time friend, with whom he has flirted at Georgina Simpson's housewarming party in 1888 (*U* 574 and 878), again at Leopardstown Races (*U* 576–8) and who, now married to Denis Breen, he meets on the morning of the novel

(U 199–200) and in guilty hallucination in 'Circe' (U 576–8). He has flirted with the maid Mary Driscoll too, as we are told in 'Oxen of the Sun' (U 535) and 'Circe', where he is tried for the offence and only the return of Paddy Dignam from the grave is enough to defend his good name (U 586–98). 'I woman is not enough for them', Molly complains (U 873).

Molly's adultery may seem most important to the structuring of the novel's actions, but Bloom's extramarital activities are more visible to us since they are narrated in a more straightforward way. They may consist in apparently trivial voyeuristic appreciations of the swinging hips of the girl next door (U 70–1) or of the grand Dublin ladies he glimpses in 'Lotus Eaters' (U 89–90) or who haunt him in 'Circe' (U 591–4). Nowhere, though, is the connection so apparent between Molly's adultery and his own as in 'Nausicaa' where, at the moment of Molly's infidelity, Bloom achieves his own simultaneous sexual release.[34] Whilst Molly's adulterous act is hidden or refracted in the novel, Bloom's is the centre of attention in the narrative.

Adams, to defend Molly Bloom against contemporary attacks on her morality, proved that few of her so-called lovers are intimate enough with her (from what we can divine of their history in the novel) to deserve that title.[35] Since then it has become common to talk of her adulterous past as one of the deliberate modernistic uncertainties of the book. It is, however, apparent that Joyce made this adulterousness or pseudo-adulterousness a persistent and structurally significant element in his novel and, far from exculpating Molly, we should perhaps recognize that it is in what is strictly extramarital sexual activity that many of the novel's characters and much of its work are involved.

In 'Circe' the brothel mirror shows the faces of Stephen and Bloom and the Shakespeare of Stephen's theory, all three crowned by the cuckold's symbol, the 'antlered hatrack' in the hall (U 671). In 'Eumaeus' the conversation turns to 'the eternal question of the life connubial'. 'Can real love, supposing there happens to be another chap in the case, exist between married folk?' asks Bloom (U 756). The answer that *Ulysses* offers is that there is always 'another chap in the case' and that no love nor any valid understanding can exist without a recognition of that fact. It is an answer that is foreshadowed in *Stephen Hero*, where Stephen makes his blasphemously Christ-like pronouncement on adultery. Neither condemnation nor approval of adultery are quite the point. 'Besides,' he says, 'it is impossible not to commit "adultery"' (*SH* 196).

The fiction of marriage

In looking at Joyce's reading both for support and for further elucidation of this interest in sexual situations which transcend or evade the formulation of institutionalized monogamy, we find, not unsurprisingly, much of that nineteenth-century European fiction that played so productively over questions of adultery.

Flaubert is a prominent presence in the Trieste library and, of course, Flaubert's relevance to Joyce has been well known since Pound drew attention to their literary relationship in his review of *Ulysses* in 1922.[36] Though Joyce's school-friend Curran, in his account of Joyce's early reading, remarks that it was *La Tentation de Sainte Antoine* that interested Joyce more than *Madame Bovary*,[37] the latter novel was at his fingertips by the time he came to write the notes for *Exiles*.

Joyce's reading of Tolstoy too is well documented and we know that he admired *Anna Karenina* as early as 1905 when, writing to his brother on Tolstoy's excellence, it seemed to him to be the natural novel to mention.[38] The record of his reading of Tolstoy, moreover, suggests that it was towards Tolstoy's treatment of marital themes that Joyce's interest was directed. There is, for instance, only a largely uncut copy of *War and Peace* which Joyce left in Paris in 1939.[39] His Trieste books contain no *War and Peace* but do include an Italian translation of *The Kreutzer Sonata*, whose terrifying examination of marital strains and conflicts is so potent; and he also owned a German translation, *Der Roman der Ehe*, whose English title is 'Family Happiness'.[40] *The Kreutzer Sonata*, in some editions, carried an 'afterword' setting out Tolstoy's rather extreme views on marriage: his belief in an ideal of chastity in relation to which marriage is only a feeble compromise. Joyce would have had access to this in his volume of Tolstoy's *Essays and Letters*, a heavily annotated volume left with the Paris books, whose markings indicate that it had been owned by Joyce since his residence in Trieste.[41]

Whilst Tolstoy's stated ideal of chastity may seem a backward-looking one, his fictions of marriage found their place in nineteenth-century examinations of the theme perhaps most of all because of their sense of the uncontrollable power of sexual passions. The apparent inability of his characters to achieve even the modest compromise of marital fidelity has its place alongside the more straightforward romantic or rationalist dissatisfactions with marriage that constitute the broader movement of the century.

Joyce was well acquainted with Balzac's work, which he ridiculed as a young man in Dublin but which he evidently had come to admire in Trieste. Once more the titles in the Trieste library listing suggest an interest biassed towards Balzac's treatment of married life. They include *Letters of Two Brides* in which two women, one conventionally married for economic security, the other following a wayward life of passion and adventure, exchange their experiences, and stand as representatives of the two alternative fates to which women seemed subjected by the marital system.[42] They include also *The Physiology of Marriage* and *Petty Worries of Conjugal Life*, companion studies of married life, of which the first offers a minute instruction to the married male in ways of avoiding or at least recognizing the inevitable 'minotaurization' or cuckolding to which he will be subject. *Petty Worries* is more fictionalized, giving an account of the progress of a marriage from early romance to an eventual sophisticated battle for domination. Both books are punctuated by urbane 'axioms' and indeed it is their knowing manner of discussing matrimonial transgressions that is one of their most striking qualities.[43] It is, at any rate, in this spirit that (echoing the title of another of Balzac's studies of marriage in Joyce's Trieste library) Stephen thinks of Anne Hathaway in the 'Scylla and Charybdis' discussion of Shakespeare as the '*femme de trente ans*' (*U* 277).[44]

For an English-language reader at the end of the century, especially an Irish one, it was George Moore who made popular the explicit treatment of adultery that Victorian taste had found so exceptionable in the French novel. Joyce read Moore in full, several titles surviving in the Trieste library[45] and, still more to the point, it is this quality of Moore as the advanced francophile author of works like *Lewis Seymour* and *A Modern Lover*, as the 'lecturer on French letters to the youth of Ireland' (*U* 275–6), that prompts his entry into the discussion in 'Scylla and Charybdis'.

Joyce's reading on the subject includes, of course, Ibsen (where men's adultery may be reprehensible in *Ghosts* but women's is the index of a new and valuable liberation for Rebecca West in *Rosmersholme*). It includes the Ibsenite drama of authors like Marco Praga (in whose *The Closed Door* the adulterous compact of an unhappily married couple is disclosed and justified to their young son)[46] and includes Wilde, in whose *An Ideal Husband* (in the Trieste library) the husband is 'ideal' because of his tolerant attitude to adultery.[47]

Joyce's interest in marriage and adultery conditioned his approach to the whole of the literary tradition. He owned, for instance, a complete Molière but the only comment of his on Molière which survives is a remark about the play which he refers to as *Le Cocu imaginaire* (its more usual title is *Sganarelle*), an economical and well-shaped comedy of errors whose theme is the mutual and interrelated suspicions of adultery between a man and his wife and a younger couple.[48]

Shakespeare by no means evades the association. It is not just that Joyce treats *Othello* as a study of jealousy in *Stephen Hero* and in the working notes for *Exiles*.[49] In 'Scylla and Charybdis', according to Stephen's psychobiographical theory of Shakespeare's plays, the theme of the false or adulterous brother was 'always with him'. 'Age has not withered it,' Stephen says, typically couching his comment in an allusion which gives a further dimension to it (*U* 272). Cleopatra, Cressida and the erotically overbearing Venus (from *Venus and Adonis*) are all brought into the theory and even a play like *The Merry Wives of Windsor* (where, with the exposure of Falstaff, marital fidelity might seem to be vindicated) is presented as a possible repository of 'deephid meanings' involving Shakespeare and the Virgin Queen Elizabeth (*U* 263). Joyce's particular kind of Shakespearean interest derives, as William Schutte first pointed out, from the contemporary popular biographies mentioned in 'Scylla and Charybdis' by Sidney Lee, Georg Brandes and Frank Harris. But in his choice of such plays as *Othello* and *Merry Wives*, and in his attention to the adultery theme in Shakespeare, Joyce shows, as much as anything, the depth of his interest in the operatic tradition which in its plots, one might say, effected a rapprochement between Shakespeare's 'psychological' drama, the neatly plotted neo-classical intrigues that inspired Mozart's da Ponte operas, and the fascination with adulterous passions that fired so much nineteenth-century literature. 'You have brought us all this way to show us a French triangle' (*U* 274) complains John Eglinton of Stephen's theory.

Joyce would inevitably have been immersed in fictions of adultery but, more remarkably, his reading of Homer has no less of a sense of the significance of these themes. This is evident not so much in specific comments that Joyce made as in the conflation of the ten-year wanderings of Odysseus with the domestic matrimonial concerns of modern bourgeois fiction that his project of recasting the myth '*sub specie temporis nostri*' seems to imply.[50] What is implicit in the larger movements of *Ulysses* is sometimes made more explicit in smaller details. In 'Eumaeus' the drunken, talkative sailor W.B. Murphy (whose correspondence to 'Ulysses Pseudangelos' in Joyce's scheme identifies him as a Ulysses in miniature)[51] has his journeyings cast explicitly into a marital context. 'She's my own true wife I haven't seen for seven years now, sailing about,' he whimpers (*U* 719).

Bloom instantly ties up his story with those of other straying husbands whose wives may be less than true, including Tennyson's 'Enoch Arden' and the song 'Ben Bolt', commenting ruefully that the stories are 'never about the runaway wife coming back' (*U* 719). Joyce may have felt the marital implications of *The Odyssey* all the more strongly through his knowledge of a poem called *The Oddity* by one 'Frank Hopewell', which is a piece of comic verse cast as a sailor's letter home to his sweetheart, one of the strangest of the many Odyssean leads he followed up. Joyce may well have remembered its short lines and repeated rhymes on '-ation' in the passage at the end of 'Ithaca', where Bloom finally returns to Molly's bed with a 'mellonsmellonous osculation' and 'a proximate erection' (*U* 867).[52]

Joyce saw even the Bible as a reservoir of material on the theme of marriage and adultery. He discussed with Stanislaus (and incorporated into *Stephen Hero*) Christ's tolerant judgement on the woman taken in adultery in John 8, and his redefinition of the Old Testament commandment against adultery in the light of the ubiquity of adultery committed in the

heart spelled out in Matthew 5.[53] Such discussions, it is sometimes suggested, show Stephen and Joyce to be 'sympathetic
aliens' to Catholicism, 'supersaturated in the religion' they
claim to reject, but there is much more modern liberalism than
strained conformity in Stephen's attitude.

There are no fewer than four separate versions in Joyce's
known reading of the eccentric theory that Joseph was literally
cuckolded at the conception of Christ (which a Mulliganian
irreverence might suggest explains Christ's tolerance of extramarital desire). These range from Leo Taxil's version in his
blasphemous *Vie de Jésus* that Joyce has Stephen remember in
'Proteus' (*U* 51)[54] to a book by Adrian Beverland, where the
notion is dignified as part of the Ebionite heresy.[55] There is a
tradition of Joseph's suspicion of Mary in the English medieval
drama which is mentioned by Herbert Spencer, and finally
Balzac compares Joseph's complaisance favourably with
Othello's absurd jealous rantings.[56]

Joyce discovered in Paul de Kock's *Le Cocu* a work of fiction
which, though he admitted its inferiority, had a theme and still
more a title which suited his purposes both for *Exiles* and for
Molly in *Ulysses*.[57] His keen eye for adultery led him to note in
the so-called *Scribbledehobble* notebook (presumably fearing the
worst in Eve's relationship with the serpent), 'Adam 1st
cocu'.[58]

Joyce also interested himself in non-fiction investigations of
the theme. Just as reformers of the marriage law came gradually
to replace the divine validation of the institution, so historians
and ethnographers interested themselves in the institution to
seek to discover its natural or original form. One of the most
frequently discussed books was Edward A. Westermarck's
History of Human Marriage.[59] Westermarck claimed to have
discovered that monogamous marriage was universal in human
societies. Even the higher apes were monogamous, he argued,
thus proving the validity and inevitability of traditional marital
customs. Westermarck was often cited by marital traditional-
ists, but his brave attempt to reconcile traditional Christian
marriage with new evolutionary thought was, to some extent,
in conflict with the main thrust of new work. Writers like
J.J. Bachofen, J.F. McLennan, Sir John Lubbock and
L.H. Morgan argued (from what they took to be the survivals of
older practices in certain customs) that monogamous marriage

was not universal but was a development from original polygamy, from marriage by capture, primitive promiscuity or
group marriage.[60]

If Westermarckian theory supported a traditional kind of
monogamous marriage, then these other theories tended to
undermine or relativize it and this radical dimension was
exploited by writers from Friedrich Engels (whose work on *The
Origin of the Family* drew on Morgan's study[61]) to Bertrand
Russell (whose *Marriage and Morals*, a classic statement of
modern sexual liberalism, drew on Malinowski's studies of
matrilineal societies).[62]

Joyce seems to have been aware of this arena of debate. In the
Scribbledehobble notebook such terms as Lubbock's 'end (ex)
ogamy' and McLennan's 'group marriage' and 'marriage by
capture' are noted.[63] As Engels explains, Morgan's theory of
earlier forms of marriage was based on the survival of unusual
terms of kinship. McLennan, however, thought that these
terms were to be understood in the same way as the modern
forms of address 'father' and 'mother' for priests and nuns.[64]
Joyce's sense of this is suggested by the *Scribbledehobble* note
'group marriage [546.13] (uncle bros. in J.C.)'.[65] He includes
the phrase in *Finnegans Wake* in a passage in Book III Chapter
3, where HCE is defending himself to the four old men, deny-
ing that his apparent involvement with the three soldiers and
two girls can be explained by an enquiry into 'the forced
generation of group marriage' (*FW* 546.13) and proceeding to
expound on the joys of faithful marriage to his 'Fulvia Flavia'.

Stephen in *Ulysses* has an idea of the history of marital
institutions too, typically claiming to prefer an Aquinas-like
view of incest and endogamy (that they represent an 'avarice' of
the emotions) to a more modern Freudian one, although just as
typically he is using his Aquinas to make a modern-sounding
defence of less 'avaricious' sexual liberalism (*U* 264). Dixon and
Lenehan in 'Oxen of the Sun' taunt Stephen with his rejection
of the priesthood and with rumours of his profligacy, alluding
to some (apparently spurious) rite of wedlock from Madagascar, where the priest enjoys a *jus primae noctis* or *droit de
seigneur* privilege over the bride's virginity.

Bloom is intrigued by polygamy in 'Lestrygonians', first
wryly thinking of the evangelist J. Alexander Dowie: 'Polygamy. His wife will put the stopper on that' (*U* 120). Then

more picaresquely he imagines a cannibal chief consuming his victims' 'parts of honour' with 'his wives in a row to watch the effect' (*U* 218). It is no surprise to find on the 'syllabus of intellectual pursuits' he envisages for his dream cottage in 'Ithaca' the perusal of 'folklore relative to various amatory and superstitious practices' (*U* 841) and two broadly ethnographic items (*Voyages in China* by 'Viator' and Ellis's *Three Trips to Madagascar*) on his bookshelf when its contents are listed (*U* 832).[66]

In Joyce's Paris library there remains a strange book by Adrian Beverland entitled *The Law Concerning Draped Virginity*, which investigates such issues with a semi-prurient interest perhaps not unrelated to that which Joyce sometimes seems to impute to Stephen and Bloom.[67] Such investigations were, however, important to contemporary discussions of marriage and there was a high level of awareness of them in literary circles. Shaw, for instance, in his Preface to *Getting Married* (which Joyce had in his Trieste library[68]) gives an account of much of the contemporary debate. A rather better-known work, also appearing in Joyce's library, is Richard Burton's seventeen-volume translation of *The Arabian Nights*. Burton was particularly interested in the sexual customs of the Arab world that were revealed in the stories, and polygamy is just one of such customs discussed in the 'terminal essay' which forms part of the tenth volume of his work.[69] No doubt it was Burton's emphasis on Arabic sexual customs that encouraged Joyce to have Bloom escape from the brothel in 'Circe' under the appropriately polygamic 'incog' of Haroun al Raschid (*U* 685). Bloom dreamt of Molly 'with red slippers on in pair of Turkey trunks' on the eve of the novel's action (*U* 199, 497 and 519) and she appears in full harem costume on his entry into nighttown (*U* 570). Yashmaks puzzle her in 'Sirens', adding a final note to this oriental flavouring of the presentation of their marriage (*U* 353 and 373).

Joyce's researches extended to a book by a French socialist, Charles Albert, entitled *L'Amour libre*. Albert's book is basically a polemic for free love and the abandonment of marital institutions, with a strong socialist and anarchist flavour. His thinking is closely bound up in evolutionist patterns and he argues his case in such terms, drawing on the work of the more serious anthropologists I have cited. Quoting Darwin and Geddes and

Thompson's *Evolution of Sex*, he argues that reproduction has evolved towards highly complex forms of courtship and sexual-object choice. In the shorter term, he argues (quoting Letourneau's *L'Evolution du mariage et de la famille* and specifically attacking Westermarck), human marriage has itself developed from primitive forms of marriage-by-purchase towards a greater dependence on the emotional choice of the partners themselves.

Love, he says, is evident neither in the Bible nor in classical literature but only came into being in medieval times, since when it has consistently opposed all forms of institutionalized monogamy which are, he claims, merely products of the desire to determine paternity for the purposes of inheriting private property. Love is consequently in conflict with capitalism but when socialism triumphs it will be at last released.[70]

Such a polemic may have been congenial to Joyce. His interest in socialism and anarchism have recently become much better known thanks to Richard Ellmann's *The Consciousness of Joyce* and Dominic Manganiello's *Joyce's Politics*. There are other works in the library which suggest an interest in free-love unions, such as the novel *The Woman Who Did* by Grant Allen,[71] a popular contemporary work which celebrated the decision of its heroine to live with her partner and have his child, despite the personal tragedy it cost her. The title of the book crops up in *Finnegans Wake* in a list of attributions to ALP, so that its melodramatic note is comically emphasized. We may nevertheless suppose that the Joyces enjoyed this vindication of their unmarried condition. Alfred de Musset's *A Modern Man's Confession*, partly based on the author's famous unmarried association with George Sand, and fictionalizing the traumas of attempting to live in the modern disillusioned sexual atmosphere of post-republican France, was also in his library.[72] Forming part of an arguably related interest (for it was translated into English by the same man and the translations published in the same year) is Pierre Loti's *The Marriage of Loti*, an exotic 1890s novel during the course of which the hero is forced to come to terms with the realities of Tahitian marriage not 'according to European ideals binding him for life'.[73]

Such reading provides a context for Joyce's life as well as for his work. For instance, according to Havelock Ellis's *The New Spirit*, in the library, both Heine and Goethe had sexual relationships which were only later solemnized by marriage,[74] and Joyce compared Nora to Heine's mistress in a letter of 1905.[75]

In Joyce's writings there are moments when an interest in and enthusiasm for free love seems very evident. *Stephen Hero* is obviously such a work. Its prefiguration of the discussions of aesthetics in *A Portrait* have always secured the greatest amount of critical attention, but just as much of the surviving manuscript deals with Stephen's rebellion against the sexual mores of his contemporaries. The most vivid scenes in the incomplete novel are arguably not those concerned with the theories of art at all but those concerning Stephen's artless attempt to court Emma, especially in Chapter 24 with which Joyce himself was pleased.[76]

Here he establishes a tentative flirtatious intimacy with Emma and discusses with Lynch the relationship that might be possible with her in relation to that which he might have with a prostitute 'in a black straw hat'. He breaks out from his Italian lesson to chase Emma and proposes wildly to her that they 'live one night together' and then 'say goodbye in the morning', and that she open her bedroom window to him at night to let him in (*SH* 203). In his outburst Stephen rejects both love and marriage: 'I do not bargain with you or say I love you or swear to you,' he says (*SH* 203).

In his claim that marriage would represent an irrelevant commerciality or 'bargain', his belief that a woman 'must sell [herself] either as a harlot or as a married woman or as a celibate or as a mistress' (*SH* 206), Stephen's argument is closely parallel to that of Albert and to other rationalist writers like W.E.H. Lecky in whose *History of European Morals*, in the Trieste library, the analogy between wife and prostitute is also drawn.[77] This sense of the conflict between love and commerciality occurs elsewhere in Joyce's works showing that the fascination of its discovery did not pass with his youth.[78] Stephen recognizes the conflict between proprietary and emotional feelings in his discussion of Shakespeare in *Ulysses* (*U* 264). It is apparent in *Dubliners*, where Mrs Mooney contrives to arrange her daughter's match in 'The Boarding House', in an evident attack on the hollowness of the marital ideal; and Mrs Kearney is no less determined in the commercial exploitation of her daughter's singing in 'A Mother'. 'Two Gallants' is a more bitter attack, with Lenehan who could 'live happily if he could only come across some good simple-minded girl with a little of the ready' (*D* 62), and Corley who cruelly exploits the affections of his servant-girl friend. We may see one aspect of the incompatibility of sexual and economic elements in the absurd 'marriage of trees' passage of parody in 'Cyclops', introduced to expose John Wyse Nolan's 'espousal' of the Irish aforestation cause. Even in *Finnegans Wake* Joyce's attack on the conjuncture of the economic and the sexual in marriage continues. Jaunty Jaun's sermon in Book III Chapter 2 insists on chastity, lest there be a 'marriage slump' (*FW* 438.21). 'Vamp, vamp, vamp the girls are merchand', we are told, as 'Izod' and the 'Floras' prepare to taunt 'Glugg' for the third and final time in Book II Chapter 1. Such courtship games are all commercial, it is implied, with some suggestive punning on the French 'dot' or dowry system criticized by Balzac: 'Now a run for his money! Now a dash to her dot' (*FW* 232.27).

The connection between free love and socialism in Albert's work[79] is remembered when we are told of Stephen that he 'was not sufficiently doctrinaire to wish to have his theory put to the test by a general [revulsion] revolution of society' (*SH* 208). But for Joyce, as we have seen already, love was by no means such a positive term as it was for Albert.[80] Stephen neither 'bargains' for Emma nor swears love to her. It seemed to Joyce that, far from being the highest form of human evolution, 'a lot of this talk about love is nonsense'.[81] Albert saw love in conflict with capitalism but for Joyce, in *Stephen Hero* at least, romance, both in the mythologizing of the Byronic poet lover (*SH* 37) and in Emma's chaste holding back (*SH* 215), is a 'burgher' or bourgeois notion. The brash, successful journalist Gallaher in 'A Little Cloud' desires to marry cynically someone 'rotten with money' (*D* 84) but, if anything, he is presented as less of a victim of the system than Little Chandler who has married his Annie for love. Romance is distrusted by Stephen in *A Portrait*,[82] and exploded in the juxtaposition of Gerty's longings with Bloom's unromantic desires in the 'Nausicaa' episode of *Ulysses*. It is thus then in *Stephen Hero* that Stephen condemns the conventional Emma with her hopes for love and marriage as 'the most deceptive and cowardly of marsupials' (*SH* 215).

Outside *Stephen Hero*, these criticisms of love and marriage are often less than whole-heartedly articulated. In 'Circe', for instance, Bloom stands for 'Free money, free love and a free lay church in a free lay state' (*U* 610), and HCE in the 'Ballad of Persse O'Reilly' is said to be a supporter of 'openair love and religion's reform' (*FW* 45.16).

We may see an appeal for unmarried union in such lines as these from *Chamber Music*:

> Gentle lady, do not sing
> Sad songs about the end of love
> Lay aside sadness and sing
> How love that passes is enough   (*CM* 32)

Here too, though, the appeal is not a straightforward one. There is, first of all, a subtle mixing of the direct modern lover's address and the erotic sensitivity, the concern for mutability and the idiom characteristic of those Elizabethan songs that Joyce so admired.[83] Such equivocation of idiom is a phenomenon that is intrinsic to the effect of the poems. Stephen himself discusses it in a passage in *Stephen Hero*, whose ideas are highly relevant to the 'feudal terminology' of his verse:

In his expressions of love he found himself compelled to use what he called the feudal terminology and as he could not use it with the same faith and purpose as animated the feudal poets themselves he was compelled to express his love a little ironically. This suggestion of relativity, he said, mingling itself with so immune a passion is a modern note.   (*SH* 179)

The 'ironic' element in the poems is indeed highly suggestive of the 'modern note' that Joyce was able to strike in his later work. It seems, furthermore, highly significant that it is in his attempts to investigate modern love that this choice of an ironically distanced 'feudal terminology', rather than a polemical attempt like Albert's (or like that of Lawrence in more familiar fictional territory), should emerge to try to articulate newly felt understandings of the sexual relationship in a new, more straightforward language. Equivocation of tone and the lack of a direct polemic is what we would expect in Joyce but that need not lead us to abandon the interest in free love that the works seem to indicate to us. It should encourage us to look for it in less direct ways.

Many of the *Chamber Music* poems make seductive appeals, self-recommendations of the lover, celebrations of the beloved and anticipations of their consummation: familiar enough themes for love poems. Towards the end of the collection however (beginning, perhaps, with poem XVII which records the parting of friends: 'He is a stranger to me now / Who was my friend') a stronger and more profound note enters. The union of the lovers becomes less the focus of attention than their isolation. The lover is 'unconsortable' (poem XXI), comparable to a bitter, isolated figure like Mithridates (XXVII) and the beloved is encouraged to be disdainful: 'as they deny, deny' (XX). Love may be passing (XXVIII) or even past (XXX, XXXI, and XXXIII) and the effect of increasing isolation is emphasized by the placing of the two final poems. In poem XXXV the lover is compared to a sad seabird 'going / Forth alone' and in poem XXXVI love has almost vanished as the principal subject and we are left with a nightmare of isolation.

This sense of isolation rather than any call for erotic indulgence seems to constitute the strongest centre of feeling in the poems and in this, as well as in the highlighting of such isolation at the culmination of the work, the *Chamber Music* volume anticipates Joyce's other works. The end of 'The Dead', which brings *Dubliners* to its close, does not provide a romantic closure in the union of two lovers so much as a new and poignant separation and isolation of the married pair. The closing sequence is foreshadowed when Gabriel thinks he sees 'a woman', strange and unnamed, in the first instance, only later recognized as Gretta (*D* 239). They are, as it were, strangers for a moment and in *Exiles*, too, Bertha and Richard rediscover each other not in everyday familiarity but as strangers once more. 'You are a stranger to me ... A stranger! I am living with a stranger,' cries Bertha when Richard refuses to condemn her meeting with Robert or to insist on her fidelity (*E* 149). Paradoxically this enforced freedom only renews their loving attachment but it is as strangers that they must come together. 'Forget me and love me again as you did the first time,' begs Bertha in her passionate closing speech.

The free-love element in the play consists not merely in the fact that Richard and Bertha have loved in an unmarried, experimental marriage or that they contemplate adultery. It consists even more in this creation of a world where individuals are shown as profoundly isolated in their interests and in their moral choices – isolated inasmuch as they can never depend or rely upon each others' actions or on traditional institutions or formulae for their relationships.

Love, for all Joyce's desire to replace romantic mystifications with biological certainties, is not solely represented as sexual passion. Indeed Robert is the apologist for 'nature's law' of passion and Richard (and by implication Joyce too) condemns such a law as mere possessiveness, saying 'I am afraid that longing to possess a woman is not love' (*E* 88). Richard leaves Robert with a tentative definition (perhaps prefiguring Bloom's definition of love in 'Cyclops'), saying that love is 'To wish her well' (*E* 88): an arduous altruistic duty according to Richard's severely philosophic view. Love is presented not as a kind of union but as a kind of separation of individuals and the play's free-love morality consists, as Joyce points out in his note, in 'the very immolation of the pleasure of possession on the altar of love' (*E* 164). As Budgen reports, 'the Joycean conception of sexual love (at any rate on the male side)' is an 'irreconcilable conflict between a passion for absolute possession and a categorical imperative of absolute freedom.'[84]

'Isolation,' Stephen declares in *Stephen Hero* 'is the first principle of artistic economy' (*SH* 37). It is a view that may owe much to Havelock Ellis's enthusiastic defence of the new spirit in literature, whose emphasis on sexual as well as literary modernity we have noted, and which celebrates Ibsen in terms of his Stockmann-like 'proud isolation and defiance of his fellow citizens'.[85] Isolation seems a suitable watchword for the proud artist, but we may find it less obviously appropriate as the first principle of the emotional life that it seems to be for Richard and Bertha in *Exiles* and for Gabriel Conroy.

Yet isolation provides the climaxes of other works. Stephen, of course, in *A Portrait*, ends on a gesture of isolation. There is a kind of isolation in the close of *Finnegans Wake* too, where Anna flows into the sea but flows, as we are told in the last half-sentence of the book, 'alone' (*FW* 628.15). Isolation is no less significant a description of Leopold and Molly Bloom in *Ulysses*, left at the end, in the distinct stylistic contrast between 'Ithaca' and 'Penelope', strangely separate in their own mental worlds. Throughout they have been given separate emotional and sexual lives, which as we have seen, are presented as hugely in excess of romantic or marital exclusiveness.

Bloom's famous tolerance in 'Ithaca', just like Gabriel

Conroy's, is based on the recognition that his wife is a separate being over whose actions neither he nor her lover have any direct form of control. Molly must be a free, active agent in any adultery, as this typically 'Ithaca-like' account of the situation, in meticulous grammatical terms, suggests, invoking:

the natural grammatical transition by inversion involving no alteration of sense of an aorist preterite proposition (parsed as masculine subject monosyllabic onomatopoeic transitive verb with direct feminine object) from the active voice into its correlative aorist, preterite proposition (parsed as feminine subject, auxiliary verb and quasimonosyllabic onomatopœic past participle with complementary masculine agent, in the passive voice'.   (U 866–7)

Marital fidelity for Bloom is an equivocal distant memory of 'Pleasants Street' or a frail dream of some utopian future residence in 'Bloom Cottage. Saint Leopold's. Flowerville', where he will do his matrimonial duty 'upholding the letter of the law' against 'all recalcitrant violators of domestic connubiality' (U 843).[86] The Blooms, in the present reality of their lives, are not so ideally united and protected, but it does not seem appropriate to their great representative normality to suggest, as many critics do, that Joyce wished to present them as a particularly or exceptionally unhappy couple. It seems, rather, that Joyce wished to show them in this light in order to point to what Bloom calls, with 'Ithaca-like' punctiliousness, 'the painful character of the ultimate functions of separate existence' (U 817).

Free love, in this sense of the recognition of the inadequacy of the matrimonial formulation of the sexual relationship and the presentation of individuals as fundamentally separate from each other, though Joyce makes little attempt to argue directly for it, runs through the understanding of relationships in all his works, whether those relationships be formalized by marriage or not.

The letter of the law

Joyce's criticism of marriage, consisting in such rationalist, socialist and individualist elements, places his work more closely in relation to the 'progressive' theories of late nineteenth- and early twentieth-century writers than is normally supposed. Though different in tone and manner, the radical moral individuality of Richard Rowan's stance in *Exiles* has a strong common link with the epigrammatic heterodoxy of Wilde's Algernon Moncrieff in *The Importance of Being Earnest*. Richard refuses to intervene just as Algernon declares that 'selfishness is not living as one wishes to live, it is asking others to live as one wishes to live'.[87]

This kind of moral individuality is fundamental to modern sexual liberalism. We may find it in Bertrand Russell's *Marriage and Morals*, for instance, where in the liberal future, we are told, 'self-control will be applied more to abstaining from interference with the freedom of others than to restraining one's own freedom'.[88] And in John Stuart Mill's *On Liberty* (of which a copy survives in Joyce's library) we are similarly instructed that 'the liberty of the individual must be thus far limited; he must not make himself a nuisance to other people'.[89] Bloom's cuckoldhood, we may suppose, is just this principle of liberalism applied to the sexual morality of his daily life.

Of the writers who may have supported such a position in Joyce's thinking there survive several traces. There is Nietzsche, of course, whose rejection of morality in *Beyond Good and Evil* is such a powerful index of the shift from tradition to modernity. Joyce, as Ellmann notes, signed a letter to Nora in 1903 'James Overman', indicating a Nietzschean interest.[90] It is Mulligan not Stephen to whom Joyce attributes such interests in the opening chapter of *Ulysses*, but we should notice that Joyce's interest was a strong and consistent one and that copies of *The Birth of Tragedy, The Case of Wagner* and *The Joyful Wisdom*, which could not have been bought before 1909, survive in the Trieste library.[91]

It would be possible to establish a compendium of contemporary liberal and advanced positions from the evidence we have of Joyce's library. Havelock Ellis, whose interest was in modern sexuality as well as modern literature, would be included as well as Shaw and Georg Brandes.[92] Spencer and Huxley would be included for their enthusiasm for empirical, scientific truth.[93] Writers like Renan, whose literary or biographical approach to the Bible and whose conversion to Hellenism fascinated Joyce,[94] have a place in such a compendium, as do more politically urgent works like Albert's *L'Amour libre*. Oscar Wilde, whose *Soul of Man Under Socialism* Joyce owned in Trieste, might serve as a suitable amalgam of ideas, for Wilde's 'socialism' was of the most eclectic kind. 'Socialism itself will be of value simply because it will lead to Individualism',[95] writes Wilde with typical paradoxical and epigrammatical energy, adding that 'the new Individualism is the new Hellenism'.[96]

Joyce's new morality may have found support further afield too, in the stoic moralists who appear in his library listings. He had a copy of Cicero's *Tusculanarem Disputationem*, and introduces Ciceronian stoicism into his parody of Sir Thomas Browne in 'The Oxen of the Sun', declaring 'assuefaction minorates atrocities (as Tully saith of his darling Stoics)'.[97] He owned also editions of Epictetus and of the *Thoughts* of Marcus Aurelius.[98] Epictetus, in fact, gets a considerable airing in *A Portrait* in the discussion between Stephen and the Dean of Studies and, though it is the lame and lifeless Dean who defends Epictetus' doctrine of tolerance to the thief, we may see elements of stoicism in Joyce's central protagonists. Stephen finds stoic-sounding moments of 'calm' (*P* 87) and of 'cold lucid indifference' (*P* 103), and when we note that Epictetus extends his toleration of the thief to include the adulterer we may be more ready to see a stoic streak in Bloom's contemplation of 'the apathy of the stars' in 'Ithaca' (*U* 867).[99]

Joyce's reading interests, and especially those interests that are highlighted in his work, are not by any means confined to works that echo what I have argued to be his own views. On the contrary, he investigated just as conscientiously those works which, as it were, pointed up the anomalies of the present established situation, rather than offering a fully worked out critique and programme for change.

He was fascinated, for instance, with the famous divorces and adulteries of the day. One of the items listed on the 1920 inventory of his books, *Nouveau scandale de Londres*, is an anonymous account of the second part of that divorce trial which named Sir Charles Dilke as co-respondent and thereby curtailed his political career.[100] The book records in some detail the examination of the witnesses and the verdict in which Crawford was granted a divorce on the grounds of his wife's confessed adultery with Dilke, though Dilke contested the claim and denied adultery with her.

In 'Eumaeus', Bloom passes to Stephen a 'faded photo' of 'a large sized lady, with her fleshy charms on evidence in an open fashion': his wife (*U* 758). Soon his association of thoughts runs on to adultery and to the lengthy public procedures of divorce that thrilled the newspaper readers of the day. He recalls 'the same old matrimonial tangle' and his account of the granting of decree nisi followed by decree absolute is (as Gifford and Seidman remark in *Notes for Joyce*) reminiscent of the Dilke case (*U* 760).

Bloom's mind moves swiftly on to Parnell, whose proven adultery with Kitty O'Shea ('that bitch, the English whore', as Skin-the-Goat called her earlier in the episode: *U* 755) likewise ended his career. Joyce's knowledge of Parnell needs no under-lining, though it may be thought that the emphasis on Parnell's significance as a proud, hunted figure corresponding to Joyce's own fictional self-portrayal has been so emphasized that the issues of sexual morality have been overlooked.[101]

Joyce had two biographies of Parnell in his Trieste library; Kitty O'Shea herself wrote one of them, which is understand-ably high-minded in its defence of their relationship.[102] Joyce mentions the book in his *Exiles* notes, commenting that 'her manner of writing is not Irish – nay her manner of loving is not Irish' (*E* 175). O'Shea himself was, no doubt, more typical of Ireland in Joyce's view, for his pursuit of the conventional solution of exposure and divorce. The second biography, by R. Barry O'Brien, was most likely acquired in connection with Joyce's article on Home Rule for *Il Piccola della Sera* in 1912.[103] It seems to be behind much of Joyce's use of Parnell material, more so than the 'St John Irvine' [*sic*] that he recommended to Harriet Shaw Weaver in 1926.[104] O'Brien has the full story of the Pigott trial, whose famous misspelling 'hesitence' Joyce uses repeatedly in *Finnegans Wake*; it has the image of Parnell as a hunted animal that Ellmann finds important and, more especi-ally, contains the vividly portrayed scene of Parnell's recapture of the *United Ireland* offices on 19 December 1890.[105] This description is behind Bloom's presence at the event, his help with Parnell's fallen hat and, no doubt also, behind his 'heroic' return home via the area railings of the next episode.[106]

Joyce had a copy of Esther Hallam Moorhouse's popular account of *The Story of Lady Hamilton*, telling of the equally famous adultery of Nelson, which (as Shaw points out in the Preface to *Getting Married*[107]) never aroused much moralistic censure. Joyce evidently found the Irish condemnation of

Parnell absurd and he subtly exposed that absurdity. In 'Hades'
the funeral procession passes the Statue of Nelson on O'Connell
Street just before it reaches the empty plinth where there was to
have been a statue of Parnell had his adultery not been condemned (*U* 118 and 9). Nelson's adultery had somehow been
overlooked, and so naturalized is the statue into Dublin's
landscape that the two 'elderly and pious' 'vestals' who climb it
on a day-trip in Stephen's bitter and ironic 'Parable of the Plums'
in 'Aeolus' have no sense of Nelson's sexual transgressions.
Stephen drives the point home, though, naming Nelson, to
Professor McHugh's delight, the 'onehandled adulterer' (*U*
187).

In 'Ivy Day in the Committee Room' the short-sightedness of
Irish morality is further exposed when Edward VII's proposed
visit to Dublin is the subject of conversation:

– But after all now, said Mr Lyons argumentatively, King Edward's
life, you know, is not the very ...
– Let bygones be bygones, said Mr Henchy. I admire the man
personally. He's just an ordinary knockabout like you and me. He's
fond of his glass of grog and he's a bit of a rake, perhaps, and he's a
good sportsman. Damn it, can't we Irish play fair?
– That's all very fine, said Mr Lyons. But look at the case of Parnell
now!
– In the name of God, said Mr Henchy, where's the analogy between
the two cases?   (*D* 148)

Joyce, of course, found the analogy quite to his taste and made
Molly Bloom, in her soliloquy, connect Lily Langtry with
Kitty O'Shea (*U* 889).

Joyce gathered and carefully incorporated into his writings
the minutiae of adulterous intrigue. Molly and Boylan communicate their passionate intentions (while strolling beside the
Tolka River in Bloom's company and apparently with his
knowledge) by means of hand signals (*U* 212, 874). Bartell
d'Arcy woos her suggestively with the song that Parnell and
Kitty O'Shea used as a code in their liaison (*U* 197 and 640) and
Molly tries, in vain, to communicate her interest to a 'medical in
Holles Street' by suggestive signs (*U* 199).[108]

If we attend to details, then even legitimate marriages can be
revealed as not quite legitimate at all. The Blooms, for instance,
as we learn in 'Ithaca', have Milly, their first child, in June 1889
though they were not married until October 1888, the marriage

'having been anticipatorily consummated on the 10 September of the same year' (*U* 869). Technically they cohabited, just like the Joyces and like Rowan and Bertha in *Exiles*, though with less sense of the radical nature of their action. The angry gesture of the early works remains as a matter of technical detail.

It is not clear, either, that the married couple in *Finnegans Wake* are married in any strict sense. HCE claims in Book III Chapter 3, defending himself before the four old men, that his wife is faithful and that their legitimacy is above reproach. 'With all my bawdy did I whorship, min bryllupswibe,' he claims: 'I was her hochsized, her cleavunto her everest.'[109] She has been possessively kitted out with 'yashmak' and 'snood' (*FW* 547.15–16). However the name he gives her when he 'bolts' around her his 'wedlock' is not his own, in any of its various manifestations, but rather 'Appia Lippia Pluviabilla' (*FW* 548.6). It is one of her ALP names, appropriately Roman, reinforcing hints of Mark Antony in *Julius Caesar* and *Antony and Cleopatra* elsewhere in the passage, but surely alerting us to the fact that though apparently married HCE and ALP do not share a surname.

'Ann' in Book II Chapter 1 is introduced not as a wife but as her children's 'little old mother-in-lieu, who is woman of the house' (*FW* 220.22–3). When she appears in this chapter she is, as we have seen, 'woman who did', 'helpmeat' and 'spawife to laird of Manna' (*FW* 242.25–6). It is not so much that they are married as that 'he harboured her when feme sole' (*FW* 243.9–10), and she is 'jackticktating' (jactitation is the technical term)[110] or falsely claiming to be married. No doubt as a result of Tim Finnegan's astonishing powers of resurrection drawn from the ballad of 'Finnegan's Wake', she is at once wife and widow and apparently makes these claims to secure her widow's rights.

Legitimate love, in these instances, is presented as intrinsically exceptional to the jesuitical eye, appropriately mirroring the adulterous loves which have been presented not as culpable exceptions so much as normal, forgiveable occurrences. There is an intentional blurring of the distinction between (as Stephen puts it in 'Scylla and Charybdis', echoing the title of a work by Swedenborg) 'conjugal love and its chaste delights, and scortatory love and its foul pleasures'.[111]

Matrimonial anomalies, in his reading interests and worked

into the detail of the books, provided Joyce with a means of sustaining his sense of the inadequacy of conventional marriage. To take such delight in anomaly, though, Joyce needed to have an especially accurate sense of the law itself, and of his interest therein much evidence remains. In *Stephen Hero* Lynch mocks Stephen for his attempt to seduce Emma by a simple and direct request to spend the night together. Marriage, he says, is a much more sane procedure, but Stephen is doubtful and asks him, 'Have you ever read the Form of Solemnization of Marriage in the Book of Common Prayer?' Stephen's retort is an interesting one, pointing out to Lynch the influence of this English Protestant service on Irish Catholic life. 'You should then,' he says, 'Your everyday life is Protestant: you show yourself a Catholic only when you discuss' (*SH* 206). But there is surely another point that Stephen is making here, and Joyce's text endorses, drawing our attention to the wording of the marriage service itself and to the rarity with which we trouble to investigate these forms of law which structure and control our lives.

Joyce, unlike Lynch, took the trouble to read the service and, in fact, two copies of *The Book of Common Prayer* survive in the collection of books he left in Paris.[112] Familiar phrases from the funeral service occur in the 'Hades' episode of *Ulysses* (*U* 120 and 145) but it was apparently the marriage service that most interested Joyce, for it is marked in pencil in the margin of his French edition,[113] and phrases from it, like the jokey rewording 'Till Breath us depart', occur several times in *Finnegans Wake*.[114]

Finnegans Wake, with its vast resources of vocabulary, is remarkably well supplied with legal terminology and other technical terms relating to the marital situation. Whenever the relationship of the parents is to the fore, or the games of the girls suggest temptations to marriage, or when Jaun preaches in Book III Chapter 2, the language is rich in such terms. 'Feme sole', the law of 'baron and feme', 'coverture of wife' and 'jactitation', along with other terms mentioned above, all arise and can be traced to the notebooks where Joyce gathered his material.[115] There are these references to English law but the Quran also gets a hearing; its notoriously strict proscriptions of adultery give rise to the comment, 'his Kuran never teachit her the be the owner of thyself' (*FW* 242.32).

It is no wonder that Joyce, giving an account to Harriet Shaw Weaver in 1930 of the composition of a fragment of Book III Chapter 1, should list among the books he was using a work on marriage law, Maud Crofts's *Women Under English Law*.[116] But Joyce's interest in marriage law did not only feed into his writing, for it was during 1930 and 1931 that the idea came to him of utilizing it in his own life and becoming legally married to Nora.

The idea arose when Joyce's letters show him to be engrossed in eye operations, in his campaign to boost the singing career of John Sullivan, in his work on *Finnegans Wake* Book II Chapter 2, and in his reworking of 'Anna Livia'. It seems to have been prompted by Giorgio's marriage to Helen Kastor Fleischman in December at which, as Joyce comments in a letter, 'the lawyer forgot to insert at the mairie the clauses of the contract of *séparation des biens* which by my son's request had been made a few days before so that my son becomes by French law the monarch of all he surveys'.[117]

Joyce's ironic tone was apparently his only voiced objection to this strikingly possessive and traditionalist gesture on Giorgio's part, but the marriage had the effect of making Joyce think about his own situation. He wrote to Harriet Shaw Weaver whilst 'reading a book on the legal position of women' (presumably the same book by Maud Crofts) which alerted him to the fact that his 'marriage by habit and repute' was legally binding in Scotland or New York and made him wonder about the situation in England and Ireland.[118]

Some consultations apparently took place with Miss Weaver's solicitors on the subject and Joyce followed up his enquiries until he was able to conceive a plan which required going to the lengths of taking up domicile in England.[119] He moved to Kensington that year, though he had been advised against it, and proceeded with his idea, which evidently required the kind of legal knowledge he shows off in his account of the wedding to Stanislaus:

It was very thrilling when the registrar refused to function saying we should go and get divorced but after production of law books by my solicitor he did the deed. While I was signing the roll the King was signing the new law the English call the Marry-Your-Aunt-Bill.[120]

The event was leaked to the London papers, which made the marriage particularly embarrassing for the Joyces. It is tempting to think that this embarrassment arose because the marriage required Joyce both to admit to and to repudiate the dissenting gesture of their elopement and cohabitation of 1904.

By 1931, however, as Hélène Cixous pointed out, 'there was no longer any risk of being suspected of conformism'[121] and Joyce's marriage plan seems to have included an elaborate artifice which prevented any likelihood of such a suspicion. The apparently deceitful idea was to suggest to the registrar that he and Nora had already been married in Trieste in a technically illegal way. As Joyce explained it, half-in-jest, to Stanislaus:

Having eloped with my present wife in 1904 she with my full connivance gave the name of Miss Gretta Greene which was quite good enough for il Cav. Fabbri who married us and the last gentleman in Europe il Conte Dandino who issued the legitimate certificates for the offspring, but their full connivance voided the marriage in the eyes of the English Law see Hargreave's Laws of England page 471–2 and the second ceremony was thought advisable to secure the inheritance under will.[122]

Somehow Joyce managed to secure the protection of the law without compromising his principled objection to its authority. In the language of *Exiles* he avoided 'giving the lie to [his] past life' (*E* 51) because the intricate ruse enabled him to avoid any reference to, or repudiation of, their cohabitation. Arguably, too, the 'second' marriage had an inbuilt element of deceit which called into question its conventionality if not its legitimacy, since the Joyces, like Anna Livia in the *Wake*, were guilty of 'jactitation', or the false claim to be married.

There is, then a consistent rejection of convention which links Joyce's marital gesture of 1904 to that of 1931. But there is also a difference in the kind of gesture between a straightforward refusal to conform in the first place and an elaborately contrived anarchic hyper-conformity in the second. To elope requires a kind of willed ignorance of convention and the law, but to re-marry in this way requires an unusually pedantic and precise attention to the letter of the law.

The emergence of such a precise interest can be traced throughout Joyce's writing from the *Dubliners* story, 'The Boarding House', whose Mrs Mooney, Joyce felt it necessary to point out, 'went to the priest and got a separation from him with care of the children' (*D* 66). Marriage law was a strongly present interest in the composition of *Ulysses* from the first idea

of a story about a Dublin cuckold, which occurred to Joyce in
1906. For this Joyce asked Stanislaus to send him information
about the divorce case of a Jewish man called Hunter,[123] and
such cases still fascinated him in 1922 when, as Arthur Power
reports, he was interested in another divorce between Bywaters
and Thompson.[124]

In 'Scylla and Charybdis', Mulligan facetiously uses the legal
term for separation (mixed up with Shakespeare's bequest of
his 'secondbest bed') *'separatio a mensa et a thalamo'* (*U* 261).
Eglinton says of Shakespeare that 'his legal knowledge was
great' (*U* 260), and Joyce no doubt wished to show that his
own was just as great. Yet it was not mere sciolism that
encouraged Joyce to introduce this kind of material so consistently and pointedly into his fiction. It was rather a reflection of
his developing sense of the relationship between his own views
and attitudes on sexual questions and those of the conventional
world (though in fact the 'conventional world' was changing
along with Joyce), which he chose to portray as increasingly
divided one from the other.

I have commented already on Stephen's characteristic habit
of talking in terms of the Bible or Aquinas when in fact the
drift of his argument seems more in tune with the spirit of
modern liberal thought. Stephen seems drawn in two direct-
ions at once, desiring on the one hand to appear more
'advanced' and 'progressive' than his interlocutors, but on the
other hand to be more knowledgeable than them of tradition
and the past. Robert Hand in *Exiles* arrives at a similar impasse
when he tries to talk to Richard about his elopement with
Bertha. 'Everyone knows,' he stammers 'that you ran away
years ago with a young girl ... How shall I put it?' He admits
defeat in the attempt to describe this action in a way that will be
acceptable to Richard. 'Excuse me, Richard, that is not my
opinion nor my language. I am simply using the language of
people whose opinions I don't share' (*E* 51).

Much has been recently said about Joyce's difficulties as an
Irishman forced to speak and think in the English language, the
language of his colonial rulers. Here, though, the difficulty that
Robert Hand feels is of a slightly different order: he must speak
in a language which seems to him to contain within it certain
implicit values and attitudes to which he might object. Whilst
Richard Rowan may be able to forge a new forthright view,

Robert is brought to a full stop, unwilling to throw off the 'language' of conventionalism and unable to accept it either.

Arguably it is this double tendency, to which Robert Hand gives voice, that makes Stephen speak in quotations; and the same habit of mind seems to be behind Joyce's own allusive and parodic manner, from the ironic 'modern note' in the *Chamber Music* poems to the more pronounced conflict between language and meaning in the later works.

As we have seen, books like Albert's *L'Amour libre*, together with a tradition of relatively modern secular liberal thought, inform *Stephen Hero*, though discussion of the marriage service arises. In *Finnegans Wake* the informing base of liberal ideas and attitudes is much less evident and the fragments of established order and convention seem all that remains. The most striking book bearing on the marriage issue that Joyce read and used during the composition of *Finnegans Wake* is surely the book of matrimonial casuistry by M.M. Matharan that he left in his Paris flat and which Connolly, in annotating those Paris books, considered worthy of an independent scholarly study.[125]

Matharan's book is an orthodox Catholic account of marital law, published in 1893. Though civil divorce was reintroduced in France in 1894 and so not strictly current, the book might have been of interest to anyone concerned to investigate the premises and traditions on which marital law was based. It consists of some 500 cases followed by approved judgements on them, drawing on a tradition of Catholic casuistry stretching back to writers like the seventeenth-century Spaniard Sanchez, whose work is best remembered for the detailed and explicit attention it pays to marital sexuality. Matharan is concerned, above all, with questions of legitimacy, recording events before, during or after the marriage ceremony that may invalidate it in the eyes of the Church. Characteristically over 200 of the cases deal with various 'impediments' in the performance of the service or in the 'consanguinuity' of the partners that may legitimize the otherwise unthinkable separation or divorce. Many of the cases deal with the sexual relations of the partners, but not within modern terms of reference where the biological or emotional well-being of the partners is the primary consideration. For Matharan the sexual act is understood as a rendering of the conjugal debt incurred in the marriage contract and the validity of specific acts is established or challenged in such terms.

Joyce may well have consulted Matharan for a Catholic Church view of his forthcoming marriage, but its most direct relevance to the fiction is to a passage in *Finnegans Wake* Book III Chapter 4 probably written in 1929,[126] which enacts a typical case in full.

The *Wake*'s English is no easier to unravel than Matharan's clerical Latin, but basically the case discusses the rights of Honuphrius (HCE) to exact the conjugal debt from Anita (ALP) and it occurs between their depiction in the copulatory 'second position of discordance' (*FW* 564.1–2) and 'third position of concord' (*FW* 582.30). It is the kind of question that Matharan deals with in cases 458–482 and, as in Matharan, a narrative of the case is given, followed by a judgement.

Joyce makes his case absurdly complicated, its background including the consanguineous infidelity of Honuphrius with his three children, here given as Felicia (the name of the heroine of an erotic novelette by André de Nerciat),[127] Eugenius and Jeremias. Anita's virtue is no less compromised, she having indulged herself with Mauritius and Magravius, who roughly correspond to Iago and Michael Cassio with Honuphrius as a complaisant Othello. Anita has been given a dispensation from her matrimonial obligations by a priest, Michael Cerularius (otherwise leader of the schism that founded the Greek Ortho- dox Church[128]), by whom she has also been seduced. Despite her further involvements with the four historians (Gregorius, Leo, Vitellius, and Macdugalius) and the twelve jurors (the Sullivani) she would accede to Honuphrius's request in order to protect the virtue of Felicia, were it not that it might lead Eugenius and Jeremias into reprehensible conduct. She has also been warned by Fortissa of Honuphrius's taste for flagellation. The narrative part of the case ends with the question: 'Has he hegemony and shall she submit?' (*FW* 573.32).

For the judgement, this Freudian family-sexual whirl is converted, in the metaphor of the debt, to the question of a cheque numbered 'DUD 1132' (*FW* 574.26). Under Judge Doyle (apparently a representative of the Irish parliament) the question becomes one of whether this debt, having been paid to the senior partner of a business (the father, or perhaps for the last sexual act), might need to be paid again to the junior partner (the son, or perhaps for the next sexual act). Anita (now called Ann Doyle) interposes that she has rendered the service in the past in exchange for extra payments of flowers ('pinkwilliams'), cosmetics ('crème-de-citron') and confectionery ('marshmallow') (*FW* 575.15–17). She offers to enter into a new contract tomorrow, but Judge Jeremy Doyle, claiming her contractual incapacity as a woman and that of HCE (now called Pepigi) as a corpse, concludes the affair inconclusively by saying that such a contract would be illegal.

Joyce's interest in working the fiendishly complex identities and relationships of his *Finnegans Wake* 'characters' into this strict casuistical formula is not, perhaps, immediately clear but it seems to me to be highly characteristic of one feature of the *Wake*. At the level of the single word or sentence, meaning in *Finnegans Wake* is so plural and indeterminable that Joyce frequently resorts to pre-existing narrative structures (whether they be the fables of ant and grasshopper or fox and grapes or the story of Buckley and the Russian General that Joyce's father told him[129]) to lend coherence in larger narrative units. We might even wish to argue that, with meaning so uncertain in Wakean neologism and word-play, the only sure way for explication to proceed is by reference to the relative fixity of words, phrases, and narratives or to pre-existing arguments either in or outside the *Wake* itself.

Rather than by the representation of some new reality or the explication of some modern, radical critique, Joyce's engagement with marital questions in this passage from the *Wake* consists in adverting our attention to the language of the law itself and investigating or disrupting it through parodic and ironic means. So strong is the impulse to penetrate to the heart of these established orders that Joyce chose what was perhaps the most pedantic and conceptually pure example of the established view that was available to him. Matharan encodes a form of law that no longer had currency even at the time it was written, a full fifty years before Joyce's use of it. Joyce's recognition of its importance in understanding family relationships has something of the force of a scholarly as well as an aesthetic discovery.

The separation between Wakean chaos and contradiction and the traditional, legalistic ordering that stands in the shadows behind it is extreme. It represents a further stage of development in the kind of argument-thorough-parody that we saw in the 'marriage of trees' section of the 'Cyclops' episode of *Ulysses*. Like parody, Wakean linguistic complexity diverts our attention away from any obvious authorial statement or position and towards pre-existing statements or positions, exposing their inner contradictions, insufficiencies, or irrelevancies, and highlighting what is called here with anarchistic amusement the 'jurisfiction' of the law (*FW* 574.34).

That Joyce's last work functions both to bring before our attention and to challenge or subvert traditional structures and orders may help us to account for one of the best-known interests displayed by Joyce in the *Wake*: the interest in Viconian theory. That interest was first suggested to readers of Joyce by Samuel Beckett in his contribution to the *Our Exagmination* collection of essays published in 1929, but Beckett paid attention to Vico's relationship with Giordano Bruno, to his sense of the importance of poetry as 'the first operation of the human mind' and did not discuss the question of marriage that forms so strong a part of Vico's theory of the origin of societies.[130]

According to Vico's system, in the earliest times man lived in a state of bestial primitive promiscuity until, surprised and frightened by divine thunder, he felt shame and hastened to copulate under covers (*nuptiae*). Ultimately, for in Viconian theory of language words and concepts evolve from their concrete indicative origins more complex and abstract forms, these *nuptiae* became the nuptial institutions that characterize all civilized societies.[131] Solemn marriage, burial and this fear of a divine authority are common elements in all societies, Vico argued, and Joyce clearly exploits such Viconian formulations in *Finnegans Wake*, referring to 'sollemn nuptialism, sallemn sepulture and providential divining' (*FW* 599.12–13).

Vico was of use for *Finnegans Wake* because of the sense, in both his philology and his ethnographic history, of the immanence of the past in the present and because of his now famous cyclic ordering of world history. But perhaps also his sense of the origin of marriage provided support for the growing sense in Joyce's later writings of the arbitrariness of such institutions. For in Vico marriage is not 'instituted by God' (or at least not in the way that a believing Christian might accept). It is not thought of as the product of natural human desires nor is it common to all ages of human or even ape society. Matrimonial institutions are not seen as evolving towards a more perfect form where the needs of society and biological nature will be reconciled. In the Viconian model marriage arises suddenly and arbitrarily from human fears and runs in inevitable contradiction to biological desires. It is not, as some kinds of liberal might like to think, eradicable, but neither is it an institution whose prescriptions can be seen as anything other than obliquely related to human needs.

As Joyce's writing developed from a relatively conventional and explicit fictional treatment of marriage questions to a more complex and elaborated linguistic and stylistic response, it seems that he did not altogether abandon his modern attitude to marriage. Indeed we have seen that to some extent modern aspects of style like irony, allusiveness and parody arose in his work whilst he attempted to treat modern sexual attitudes. We might say that his critique changed from a relatively direct one, or one couched in the affective appeal of his writings, to one which functions in relation to the language and detail of established laws and concepts, and which, through devices of semantic play, seems both to bring before our attention and to ridicule and disrupt the forms of order that his youthful mind had rejected.

2 *Emissio seminis inter vas naturale*

The new science of sexuality

The institution of marriage, as I outlined in the last chapter, was increasingly challenged throughout the nineteenth century, its prescriptive ideals falling foul of the newer rational-istic and humanistic mood of the times. Marriage was a focus for a wide variety of contemporary concerns but the debates about its nature and validity were not isolated. They were allied to equally important changes in attitudes to the whole of the sexual life. We might say that it is a new emphasis on questions of sexuality, as opposed to questions of marital legitimacy, as well as a new understanding of what sexuality might be, that most characterizes the modern scene.

One way in which writers like Freud, Krafft-Ebing and Havelock Ellis may be seen as inaugurating a modern under-standing is in their common desire to establish a new scientific or pseudo-scientific basis for the investigation of sexuality. Such movement towards scientificity is, in Foucault's account, a more significant development than any change from Vic-torian 'repression' to modern 'toleration'. However it is also important to note that the work of these writers seems to recognize the importance of a new idea of sexuality: an idea that seemed somehow unavailable to the previous generation of writers.

In a characteristically Victorian work, like William Acton's much discussed *Functions and Disorders of the Reproductive System*, there is no real concept of sexuality as distinct from reproduction. 'In the following pages,' Acton remarks in a revealing footnote, 'the words, "generative", "sexual", "repro-ductive", will be used synonymously.'[1] Youthful sexual feelings and masturbation, for example, are treated by him as clinical disorders in their deviation from the strict reproductive norm. On the other hand, at the root of a modern attitude is Freud's notion of an erotic instinct not bound by reproductive utility but developing, by its own laws, from perfectly normal childish sensuality, and only arriving at reproductive maturity through a number of developmental stages, in response to both unconscious and external forces. The *Three Essays on the Theory of Sexuality* (though Freud denied that they should be considered an adequate sexual theory in themselves[2]) nevertheless provided the concept of a 'polymorphously perverse' sexual instinct, and a radical shift of attention away from *phylogenesis* (the development of the race) to *ontogenesis* (the development of the individual).

Even more typical of a modern sexual attitude, though less central to the Freud canon, is the essay written in 1908 entitled 'Civilised Sexual Morality'. Here Freud spells out the difference between the sexual instinct and reproduction, arguing 'that man's sexual instinct is not at all primarily meant to serve purposes of reproduction but is intended to furnish certain forms of gratification'.[3] In order to make clear that the part of sexual experience which relates to reproduction (and which had hitherto been recognized by orthodox opinion) was only a small and specific part, Freud invented an appropriately qualified term to describe it: 'heterosexual genital love'.

The discovery of this new and enlarged concept of sexuality was partly the result of contemporary investigations of sexual perversity. Krafft-Ebing's *Psychopathia Sexualis* is precisely this: one of a number of sexological investigations of the perverse carried out, as one historian of the subject points out, in the decadent atmosphere of Germany under Kaiser Wilhelm II.[4] Krafft-Ebing, to whom we owe the familiar taxonomy of perverse sexual acts, set out to categorize such activities within a traditional frame of reference and not in any sense to inaugurate new ideas of normality. For him the perversities were 'functional signs of degeneracy',[5] the precise function from which they 'degenerated' being that of reproduction. Yet in Freud's eyes this concept of 'functional degeneracy' was shown up as unsatisfactory, and the familiar catalogue of abnormalities came to be seen as relatively normal, or at least as credible and explicable parts of the erotic life.

In the work of the best-known English sexologist, Havelock Ellis, we can see a similar interest in the perversions as the key to a new understanding of sexuality. It is significant that he began his famous *Studies in the Psychology of Sex* as an attempt to mount, with J.A. Symonds, a defence of homosexuality.[6] In the later volumes, where Ellis tries to conclude a theory of the range of sexual experiences he has described, he chooses a term, 'sexual symbolism', which, though it retains the sense that these experiences are somehow secondary or derivative in character, goes some way to accommodate them within the bounds of normal or acceptable experience.

There are, then, several aspects of the transition from nineteenth- to twentieth-century attitudes to sexuality that seem particularly relevant to Joyce's fiction: this sense of new interest in sexuality; the growth of a sexual science; and the development of a new concept of sexuality worked out in distinction from traditional associations between sexuality and reproduction and in relation to new enquiries into sexual perversity.

Joyce, I have argued, was interested in medicine, not only in relation to his shortlived hopes for a medical career or out of a negligible or insignificant 'taste for the medical vocabulary',[7] but as an important part of his artistic self-image. Medical science, I have argued, offered him a more satisfactory way of understanding his human nature than the Church. It is hardly surprising, then, that the medical terminology that appears in the fiction is frequently related to sexual medicine, from the word '*foetus*' that Stephen sees scrawled in the anatomy theatre of his father's old college (*P* 92) to the pseudo-Ibsenite desire to examine the 'syphilitic contagion of Europe'. In the early works and letters medical metaphors provide Joyce with the means by which he articulates his criticisms of society. Stephen's use of the language of reproductive medicine is evident at some of the most crucial moments in his theorizing about art, or, as he puts it, 'the phenomena of artistic conception, artistic gestation and artistic reproduction' (*P* 214).

In *Ulysses* the medical interest ceases to be so clearly metaphorical and takes on more of a life of its own. Bloom is frequently exercized by issues relating to childbirth, remembering Molly's labour and taking the trouble to visit Mina Purefoy, so that one whole episode takes place in a maternity hospital. Sex doctors seem to turn up with frequency, from the Dr Hy Franks who advertises in 'Lestrygonians' (*U* 193) and Molly's midwife Mrs Thornton, whom Bloom recalls (*U* 205), to the Dr Collins that Molly remembers in 'Penelope': 'that dry old stick Dr Collins for womens diseases on Pembroke road your vagina he called it' (*U* 915). A birth is an institutionalized occasion in Joyce's works, from that of the Purefoy child to that of Finn MacCool who, as we are told at one point in *Finnegans Wake*, was not so much born as 'took place before the inter-natural convention of catholic midwives' (*FW* 128.25–6). Bloom is intrigued by the aphrodisiac qualities of oysters (*U* 222 and 632–3) and of chocolate (*U* 640–1) and marchpane (*U* 649). Sexological discourse is plentiful not just in 'Oxen of the Sun' but in 'Cyclops', for instance, where one of the parodic inserts apes a medical report on the supposed orgasm of the hanged man (*U* 394) and in 'Circe' where Bloom's sexual personality is diagnozed by Mulligan and Dixon (*U* 613–14). Bloom's father Virag appears down the brothel chimney in 'Circe' and, before he finally unscrews his head and departs with Bloom's erotic alter ego Henry Flower, he offers a magnificently sage and spurious commentary on the scene, peppered with sexological terminology. He has, we are told, written a 'Fun-damentals of Sexology or the Love Passion' in seventeen volumes (*U* 632).

It is often a kind of popular or pseudo-science that informs *Ulysses*. One book Joyce had in his library was by a French doctor called Galopin and was entitled *Le Parfum de la femme*, a loosely psychosexual account of the importance of the sense of smell.[8] Galopin describes the smell of the onanist as like rancid butter, and Joyce evidently felt the need to go one step further in descriptive precision and in culinary analogy, having Bloom think, in the second half of 'Nausicaa' that Molly gives off a smell during her menstrual period like 'potted herrings gone stale' and that his own recently shed semen is like 'celery sauce' (*U* 489).

Interest in the science of sexuality makes Joyce's writing modern in the first way I defined but what of its modernity in relation to the new concept of sexuality? Stephen defines his aesthetic modernity at one point in *A Portrait* in a way that may help us here.

– The Greek, the Turk, the Chinese, the Copt, the Hottentot, said Stephen, all admire a different type of female beauty. That seems to be a maze out of which we cannot escape. I see however two ways out. One is this hypothesis: that every physical quality admired by men in women is in direct connection with the manifold functions of women for the propagation of the species. It may be so. The world, it seems, is drearier than even you, Lynch, imagined. For my part I dislike that way out. It leads to eugenics rather than to esthetic. It leads you out of the maze into a new gaudy lectureroom where MacCann, with one hand on *The Origin of Species* and the other hand on the new testament, tells you that you admired the great flanks of Venus because you felt that she would bear you burly offspring and admired her great breasts because you felt that she would give good milk to her children and yours. (*P* 212–3)

One part of Stephen's argument is designed to elevate purely aesthetic over biological conceptions of beauty but there is another sense in which his rejection of a reproductive utilitarianism, his determination to define beauty in terms of the 'relations of the sensible' (*P* 213) and the 'enchantment of the heart' (*P* 217), if applied not just to artistic questions but to questions of sexual-object choice, make a convincing parallel to twentieth-century notions of sexuality.

In what remains of this chapter I shall investigate Joyce's reading of scientific and other literature of sexuality with this sense of modernity in mind, though, as we found in his reading on marriage and of his use of these books in the fiction, the sources of his modernity and his means of expressing it are not always straightforward.

Specific and generic onanism

In a letter to Grant Richards on the printer's censorship of *Dubliners*, Joyce commented on the arbitrariness of the objections that had been made to his work. Certain passages had been condemned but exceptional parts of others had apparently passed without objection. 'The more subtle inquisitor,' Joyce noted, 'will denounce *An Encounter* the enormity of which the printer cannot see because he is, as I said, a plain blunt man'.[9] In making this complaint Joyce did not, of course, wish his work to be censored any more stringently than it had been, but his attack on the 'plain blunt man' and his approval of 'the more subtle inquisitor' is highly revealing. It shows that Joyce realized that the Church and its inquisitors were indeed rather sophisticated in their knowledge of sexual enormities. This is a phenomenon observed by Havelock Ellis, who commented that the Jesuit Sanchez had paved the way in the examination of sexual perversity. Joyce's attitude to the inquisitor also helps us to understand the presence of certain items in his library.

The work that stands out in this connection is a book entitled *Onanisme* by Dr Paul Garnier. Ellmann noticed this book in his account of Joyce's library and talks of it as if it were interesting to Joyce merely as a convenient source of information for his description of masturbation in the 'Nausicaa' episode of *Ulysses*.[10] However Garnier, on closer inspection, offers little information on what we might call masturbation. What strikes a modern reader most forcibly is the way he organizes his material and the understanding of sexuality that such an organization seems to imply.

Garnier's ideas on the subject are dependent upon two, arguably related, traditions. The first is the disturbing theory of masturbatory insanity which achieved prominence with Tissot's *L'Onanisme* in 1760, outlined by Edward Hare in a now famous article in *The Journal of Mental Science*.[11] According-ing to this theory masturbation is held both to be a disease itself and the cause of a wide variety of other physiological and psychological disturbances. Even William Acton was sus-picious of its most extreme manifestations in work like that of John Laws Milton on 'spermatorrhoea'.[12]

The other tradition is the Catholic orthodoxy of condemning all kinds of non-reproductive sexuality, which is given an added spice in Garnier's treatment where all are condemned as types of the sin of Onan in Genesis. In this Garnier's immediate pre-decessor is Louis Bergeret, whose *Des Fraudes dans l'accomplisse-ment des fonctions génératrices* was widely known for its opposition to birth control.[13] Garnier's book, then, is not merely about masturbation but seems to present or reflect a whole theory of sexuality. He writes against '*tous les obstacles artificiels apportées à la génération humaine*' ('all artificial obsta-cles to human generation') and these do not just include contraceptive practices. There is no distinction drawn between the conscious planning of the contraceptive act and what we usually understand as the unconscious compulsions of the sexually perverse act.

As in Krafft-Ebing, perversities are classified but they are not, as in Krafft-Ebing, held to be kinds of particular deviant personality. In Garnier perverse or non-reproductive sexual acts are all described as different forms of onanism whether 'vulvo-vaginal', 'buccal', 'mammary', 'anal', or 'bestial' in their working. Garnier's is a theory, then, not of specific but of generic onanism, an almost hysterical, hyper-Catholic Krafft-Ebingism, combining an investigation of perversity with a strong-principled objection to contraceptive intent.

In the course of the book there arises a term which distinguishes between legitimate and non-legitimate sexual acts quite as precisely as the Freudian notion of 'heterosexual genital love'. This phrase, Garnier says, is borrowed from the theologian Nardi and it defines the onanistic act as '*effusio seminis extra vas per voluntarium et violentam copulae interruptionem ad generationem impediendam*' ('the ejaculation of the semen outside the vagina by the voluntary and violent interruption of copulation to impede reproduction'). For Garnier this is more than just the contraceptive practice of *coitus interruptus*. It includes all perverse or indulgent sexuality.

Garnier was not, of course, Joyce's only source of information on Catholic Church attitudes to sexuality. Joyce had his own casuistical authority in Matharan's book on marriage. Matharan, too, condemns non-reproductive sexuality and has a precise formulation for distinguishing between legitimate and illegitimate acts. He says '*Mortale est quidquid per se inducit ad effusionem seminis extra conjunctem naturalem*' ('whatever of itself leads to the ejaculation of semen outside of natural coupling is a mortal sin'). Cases 483–497 of Matharan's book all deal with the problem of distinguishing legitimate from illegitimate sexual acts in these terms.[14]

Joyce was apparently fascinated with this kind of discussion and introduced into his working notes for *Exiles* a brief inquisition into whether Bertha commits a sexual act with Robert and, if so, what kind of act she commits.

Bertha is reluctant to give the hospitality of her womb to Robert's seed. For this reason she would like more a child of his by another woman than a child of him by her. Is this true? For him the question of child or no child is immaterial. Is her reluctance to yield even when the possibility of a child is removed this same reluctance or a survival of it or a survival of the fears (purely physical) of a virgin? It is certain that her instinct can distinguish between concessions and for her the supreme concession is what the fathers of the church call *emissio seminis inter vas naturale*. As for the accomplishment of the act otherwise externally, by friction, or in the mouth, the question needs to be scrutinized still more, would she allow her lust to carry her so far as to receive his emission of seed in any other opening of the body where it could not be acted upon, when once emitted, by the forces of her secret flesh?   (*E* 173)

The primary concern of the passage is to investigate what is rather delicately called Bertha's 'reluctance' and it is important to note that Joyce, when he came to write the play, achieved his most striking dramatic effects precisely by leaving unstated and mysterious the nature of Robert's and Bertha's desires and acts. There is, however, something peculiarly Joycean about this impromptu sexual confessional which helps place his writings in relation to Garnier's and Matharan's scheme of reference.

It is, first of all, rather striking that Joyce uses the identical terms which are offered in Garnier to distinguish between sexual acts, quoting, like him, the casuistical formula and referring to non-reproductive acts in a very similar language.[15] Robert Hand is characterized as sexually modern in our precise sense since 'for him the question of child or no child is immaterial'. Though Joyce may not present him as an especially heroic character for this indifference to reproduction, it is evident that he avoids a Garnier-like condemnation of Robert and is fully conscious of the implications of these terms of reference not just for condemnation within the established morality but for defining modern liberal sexual mores. The investigation of Bertha's feelings also involves a kind of inversion of the Catholic hierarchy of sins since, for her, in the modern situation of an adulteress, a 'lustful', 'perverse', 'onanistic' or non-reproductive sexual act is less of a 'concession' than a more conventionally legitimate one.

The validity of the casuistical phrase with its precise denomination of the legitimate sexual act is recognized here, but the condemnatory connotations are distanced through the phrase 'what the fathers of the church call'. When the phrase '*emissio seminis inter vas naturale*' reappears in *Ulysses* that distancing is made more apparent, for in *Ulysses* it is Father Conmee who is shown pondering the confessional implications of a fiction he might write about the adulterous Countess of Belvedere:

Who could know the truth? Not the jealous Lord Belvedere and not her confessor if she had not committed adultery fully, *eiaculatio seminis inter vas naturale mulieris*, with her husband's brother. (*U* 286)

Here, unlike in *Exiles*, the reader's interest is aroused not just by the nature of the act and the participants' feelings; Conmee's casuistical phrase alerts the reader's attention to an unfamiliar codification of sexual practices. Joyce's knowledge of and interest in the phrase, his sense of its importance to the conceptualization of sexuality, is confirmed and there is the extra sense, characteristic of the operation of *Ulysses*, that part of his artistic intention is to highlight the phrase itself and its implications for the upheaval in contemporary ideas.

Joyce had, in fact, long been interested in specific as well as generic onanism. No doubt he and his brother talked over the question, for Stanislaus records thoughts on his own experience in his diary in a number of entries on 'involuntary emission' and 'orgic dreams', and 'a certain sexual aberration which once obsessed me'.[16] Stanislaus was a little anxious about these aspects of his sexual experience. 'I find involuntary emissions, besides being painful in their after-effects, very upsetting,' he writes; 'I do not feel physically weaker or ill, but my energy is deranged, my nerves uncontrolled.' He thought (if we can judge by a parody of the song 'Mr Dooley' which he wrote some years before Joyce's more celebrated version called 'Dooleysprudence') that masturbation could have damaging effects on society as well as on each individual constitution:

> For 'it's masturbation
> That kills a nation,'
> Said Mr Dooley-ooley-ooley-oo.[17]

There must have been some difference of opinion between the brothers for Joyce, in a letter written only a few months after Stanislaus's diary entries, reports approvingly of Nora's sexual life: 'she has told me something of her youth, and admits the gentle art of self-satisfaction'.[18] The well-known letters that Joyce wrote to Nora in 1909 testify to the continuation of an interest in this subject between them, uninhibitedly celebrating an indulgence in 'frigging' without a thought for its sinfulness in the eyes of writers like Garnier.

When it came to his fiction Joyce used his interest in the subject to good effect. In *Stephen Hero* the sexual propagandist in Stephen emerges to explode the nationalist Madden's pious belief in the chastity of the Irish. They are chaste 'because they do it by hand', he says, with a characteristic combination of periphrasis and outrageousness (*SH* 60).

That chastity is an impossibility and that the prevalence of masturbation cannot be denied, seem to be the two motivating ideas for Stephen and it is that kind of attitude that surely underlies *A Portrait of the Artist*, though (no doubt as a result of the experience of trying to publish *Dubliners*) in *A Portrait* the periphrasis is more marked and Stephen's anxieties are highlighted more than his radical convictions. As in Stanislaus's diary, the term 'orgies' is used (an interesting conflation of a lonely and a group experience repeated in 'Eumaeus': *U* 748) to describe masturbatory sexual fantasies. Stephen's masturbation is, no doubt, the 'wretched habit' which the Priest to whom he confesses at the end of Chapter 3 singles out for attention (*P* 148).

Masturbation is a frequent issue in *Ulysses*. Mulligan reductively satirizes Stephen's theory that the sexual personalities of all Shakespeare's characters have their roots in Shakespeare himself by staging an impromptu 'immorality' play entitled 'Everyman His Own Wife or A Honeymoon in the Hand' (*U* 278). Mulligan's irreverence is at issue here more than any consideration of the dangers or delights of solitary vice. Such considerations do, however, have their place in *Ulysses*. Bloom finds himself in a hallucinatory exchange with the picture of the nymph over Molly's bed, which reappears in 'Circe'. He is accused of having 'profaned our silent shade', like Onan committing his indiscretion 'on our virgin sward'. The hallucination apparently recalls some youthful incident excited by 'a price list of their hosiery' and a girl called Lotty Clarke. Bloom replies that he was 'simply satisfying a need' (*U* 657–9).

The suspicion of masturbation is never far away in *Finnegans Wake* either. We hear of 'Bygmester Finnegan, of the Stuttering Hand' (*FW* 4.18) and his fall from the ladder echoes 'mastabatoom, mastabadtomm, when a mon merries his lute is all long. For whole the world to see' (*FW* 6.10–13) and Hosty is 'on the verge of self abyss' (*FW* 40.23). The practice extends beyond boundaries of social class: 'secret satieties and onanymous letters make the great unwatched as bad as their betters' (*FW* 435.31–2). Indeed the ubiquity of auto-eroticism matches that of adultery which we noted in the last chapter, for in the *Scribbledehobble* notebook Joyce (in a rather reductive version of the creation of Eve) notes that 'Adam fucked himself'.[19]

The theme is a widespread one in Joyce but nowhere more prominent than in the 'Nausicaa' episode of *Ulysses* which is renamed, in the recapitulation of the day's events that we are given in 'Ithaca', the 'rite of Onan' (*U* 860). Bloom's masturbation has often seemed a puzzle to critics, both those who find it unequivocally exceptionable and proof of either Joyce's or Bloom's moral bankruptcy and those who find it rather poignant and sad. The view offered by Fritz Senn in Hart and Hayman's collection of critical essays on *Ulysses* may serve as a typical attitude to the events in the episode. 'Bloom resorts to the most isolated form of sexual gratification,' writes Senn, 'an event made more poignant by his realization that a more vital and more mutually fulfilling embrace has recently been staged at home.'[20] For Senn it is 'cheap satisfaction brought out in a style of cheap fiction' and yet Bloom somehow retains our sympathy and some integrity from the episode, so much so that Richard Ellmann describes 'Nausicaa' as an episode of 'heroic naughtiness' where 'for the first time in literature masturbation becomes heroic'.[21] Ellmann's view may seem a little overstated for, if we are to think of *Ulysses* in terms of literary genre and tradition, then it is surely mock-heroic here. If we are, on the other hand, to find Bloom's masturbation sympathetic, then some further justification beyond Ellmann's observation of Bloom's age and Gerty's youth and his praise of the act as 'a way of joining ideal and real' must be provided to support the claim. Yet Ellmann's view of the episode is an attractive one, not least because it implicitly recognizes that, just because Joyce describes Bloom's masturbation in terms of the sin of Onan, his discursive liveliness does not necessarily lead us to think of it as a sin.

Heroic or not, we must first of all realize that Joyce presents Bloom's act as a fundamentally modern one in the terms that I have outlined. The whole structure of the chapter is organized (and described on the plan Joyce sent to Gorman and Gilbert) according to an opposition drawn from sexual science, not from past models of literary form. The contrast in styles is explained as a contrast between 'tumescence' and 'detumescence'.[22] These are the identical terms that Havelock Ellis used to describe the character of sexual pleasure and they are evidently highly modern in their attention to the endosomatic gratificatory

aspect of the act rather than its possible reproductive consequences. In this we might see Bloom as a proper hero of sexual
modernity for, since Masters and Johnson, masturbation has
become a familiar index of sexual normality, or, as one historian
puts it, 'the ultimate criterion of correct sexual behaviour'.[23]

Bloom's masturbation may be lonely in this precise sense but
we do not need to think of it as sadly or traumatically isolated
from any form of human contact. On the contrary, one of the
most remarkable features of Bloom's onanism, though no one
has cared to make anything of it, is that this act is pointedly
performed with another person. In this sense it is not just as a
masturbatory act that we need think of it but as what Garnier
calls an *onanisme à deux*. Gerty is not merely a passive object of
Bloom's voyeurism or complicit through her coquetry and
exhibitionism alone. We are told that she 'swung her leg more
in and out in time' (*U* 470) and that she felt 'that irritation
against her stays' (*U* 470).[24] Ultimately she shares a sort of
minor key bodily gratification: 'they were all breathless with
excitement as it went higher and higher and she had to lean
back more and more to look up after it, high, high, almost out
of sight, and her face was suffused with a divine, an entrancing
blush from straining back' (*U* 477). Bloom recognizes her
coincident self-stimulation and has a curiously Garnier-like
technical term for it, thinking of 'friction of the position' (*U*
491). In 'Circe', where exaggeration is the norm, we are told
that she lost her virginity during the course of the act (*U* 572).
Many of these specific details could have been drawn from
Garnier who describes female mechanical stimulations of
various kinds, but, more importantly, armed with the concept
of 'generic onanism' that we need to understand Garnier, we
can, I think, get a sense of what Joyce was trying to do in this
episode.

Once we recognize that for Garnier and Matharan, as indeed
for Freud, the fundamental distinction is not between sexual
acts performed singly and those performed by two people
together, but between the endorsed reproductive act and all
others, and once we recognize that, in the modern sense, almost
all sexuality is to be understood as onanistic inasmuch as its goal
is gratificatory not reproductive, then there seems to be an
important similarity between the act performed by Bloom and
Gerty and that performed simultaneously by Molly and Boylan

at 7 Eccles Street. Both couplings are onanistic in Garnier's sense. So broad is the term that we might even employ it to say that, in the simultaneity (and of course the degree of complicity) of their acts, Bloom and Molly experience a kind of *onanisme à deux* across Dublin. 'Nausicaa' might be read not as a poignant moment of loneliness and alienation for Bloom but as a perversely triumphant extension of his marital sexuality: a shared gratificatory act (albeit one that includes other partners) performed on a huge geographical scale.

The partly private, partly public act has a number of analogies in Joyce's work. These include moments whose import is obviously sexual, such as the observed sin in the park that is endlessly discussed in *Finnegans Wake*, or the sordid observed masturbation in 'An Encounter':

> – I say! look what he's doing!
> As I neither answered nor raised my eyes
> Mahoney exclaimed again:
> – I say … He's a queer old josser!   (*D* 26)

We may not need to go as far as David Hayman and see a masturbatory incident in the scene where Stephen reclines on the beach in 'Proteus'.[25] However Stephen's climactic vision on the beach at the end of Chapter 4 of *A Portrait* has often been discussed as analogous to 'Nausicaa'. Usually 'Nausicaa' is thought of as an ironic deflation of the earlier incident but both might be seen as sexual acts presented in the guise of *onanisme à deux*. Stephen's experience is indeed one of relationship with a girl and yet of profound solitude, a lyrical form of the contradiction that is exploited in 'Nausicaa', where the language of romantic idealism is starkly set against the extreme form of individual organic gratification in which Bloom and Gerty are engaged. Richard Ellmann says of Molly's lovers that 'only the most rigorous interpretation of infidelity' would allow them to be classed as partners in adultery.[26] In the last chapter I argued that Joyce's fiction relied upon our recognition of such rigorous definitions to a considerable extent but, rather than using them as a means of condemning his characters' failings, Joyce showed the inadequacy of the definitions. A similar situation greets us here. Joyce needed the precise definitions provided by casuistical investigations of sexuality to allow him to imagine characters and situations like these and his fiction turns our attention not just to these characters and situations but to those definitions themselves. The fiction is not tied to the moral values implicitly carried in the terminology it employs. It was by applying the most rigorous definition of '*emissio seminis inter vas naturale*' that Joyce managed to display the extent of everyday, observable sexual experience that falls outside this narrow ideal. Likewise, by borrowing the curious notion of *onanisme à deux*, he was able to present kinds of sexual relationship in which masturbatory acts could be shown to be normal, if not ubiquitous, and apparently normal acts inherently or fundamentally onanistic.

Copulation without population

For Joyce, as for the traditionalist Catholic writers in his library, onanism served as a focus for a whole new attitude to sexuality. Yet masturbation (which I have called specific onanism) was not the only important part of that new attitude. The most apparent threat to writers like Garnier and Matharan was not a campaign of enthusiastic and vociferous masturbators, so much as the increasing public acceptance of the techniques and justifications of the birth-control movement. That movement, founded in the rather inhumane economic theories of the Reverend Thomas Malthus,[27] gained a boost from the rationalists and feminists of the nineteenth century[28] and its principles are now entrenched as an intrinsic part of the personal, family and social planning of modern society.[29] Bertrand Russell put a strong emphasis on the role of advances in contraception in shaping new thinking: 'Contraceptives have altered the whole aspect of sex and marriage,' he claimed, 'and have made distinctions necessary which could formerly have been ignored.'[30] Whether we think of the technology, morality and publicity of contraception as cause or effect of modern liberal morality, the two are inextricably tied together.

Joyce could not but have had a strong awareness of the birth-control issue. It was high on the agenda in those literary circles where his work found an audience. Harriet Shaw Weaver, as her biographers tell us, was in 1912 a regular attender of the 'Freewoman Discussion Circle', whose programme 'included talks on eugenics by Mrs Havelock Ellis'.[31]

In his Trieste library, Joyce had a number of books which reflect the contemporary discussions on the subject. Shaw, for instance, in his Preface to *Getting Married*, refers to the 'present sterilization of marriage' and the resultant dangers of a population of reduced quality and vigour.[32] Joyce's bound collection of Fabian Tracts includes one by Sidney Webb on 'The Decline of the Birthrate' written in 1907. Webb attributed this decline to 'a deliberate volition in the regulation of the married state'. He thought that it was the abler sections of the community who were most likely to employ this regulation and, like Shaw, feared that 'race deterioration' might be the result. He nevertheless concluded broadly in favour of contraception, finding it 'difficult on any rationalist morality to formulate any blame of the married couple for the deliberate regulation of their family'.[33]

These reasonable, largely progressive Edwardian attitudes were not Joyce's only reading on the subject. Among his volumes there were the principled objections to all non-procreative sexuality voiced by Garnier and Matharan. There were also Tolstoy's fundamentalist objections to the iniquities of modern marriage. Of child-bearing Tolstoy complains that 'instead of being the aim and justification of marriage it has become an impediment to the pleasurable continuance of amorous relations and consequently, both among married and unmarried people (instructed by exponents of medical science), the employment of means to prevent the birth of children has spread'.[34]

Such an attitude on the part of a writer with radical moral instincts and from such a comparatively recent time may seem strange to modern ears. The work which, perhaps equally surprisingly, comes closest to the modern attitude to contraception is an elegantly shaped, epistolary, erotic novel which Joyce listed on the 1920 inventory of his books, entitled *The Curtain Drawn Up*. This book, written on the eve of the French Revolution, which Joyce had in an English translation, is thoroughly libertine in its attitude to sexuality. 'Rose', the narrator of the first part, has been sexually instructed and debauched by her own father and, now in a convent, she cheerfully passes on her knowledge of contraceptive sponge and spermicidal fluid (among a variety of other aids to lubricity) to another apparently far from chaste and obedient nun.

'My dear Eugenia,' she writes, 'I have made you a participator of the discovery, enabling you to enjoy your lover without fear and to give yourselves up to your mutual transports without restraint.'[35] The freedom to enjoy sexual experiences, albeit usually married ones, has been a fundamental aim of birth-control propagandists since Marie Stopes.

We might not expect the owner of a novel like *The Curtain Drawn Up* to have many reservations or anxieties about contraception though Joyce, in one of the heated letters he wrote to Nora in 1909, did strike a discordant note, indicating that he and Nora did not, for whatever reason, use any kind of contraception when they first ran away together, and apparently revealing a kind of unease or unfamiliarity in his naming of 'French letters' to her.

Is Georgie my son? The first night I slept with you in Zurich was October 11th and he was born July 27th. That is nine months and 16 days ... You told me that a gentleman named Holohon (a good Catholic, of course, who makes his Easter duty regularly) wanted to fuck you when you were in that hotel, using what they call a 'French letter'.[36]

Yet such unease is not as striking as the attack made here on the hypocrisy of a Catholic and it is rather typical of Joyce to insist on such remorseless attention to these issues. He did so in *Dubliners*. In 'Two Gallants' we hear the cynical, exploitative morality of Corley as he boasts about his conquests to the appreciative Lenehan. 'I was afraid, man, she'd get in the family way. But she's up to the dodge' (*D* 54). Corley is delighted that his girlfriend's prudence plays into his hands but he gets none of the reader's sympathy for that.

Another side of the birth-control debate comes up in *A Portrait* where Cranly probes rather sensitively into Stephen's family life. He asks.

–Has your mother had a happy life?
–How do I know? Stephen said.
–How many children had she?
–Nine or ten, Stephen answered. Some died.   (*P* 245)

There is no explicit point about contraception made here but Cranly, later in the conversation, says that she 'must have gone through a good deal of suffering' and Stephen, though he is abrupt and argumentative, recognizes that Cranly 'felt then the sufferings of women' in a way that he himself does not (*P* 249).

From these beginnings it might have been hard to guess that the issue would loom large in *Ulysses*. Yet the sordidness of Corley's interest appears transfigured in the indulgently grotesque manner of the later book. The ubiquity of 'French letters' keeps the tone low, appearing in 'Scylla and Charybdis', when George Moore is identified as 'lecturer on French letters to the youth of Ireland' (*U* 275–6), and again in 'Oxen of the Sun' (it is rather typical of the psychological verisimilitude of *Ulysses* that Stephen should recycle Mulligan's joke), where Zarathustra is 'sometime regius professor of French letters to the university of Oxtail' (*U* 513). Grotesquery is characteristic of the 'two partly uncoiled rubber preservatives' that appear in the indecorously honest inventory of Bloom's drawer in 'Ithaca', 'purchased by post from Box 32, P.O., Charing Cross, London, W.C.' (*U* 850). Bloom's 'bodyguard' distributes 'rubber preservatives' in a hallucinatory passage in 'Circe' (*U* 607). Molly's revelation that Bloom's 'French letter', kept secretly in his pocket book (*U* 483), is no secret at all (*U* 918) must strike us as grotesque, though rather poignantly so. Presumably the two 'preservatives' in the drawer are replacements for this one were it ever used. In 'Circe' the Blooms' bedroom picture, 'The Bath of the Nymph', comes to life and 'lightly clad in teabrown art colours', descends from her 'grotto' among an entourage of cheap advertisements for 'useful hints to the married' and 'Rubber goods' (*U* 656). Mildly erotic magazines like *Photo Bits*, from which the picture is said to derive, were indeed among the most common popular sources for contraceptive information and for the purchase of contraceptives. The 'useful hints to the married' sounds like a well-known birth-control pamphlet produced originally by Francis Place, which was advertised in *Photo Bits*, along with 'rubber goods' at the address of one 'P.B. Jackson, 95 Charing Cross Road, London W.C.2.'[37] Joyce evidently enjoyed the equivocal tone of the birth-control movement, partly reformist and partly indecent, and, in the 'Ballad of Persse O'Reilly' in *Finnegans Wake* he has HCE support, among a variety of other liberal schemes, 'immaculate contraceptives for the populace' (*FW* 45.14).

These items may seem little more than details of comic

decoration, yet Joyce took serious pains to ensure that his readers would be supplied with information about the contraceptive practices of his leading characters, and critics have found the issue important enough to need explanation and to be fraught with interpretative difficulties. The key passage in *Ulysses* is the answer to the question posed towards the end of 'Ithaca' about the Blooms' 'limitation of fertility'. Here the revealing phrase noted in the *Exiles* notes and in 'Wandering Rocks' reappears in an English version, its conceptual purity and precision sitting well with the style of Joyce's 'Ithaca' narrator. We learn that from the Blooms:

complete carnal intercourse, with ejaculation of semen within the natural female organ, having last taken place five weeks previous, viz. 27 November 1893, to the birth on 29 December 1893 of second (and only male) issue, deceased 9 January 1894, aged 11 days, there remained a period of 10 years, 5 months and 18 days during which carnal intercourse had been incomplete, without ejaculation of semen within the natural female organ.   (*U* 869)

Along with Bloom's sad thought in 'Lestrygonians' that they 'could never like it again after Rudy' (*U* 213), this passage has been taken to imply that, as Harry Levin puts it, the Blooms have become 'physically and mentally estranged',[38] though it is not, of course, clear whether Bloom's 'it' refers to sex, or having children, or even to their Lombard Street residence. David Hayman is very close to the sense of the 'Ithaca' passage when he points out that the formulation 'does not preclude coitus interruptus, cunnilingus (773), or mutual stimulation (74)' but he too writes as if it represents 'ten years of virtual abstinence'.[39] Molly's memory in 'Penelope' of 'the last time he came on my bottom' (*U* 874), gives us ample indication that their 'estrangement' is hardly one which excludes sexual contact and should be enough to assure us that the formula is an 'Ithacan' way of describing a contraceptive sexual relationship rather than sexual abstinence. Used with all the rigour, though none of the moral outrage, of the Jesuit theologians, it hardly entitles us to assume, as most critics of *Ulysses* do, that their marriage is an especially unhappy one.

It is certainly the case that Molly allows Boylan higher 'concessions' (on the scale proposed in the *Exiles* notes) than Bloom. Boylan's act with Molly is very nearly 'complete carnal

intercourse' and the thought even crosses her mind of reproduction: 'supposing I risked having another' (*U* 877).
However, here too it is carefully indicated to us that their sexual
contact is of the modern onanistic kind. Molly records her
gratitude for the paucity of Boylan's ejaculation 'in case any of it
wasn't washed out properly the last time I let him finish it in me'
(*U* 877).[40] Though from the point of view of a traditional
morality Bloom's masturbation in 'Nausicaa' is a mortal sin, in
terms of contraceptive modernity it is an outstandingly, even
commendably safe variety of mutual sexual pleasure. In terms
of Joyce's jesuitical modernity it shares a moral and psychological equivalence with Boylan and Molly's encounter and, for that
matter, with Bloom's own sexual congress with Molly,
achieved at the end of 'Ithaca', in the form of 'prolonged
provocative melonsmellonous osculation' and 'proximate erection' (*U* 867).

A similar controversy has arisen in the criticism of *Finnegans
Wake*, in relation to the passage in Book III Chapter 4 where
Earwicker and spouse are graphically depicted in four succes-
sive copulatory positions, blasphemously analogous to the
four-fold narrative of the gospel writers of the New Testament.
Their third kind of encounter is partly military in its metaphor:
'Poor little tartanelle, her dinties are chattering, the strait's she's
in, the bulloge she bears!' (*FW* 583.3–4). In part it is a cricket
match: 'Tipatonguing him on in her pigeony linguish, with a
flick at the bails for lubrication, to scorch her faster, faster'
(*FW* 584.3–4). After a cock crows there is a paragraph which
reads partly as a prayer of thanks and partly as a list of theatrical
credits or acknowledgements, thanking the candle ('modest
Miss Glimglow': *FW* 585.4–5) and the mattress ('neat Master
Mettresson': *FW* 585.5–6) that made the act possible. In this
paragraph it is made clear that they are using a form of
contraception: 'As well as his auricular of Malthus, the prome-
thean paratonnerwetter which first (Pray go! pray go!) taught
love's lightning the way (pity shown) to, well, conduct itself
(Mercy, good shot! only please don't mention it!)' (*FW*
585.10–14).

Bernard Benstock in *Joyce-Again's Wake* seized upon the
following paragraph and the lines, 'Withdraw your member'
(*FW* 585.26) and 'You never wet the tea' (*FW* 585.31). He
argued that the sexual act is a 'failure' and HCE a 'sexual

has-been'. Yet once we bear in mind the kind of precise distinctions that fascinated Joyce in this area then, once again, a contraceptive act rather than an incomplete or unhappy one seems to be at issue.[41]

Critics may have been less prompt to speculate on these aspects of the Blooms' and Earwickers' sexual life and to conclude that they are in some way unsatisfactory, if it had not been for the 'Oxen of the Sun' episode. As masturbation might be said to be the main issue in 'Nausicaa', so in 'Oxen', set as it is in Holles Street Maternity Hospital, questions of birth and birth-control are at the centre of the stage. Joyce indicated to Harriet Shaw Weaver that he found this 'the most difficult episode in an *Odyssey*, I think, both to interpret and to execute'.[42] In part Joyce's difficulty arose because Homer's incident gives relatively little prominence to Odysseus himself who, after passing on the warnings of Tiresias and Circe, does little more than wander off to a distant part of the island and fall asleep whilst his comrades commit their sacrilegious act. Bloom too falls into a dream in part of the 'Oxen of the Sun' episode, mesmerized (not unlike his contemporaries Braque and Picasso[43]) by the label on a Bass beer bottle. The dead oxen about which he dreams are the herds conjured up in his imagination by the Agendath Netaim advertisement he picked up in the butcher's shop in 'Calypso' (*U* 72–3), conflated with the cattle he has seen later in the day (*U* 122), which he now knows to be threatened by foot-and-mouth disease (*U* 520–2). While Bloom is dreaming, his interlocutors commit little obvious sacrilege, except the near attempt by Lenehan (restrained by the uncharacteristically solicitous Mulligan) to take the beer bottle for himself. Eurylochus, the sailors' spokesman in Homer, has no part in Joyce's version, whilst Hyperion's daughters who tend the cattle appear as nurses. Zeus sends a thunderbolt to strike Odysseus' ship in Homer; and Joyce has a storm burst outside the hospital, much to Stephen's alarm.

These are the bones of incidental correspondence but they tell us little about the most striking characteristic of the episode, which has no obvious justification in the Homeric plan: the technique of using a chronological sequence of prose parodies, providing an analogy with the development of the foetus in the womb. Frank Budgen's report suggests that Joyce felt the need to justify this prose extravaganza as an 'interpretation' of Homer: 'I interpret the killing of the sacred oxen as the crime against fecundity by sterilizing the act of coition. And I think my interpretation as sound as that of any other commentator on Homer.'[44] It is, of course, a deliberately eccentric interpretation (though we may note that in Cowper's translation, surviving in the Trieste library, Odysseus warns his men against what he calls 'appetite profane'[45]). Yet Joyce evidently found the idea important, for the letter from which Budgen's account is presumably drawn reads 'Am working hard at *Oxen of the Sun*, the idea being the crime committed against fecundity by sterilizing the act of coition'.[46] The idea that the episode had a 'crime' and that this crime was 'fraud' (a common term for contraception[47]) is included on the list of correspondences sent to Gorman and Gilbert and the schema sent to Carlo Linati in 1920 when the episode was complete.[48]

What is surprising in the criticism is the ease with which it is assumed that Joyce meant contraception to be understood as a 'crime'. Ellmann in *'Ulysses' on the Liffey* condemns the profanity of the medical students and the 'inner sterility' of Mulligan, arguing for an analogy between literary and biological fecundity.[49] Peake talks of the 'sterilizing and abortifacient influence of Stephen's companions' and celebrates Bloom as 'defender and advocate of fertility'.[50] Some take the extravagantly Carlylean congratulations of Theodore Purefoy as an indication of Joyce's deeper intentions here. 'Sexual intercourse without impediment,' writes Marilyn French, 'is the genuine encounter with the real, the not-self.'[51]

Relatively few have commented on the glaring incongruity that Joyce should have written an episode designed to celebrate fertility immediately after one in which his central character masturbates.[52] Yet that incongruity is highlighted not only by Joyce's juxtaposition of the episodes but by explicit narrative comment. When Bloom tries to criticize Crotthers and the others, the narrator questions his right to make any moral pronouncements, since his wife 'has been too long and too persistently denied her legitimate prerogative' (*U* 535) and 'a habit reprehensible at puberty is second nature and an opprobium in middle life' (*U* 536). The values of narrator and character cannot be assumed to be identical, and it is highly dangerous to base an interpretation of the author's views on the narrator's words.

We might start to tackle these problems by asking whether it is indeed the case that the medicals gathered in Holles Street are advocates of 'infertility' and whether Bloom or Stephen are significantly seen to be defenders of it. Discussions of 'birth and righteousness' begin just after Bloom has been persuaded to join the company, and it is perhaps chronologically appropriate that in this medieval stylistic parody a traditional scholastic problem should emerge concerning the respective rights to life of mother and child, should some complication during the birth make it necessary to choose between them. Most of those present, led by the student Madden, share the modern view that the mother should live before the child. They swear so by 'our Virgin Mother' though the Church, as Stephen promptly explains, takes the opposite view. 'We are means to those small creatures within us and nature has other ends than we' (U 508), says Stephen, in a conflation of Catholic and Darwinist views. Arguably his companions are 'against fertility' or against fertility at any cost here, whilst Stephen expounds the orthodox view. However, in his reference to the 'Godpossibled souls' that we 'impossibilise' by fornication or masturbation he is, interestingly, pointing to an element of the traditional Church teaching that Marie Stopes successfully ridiculed in her book *Married Love*.[53]

The issue returns to prominence in the passage of Bunyan parody after the first clap of thunder is heard. Stephen is frightened by the noise, interpreted through his (and of course Bunyan's) eyes as the voice of the 'god Bringforth'. Stephen is not much of a Christian Pilgrim, since he does not believe in a benign God, nor does he follow the pointers of 'Pious' and 'Chaste'. He has been led astray by 'a certain whore of an eye pleasing exterior' and indeed 'all that company' are prey to such distractions, caring little for the consequences, since 'Preservative' has given them 'a stout shield of oxengut ... that they might take no hurt neither from Offspring that was that wicked devil by virtue of this same shield which was named Killchild' (U 517). Here Stephen, as well as his companions, seem to be in favour of contraception. It is the narrator, who evidently has both Bunyan's style and his morality, who ticks them off:

Wherein, O wretched company, were ye all deceived for that was the voice of god that was in a very grievous rage that he would presently lift his arm and spill their souls for their abuses and their spillings done by them contrariwise to his word.   (*U* 518)

Bannon, who arrives with Mulligan half-way through the episode, and confides in Crotthers about his flirtation with Bloom's daughter Milly, is also evidently in favour of contraception. 'Would to God that foresight had remembered me to take my cloak along,' he comments, giving Mulligan and Lynch the opportunity to joke about 'cloaks' and 'umbrellas', whose prevention of 'wetting' has obvious prophylactic connotations. Lynch boasts of his conquest earlier in the day, when he emerged from behind a hedge with a girl, only to be greeted by Father John Conmee. Lynch's girl has just been 'ill' but today was 'free, blithe and mocked at peril'. The implication is, presumably, that they are hoping to enjoy the relative contraceptive safety, according to the 'rhythm' method, of the days immediately after her menstrual period.[54]

The medical company are sometimes 'against fertility' but they are by no means all or always so. Mulligan, though he may clothe himself in exaggerated Gothic villainy as the murderer Childs to make his exit from the hospital,[55] poses for most of the time he is present as an extreme advocate of fertility. He becomes a stud Juan who, under the name of *le Fécondateur*, offers to impregnate 'any female of what grade of life soever', so bitter is his objection to the sterility and genital fraud of the age (*U* 525–6). Dixon, the 'junior medical officer in residence' (*U* 536) at the hospital, when called out to help after the birth of Mina Purefoy's child, makes another rousing speech in favour of fertility, defending Nurse Callan and motherhood. 'I shudder to think of the future of a race,' he says, 'where no right reverence is rendered to mother and maid in the house of Horne' (*U* 532). Far from attacking fertility, he makes his professional dependence on fertility quite evident here.

The crowd can be as soon celebrants as attackers of fertility. They rejoice at the news of the birth, 'hoping that the joyful occurrence would palliate a licence which the simultaneous absence of abigail and officer rendered easier' (*U* 536). It is Bloom who tries to restrain their jollity, though they break out with a long and unrestrained discussion of monstrous births of all kinds. They keep up their spirits with great commendation of Purefoy and his 'doughty deed' and equal condemnation of 'Malthusiasts' and 'Population without Copulation', until they leave Burke's public house.

The Catholic Church, whose defence of the principle of fertility might seem incontrovertible, is presented in a more equivocal light here. In that passage of brilliant blasphemous play between Lynch, Dixon and Stephen on Bulls and Papal Bulls, the Church is presented as an institution which, far from promoting chaste fertility, has found a way of seducing 'maid, wife, abbess and widow' from the 'strapping young ravisher' to the 'spermacetic', and eminently spermicidal joys of the confessional' (*U* 521–3). This astonishing vision of the confessional as a kind of contraceptive sexual institution carries through into *Finnegans Wake* where Jaun's sermon in Book III Chapter 2 is full of references to birth-control. Jaun remembers the equivocal advice he was given by his parish priest: 'What a lawful day it was, there and then, for a consummation with an effusion' (*FW* 432.13–14). Annie Besant who, before her theosophical work which Joyce knew,[56] was a well-known birth-control campaigner is men tioned (*FW* 432.32), as is 'Population Peg' (the American pioneer Margaret Sanger: *FW* 436.10) and Marie Stopes (*FW* 444.6–8).[57] Jaun's overt advice is for orthodox reproductive sex, 'love, through the usual channels, ... taken neat in the generable way' (*FW* 436.14–15), yet somehow forbidden contraceptive information leaks out and the extravagant Joycean paradox that the confessional is an institution which encourages flirtatious sexuality is confirmed.

The God that Stephen puzzles over in 'Oxen of the Sun' may in one guise be a reproductive 'god Bringforth' but in another is a murderous and vindictive deity who not only effects the cruel Malthusian 'checks' to population, vice and misery, but who actually delights in infant mortality. Stephen's 'morbid-minded conceit' is that God omnivorously consumes the bodies of the dead: 'of cancrenous females emaciated by parturition, corpulent professional gentlemen, not to speak of jaundiced politicians and chlorotic nuns'. He demands newborn infants as an horrendous aid to his digestion, just as some victuallers offer the flesh of a newborn calf or 'staggering bob' (*U* 538–50).

Stephen does not so much defend the Church view as construct a 'perverted transcendentalism' all of his own and, through his eyes at least, the Church really has no simple view on contraception, but is riddled with contradictions. Bloom's position is no easier to understand. We hear at one point the tale of his first sexual encounter with a whore called Bridie Kelly. It was unsatisfactory and does not result in fertility but, despite the sentimental tone of the narration here, it would be absurd to suggest that the encounter would have been more satisfactory had the girl become pregnant (*U* 541). In the discussions that take place Bloom is quiet and withdrawn into his own reveries. His dissatisfaction with the talk around him seems to arise more from the wildness of their manner than from any substantive objection to their irreverence towards fertility. 'Their testiness and outrageous *mots* were such that his intellects resiled from', we are told in the exaggerated sensibility of this parody of Burke. Stephen may momentarily seem to endorse the Church's implicitly anti-contraceptive view that the mother give life to the child 'at risk of her own', but not Bloom. 'At the risk of her own was the telling rejoinder of his interlocutor none the less effective for the moderate and measured tone in which it was delivered' (*U* 550).

That Bloom chooses to visit Mina Purefoy has been taken to imply some stand on fertility but it is not principled enthusiasm for reproduction that takes him there. Compassion or 'stark ruth of man', as it is called in an early Anglo-Saxon passage, is what leads him, and this would seem to imply a shared attitude with Molly who, in 'Penelope', scorns Purefoy 'filling her up with child or twins once a year as regular as the clock' (*U* 877), rather than the enthusiasm for his achievement expressed in 'Oxen'. Earlier in the day Bloom, like Cranly in *A Portrait*, noticed the large Dedalus family and, a little more explicitly than Cranly, made sympathy for Stephen's mother an opportunity for criticism of the Church view of contraception. 'Fifteen children he had. Birth every year almost. That's in their theology or the priest won't give the poor woman the confession, the absolution. Increase and multiply. Did you ever hear such an idea?' (*U* 191). This is surely the attitude that takes him through 'Oxen of the Sun' and one that his masturbation of the previous episode, and the sexual modernity it implies, helps to prepare him for, enabling him to see Mina Purefoy as an individual rather than as subordinate to a larger reproductive scheme.

If there is an agency in the 'Oxen of the Sun' episode that is consistently in support of reproduction, the birth-rate and fertility and seems mostly opposed to contraception, it is none of the characters but the voice or points of view of the narrator, or many narrators, from different periods of English prose who tell us what takes place. These narrators are, of course, difficult and periphrastic. They are, as we expect in modernist fiction, unreliable, not in the sense that they are ignorant of important facts or blind to significant events, but in that they may insist on a moral perspective, which is inappropriate to the events and characters described.

The episode opens with a kind of hymn or prayer to fertility, where the phallic and reproductive 'Horhorn, quickening and wombfruit' (U 499) are inextricably tied. The long 'latinate' section which follows praises the 'procreating function' in the most insistent of terms. Passages whose sentiments seem to be those not of any character but of a narrative voice include the admonishment of the Bunyanesque narrator against seed-spillers (U 518), the outright condemnation of Bloom as 'stagnant, acid and inoperative' (U 536) and the final celebration of Purefoy. The Dickensian passage with its overblown sentimentality cannot fail to alert our suspicions of narrative moral stance. The irony of the catalogue of Purefoy offspring is unmistakable: 'Charley, Mary Alice, Frederick Albert (if he had lived), Mamy, Budge (Victoria Frances), Tom, Violet Constance Louisa, darling little Bobsy (called after our famous hero of the South African War, Lord Bobs of Waterford and Candahar)' (U 551). The absurdity of Purefoy's congratulations grow from the tribute to his 'modicum of Man's work' to the gross injunction for him to 'Drink, man, an udderful! Mother's milk, Purefoy, the milk of human kin' (U 555). The narrator (or succession of narrators) becomes increasingly extravagant in this celebration of fertility. At the end we have the voice of the evangelist J. Alexander Christ Dowie still ranting on about 'frauds': 'You'll need to rise precious early, you sinner there, if you want to diddle the Almighty God' (U 561). No reasonable critic would hold that these sentiments coincide with those of Bloom, any more than do the sentiments of the 'Cyclops' narrator. Nor do they seem any kind of basis on which to establish an interpretation of the episode as a whole.

What has been noticed about the episode from a stylistic point of view has hardly been taken into consideration for the purposes of interpretation. The parodies, it is suggested, were done for the delight in virtuosity that they evidently show, or even as some kind of tribute to the writings parodied. Stuart Gilbert, for instance, dislikes the idea that the parodies had any satiric element; 'the effect is rather of pastiche than of travesty', he claims.[58] Most readers would agree that there is both enjoyment and satire in Joyce's versions of the styles of Malory, Bunyan, Carlyle or Dickens. Yet the passages in the episode have content as well as style. The two can hardly be separated, in fact, and the moral injunctions that are voiced are, I have argued, ones that we should see as significantly divorced from both the characters' and the authors' points of view.

In part the effect is one of relativization of moral standpoint, but it is important to recognize that this relativization does not have only a formal or abstract importance. To follow up the hint of Bloom's Bass bottle, the 'Oxen' episode is analogous to a cubist picture in its displacement of an assured perception of the object. The displacement, effected in cubist painting by an abstraction and combination of elements of plane, surface and colour, is worked, in 'Oxen of the Sun', by the abstraction of certain attitudes or interpretations from the past. The episode functions in a typically Joycean maner, focussing our attention at once on the important contemporary issue of 'birth and righteousness' and on a variety of past and present understandings of that question.

Such an argument rests on the understanding that we may take the interest in birth and foetal development in the episode as itself a significant interest and not merely as a convenient analogy or a literary experiment. It rests also on the understanding that Joyce knew something of the variety of possible moral and intellectual positions that the history of writing on such matters afforded. There is little explicit help for us in Joyce's letters or his library here. His stated intentions hardly touch on these points. However it is apparent that in the texture of reference the episode exploits much scientific and pseudo-scientific literature.

It might be argued that Joyce's main interest was in gathering anything that offered some further punning or playful extravagance to his theme of conception. The language of the episode is full of such verbal play. Oliver Gogarty was outraged at the suggestion that Joyce should be considered some kind of expert in the field.[59] Yet at one point in the episode the narrator, in Huxleyan scientific mood, reels off a list of names 'such as Culpepper, Spallanzani, Blumenbach, Lusk, Hertwig, Leopold and Valenti' (*U* 547). The list suggests a familiarity with the history of the subject from Culpeper's practical medley of folklore and classical authority in the seventeenth century,[60] through eighteenth-century theories of 'epigenesis' (the idea that the form of the embryo is created after fertilization) and 'preformation' or 'evolution' (the idea that the sperm already carries the formative agent), up to the more modern and authoritative textbooks of Leopold and Valenti.[61] On the 'Oxen' Notesheets he jotted down the names of yet more figures in the history of this branch of medicine, suggesting an interest that went beyond a desire to gather vocabulary for the mere colouring of a medical debate.[62]

Such a range of reading suggests that Joyce was aware of up-to-date medical discussions of obstetrics, yet the compendium of outdated issues and understandings that are discussed in 'Oxen' suited his fictional purposes better. The episode might almost be said to provide a history of the science of birth as well as a history of English prose style. Emphasis is on the outrageous, such as Molly's memory of the birth of Pantagruel from Rabelais in 'Penelope'[63] or the book *Aristotle's Masterpiece*, whose classification of 'monstrous births' and assembly of pseudo-scientific sexual folklore recur throughout *Ulysses*.[64] There is enough discussion of such matters among the company to indicate that Joyce had something substantial in mind. There is certainly enough to indicate that the birth and birth-control issues were not ones which Joyce used only as structuring devices, or even primarily as the basis of an analogy for artistic process. They emerge as motivating issues in an episode like 'Oxen', the effect of Joyce's method being at once to respond to the contentiousness of the issue as felt by Catholics and to offer his contribution in a language which directs the reader's attention to, or filters that attention through, a variety of past formulations and attitudes.

Once these implications of Joyce's parodic method in 'Oxen' are grasped, it becomes much less possible to sustain any interpretation of the episode which sees contraception as a crime. On the contrary, Joyce's purpose seems to be to give us a strong taste of militantly and rather oppressively 'reproductive' doctrines and show sympathetic characters like Bloom and Mina Purefoy on the receiving end of such views.

Perversity

It has become familiar to talk about the sexuality presented in Joyce's works as fundamentally perverse. According to Tony Tanner, *Finnegans Wake* is a type of novel where sexual perversity and such linguistic perversions as punning coexist as parts of a greater collapse of linguistic and personal relationships associated with the breakdown of bourgeois society.[65] Colin MacCabe takes up the theme, describing both Joyce's manner of writing and the presentation of sexuality in his work as perverse.[66]

Joyce deliberately sought out and exposed the perverse and the anomalous in his presentation of sexual relationships. He chose to depict a married couple whose sexual life sits uneasily with narrow definitions of sexual normality, and highlighted those definitions so that their narrowness might be made plain. Through his reading of Catholic Church writings on sexuality he constructed an idea of sexuality which fits post-Freudian shifts in our conceptions, and focussed the attention of his fiction on issues like masturbation and contraception where that shift in sexual ideas was most significantly felt.

In terms of the close definitions of heterosexual, genital and reproductive normality which his authorities offered, most kinds of sexual experience, even the far from unusual experiences of Leopold and Molly Bloom, must be classified as perverse, but along with these apparently normal sexual activities that are seen to be perverse under the microscope of casuistical definition, Joyce's fiction parades an interest in more obviously or outrageously perverse types of sexuality. Ellmann notes that the element of sexual perversity in the Hunter divorce case added to Joyce's interest in it. In its investigation of sexual perversity the fiction is significantly contemporary with the scientific 'discovery' and classification of sexual experience which, I argued at the start of this chapter, was a striking part of the growth of sexual science at this time.

Which perversions does Joyce's fiction treat, and what was his reading and interest in the field? Perhaps the first area of

sexual perversity which commands attention is that of homosexuality, which had a special status in many accounts of
sexuality. For Havelock Ellis there was a difference of quality
between the 'perversion' of the sexual instinct and what he
called its 'inversion'.[67] Freud borrowed and sharpened the
distinction, differentiating between deviations of erotic 'aim'
and those of erotic 'object'.[68] Joyce, we may feel, might reflect
this special status of homosexuality in his work.

Stephen's relationships with Cranly and with Mulligan have
sometimes been felt to display a latent or repressed kind of
homosexuality.[69] Richard and Robert in *Exiles* have a highly
charged relationship. In his working notes Joyce says that
Bertha 'wishes for the spiritual union of Robert and Richard
and *believes* (?) that union will be affected through her body'
and that 'a faint glimmer of lesbianism irradiates' her own
mind. In 'Scylla and Charybdis' the homosexuality in Shakespeare's sonnets is discussed (*U* 259 and 260–1). Mulligan
claims, in a resonantly Swinburnean passage, that Bloom is
'Greeker than the Greeks' and when he warns Stephen later in
the episode to 'get thee a breechpad', the homosexual joke is
unmistakable (*U* 279). Margaret Solomon pointed to the anal
punning in the story of Buckley and the Russian General in
Finnegans Wake (*FW* 338–55), though, as Glasheen suggests,
it seems primarily scatological rather than sexual.[70] Fritz Senn
has collected references to sexual inversion and conjectured
upon their relationship to all kinds of inversions in the book,
which is close in spirit to the *Wake* but tells us relatively little
about the attitude the fictions take to homosexuality itself.[71]

Joyce's library contained some material on the question.
Huysmans's *A Rebours* and Gide's *L'Immoraliste* represent two
aspects of the *fin-de-siècle* literary interest in exotic pleasures.[72]
He had access to a well-known, if rather unscientific, theory of
homosexuality in Richard Burton's 'Terminal Essay' to *The
Book of the Thousand Nights and a Night*, where Burton argued
that there were certain 'sotadic zones' where climactic conditions encourage sexual aberrations like homosexuality, a
notion half-remembered by Bloom in 'Eumaeus' when he
attributes Spanish passion to 'the great heat, climate generally'
(*U* 737). In the course of his argument Burton acknowledges
and outlines other theories, such as the idea that there was
originally a third sex. He points to the difficulty of identifying

what is natural or unnatural in sexual life, describing homosexuality as '*le vice contre nature* – if anything can be against nature which includes all things'. And he even echoes Garnier's sense of the identity of sexual perversity and contraception when he condemns homosexuality not as some kind of psychological illness or eccentricity of taste, but as 'a great and growing evil deadly to the birth-rate – that mainstay of national prosperity'.[73]

Most prominent of all, in Joyce's reading on the subject and in his writing about it, is the case of Oscar Wilde, to whom Joyce responded strongly in letters, reviews, *Ulysses* and *Finnegans Wake*. Joyce's interest in Wilde was apparently not so much an interest in the work as in the Wilde phenomenon. He wrote in 1906:

I have just finished Dorian Grey [sic]. Some chapters are like Huysmans, catalogued atrocities, lists of perfumes and instruments. The central idea is fantastic. Dorian is exquisitely beautiful and becomes awfully wicked: but never ages. His portrait ages. I can imagine the capital which Wilde's prosecuting counsel made out of certain parts of it. It is not very difficult to read between the lines. Wilde seems to have had some good intentions in writing it – some wish to put himself before the world – but the book is rather crowded with lies and epigrams. If he had had the courage to develop the allusions in the book it might have been better. I suspect he has done this in some privately-printed books.[74]

Any interests Joyce may have had in Wilde's style are passed over here and the attention directed to his work as an expression of his sexuality.

Three years later, when Joyce was commissioned to write on Wilde for the Triestine newspaper, *Il Piccolo della Sera*, he took a similar approach, mixing life and work in his interpretation. Indeed his article shows strong traces of R.H. Sherard's well-known biography in its psychological defence of Wilde and in stylistic features such as the affected use of the word 'unhappy'.[75] 'There are circumstances regarding the pregnancy of Lady Wilde and the infancy of her son,' Joyce writes, 'which, in the eyes of some, explain in part the unhappy mania (if it may be called that) which later dragged him to his ruin' (*CW* 202).

Sherard's conciliatory idea is that Wilde had an 'epileptiform' madness,[76] and Joyce also talks of the 'epileptic tendency of his nervous system' (*CW* 203). But he goes beyond Sherard in explicitly condemning the puritanical public outrage against Wilde and in offering a provocatively tolerant explanation of his homosexuality. For Joyce, 'far from being a perverted monster who sprang in some inexplicable way from the civilisation of modern England', Wilde's homosexuality was 'the logical and inescapable product of the Anglo-Saxon College and University system, with its secrecy and restrictions' (*CW* 204).

Joyce evidently identified with Wilde in the same kind of way that he identified with Parnell: both, for him, were Irishmen condemned for sexual crimes by an unjust, hypocritical morality. It is, perhaps, with intentional irony that Joyce makes Wilde a subject in the literary conversation of his Irish characters: part of Mulligan's hyperborean Hellenism in 'Telemachus' (*U* 6), of Stephen's mental furniture in 'Proteus' (*U* 62) and the central literary enthusiasm of Richard Best in 'Scylla and Charybdis' (*U* 254 and 274). In *Ulysses* the Wilde trial appears hardly at all; there is little more than a hint of it in 'Eumaeus', where Bloom associates his masturbation with the sexual scandals of the day (*U* 748–9). It is that trial, though, that forms one of the most recurrent themes of *Finnegans Wake*, where Earwicker's sexual crime is strongly identified with Wilde's.

The identification begins in Book I Chapter 2, where a 'baser meaning' (*FW* 33.14) is offered for HCE's fall and it is suggested that he (like Wilde condemned by Lady Colin Campbell) is 'a great white caterpillar' (*FW* 33.23). The rumour spreads, despite HCE's denial of the 'fibfibfabrications' (*FW* 36.34), via Treacle Tom and Frisky Shorty who are perhaps implicated in some homosexual crime since the former, we are told, sleeps naked 'in strange men's cots' (*FW* 39.32). The identification recurs in Chapter 3 where, among the hubbub of voices offering their comments on HCE, 'Sylvia Silence' asks in lisping 'vowel-threaded syllabelles': 'Have you evew thought, weputew, that sheew gweatness was his twagedy?' Nevertheless like Wilde he should be subject to 'Subsec. 32, section II, of the C.L.A. act 1885' (*FW* 61.6–10). The material is rehearsed and expanded in Book III Chapter 3, where a witness at the inquest is accused of a kind of homosexual complicity with HCE: 'homosexual catheis of empathy between narcissism of the expert and steatopygic invertedness' (*FW* 522.20–1). Once again the effete defence of HCE is heard: 'the evil what though it was willed might nevewtheless lead somehow on to good towawd the genewality' (*FW* 523.2–4). Plays on passivity, androgyny and invertedness continue, with HCE described as 'deponent' (both a witness to a court and, in Latin grammar, a passive or middle-voiced verb used in an active sense). He is a racehorse whose presence at Dublin Bay 'vites inversion' (*FW* 523.17) and Treacle Tom launches into a lengthy, involved, legalistic enquiry into HCE as 'the old middlesex party' (*FW* 523.27–8), his 'epscene licence' (*FW* 523.34) and evidence of 'early bisectualism' (*FW* 524.12, 36).

It is the curious condition of the 'passive' sexual offender that he 'may be been as much sinned against as sinning' (*FW* 523.9–10). Joyce chooses the famous line from *Lear* because of its humorous implications for the homosexual, yet it also points up a serious part of Joyce's attitude on these questions. Atherton, collecting Wildean homosexual references in *Finnegans Wake*, concluded that Joyce's attitude endorsed the 'contempt and loathing' that is voiced throughout the book. The point though is surely that Joyce re-enacts that condemnation whilst retaining the attitude of his 1909 article, that 'whether he was innocent or guilty of the charges brought against him' Wilde 'was undoubtedly a scapegoat'.[77]

It is also the case that whilst HCE may be homosexually involved in his crime in the park, he is not to be characterized exclusively in terms of sexual taste or stereotyped personality as a homosexual. The same is true of Bloom. Though he may be accused of homosexuality by Mulligan in 'Scylla and Charybdis' and is diagnosed in 'Circe', like Sherard's Wilde, as epileptic, as 'bisexually abnormal' and again as 'more sinned against than sinning' (*U* 613), he is evidently not characterizable as homosexual rather than heterosexual.

The problem is partly one of a changing understanding of these issues. The idea that sexual tastes and personalities may be identified one with the other – that whole characters may be categorized as homosexual – is one which has been prominent in this century both among those who condemn and those who defend homosexual activity. Its origins are now largely recognized to be the sexual theories of Krafft-Ebing, to whom we are indebted for some of the familiar names for kinds of sexual perversity. Joyce apparently knew Krafft-Ebing, since he puns with his name in *Finnegans Wake* and Joyce critics have been quick to use Krafft-Ebing in their attempts to gloss, for instance, those passages in 'Circe' where sexual perversity is most apparent.[78]

Yet, for all the attention to the perverse in Joyce, there is no single character, except perhaps the man in 'An Encounter', who might be called sexually deviant in the Krafft-Ebing sense. On the contrary, Joyce is most keen to present his central characters with a variety of shades of sexual taste as if to suggest that such varieties are intrinsic to human psychology. Neither his attitude nor his terminology are suggestive of Krafft-Ebing so much as of a wide knowledge and reading of the available writings, some serious and scientific, but others, like Sherard's book on Wilde, used for the very unreliability of their understanding.

The idea that sexual psychology consists in such a variety of erotic taste has most in common with the Freudian notion of the 'polymorphous perversity' of the sexual instinct, explained in Freud's *Three Essays on Sexual Theory*. Joyce's knowledge of Freud has been much discussed. It is at any rate the case that Joyce's library contains such psychoanalytic work as Freud's *Psychopathology of Everyday Life*, his essay on Leonardo da Vinci's childhood memory[79] and Ernest Jones's interpretation of *Hamlet*.[80] Joyce may have picked up an important lead for the episode in *Psychopathology*. Freud discusses the meeting of Odysseus and Nausicaa in terms of exhibitionism, and this is the very word Joyce used in describing his own 'Nausicaa' episode retrospectively in 'Ithaca' (*U* 865).[81] Yet sustained use of psychoanalytic terminology is no more a feature of Joyce's writing than is the use of Krafft-Ebing. If there is a contemporary sexual psychologist with whose work Joyce's fictional examination of these issues seems most closely allied it is Havelock Ellis. Ellis's work is scholarly rather than scientific, more anxious to include a range of material evidence than to construct a clear theoretical case. Joyce's surviving library contains only Ellis's literary critical work, yet there are a number of coincidences of information and terminology which suggest a deeper knowledge of *Studies of the Psychology of Sex*. Both writers mention the legend of Aristotle's masochism,[82] the orgasm that is supposed to be experienced by the hanged man,[83] and the idea that sows eat their offspring which Stephen finds such an apt image of Ireland.[84] When Mulligan diagnozes Bloom's bisexuality, saying that 'ambidexterity is also latent' (*U* 613), he is echoing one of Ellis's less scientific suggestions that 'bisexuality would thus in a large number of cases be comparable to ambidexterity'.[85] Ellis reports the case of a man who was sexually attracted to lame women, clearly quite relevant to the 'Nausicaa' episode.[86]

Joyce did not apparently wish to make a special case for 'inversion' or homosexuality. In Ellis, as in Wilde and Huysmans, homosexuality is central; in Joyce it is peripheral. But there are ways in which their ideas of other significant perversions concur. Ellis was particularly interested in 'the relation of sexual and vesical excitation' as he puts it. The term 'vesical pressure' is one which occurs in 'Ithaca' during the description of Stephen and Bloom's comradely urination, an incident not unlike several that are described by Ellis.[87] Ellis connected his interest in eroticism and urination with more general sexual fondness for water and bathing for which he coined the term 'Undinism'.[88] There might seem to be plenty of this in Joyce's work, from Stephen's bed-wetting and the wading girl in *A Portrait* (*P* 7 and 171), and Bloom's bath in 'Lotus-Eaters' (*U* 107), to 'St Kevin Hydrophilos' in Book IV of *Finnegans Wake* (*FW* 605–6). Perhaps it is no coincidence that Joyce had a copy of de la Motte Fouqué's German romantic novel *Undine* in his Trieste library.[89]

Most sexologists, indeed most writers on sexual attraction, have recognized and wished to discuss the phenomenon whereby looking can become a sexually exciting or satisfying act. Ellis's term for what we now most usually call 'voyeurism' is 'mixoscopy'. Bloom is especially given to mixoscopy, whether it is in the erotic contemplation of the girl in Dlugacz's butcher's shop in 'Calypso' (*U* 70–1) or the sight of an imperious female figure at the door of the Grosvenor Hotel, when he thinks 'Watch! Watch! Silk flash rich stockings white. Watch!' (*U* 89–90). His voyeuristically inspired masturbation in 'Nausicaa' was anticipated by many years since, as we learn in 'Circe', the Nymph from the picture above his bridal bed and the sight of a girl called Lotty Clarke 'through illclosed curtains' have inspired similar responses (*U* 658–9). That Joyce saw voyeuristic excitation as a full sexual act, differing from what is understood to be legitimate sexuality inasmuch as it is non-reproductive, can be seen by the emergence of 'Staggering Bob' at this point in the drama as a representative of the potential child unfertilized in this onanistic act (*U* 659).

Joyce dealt with a kind of voyeurism in 'A Painful Case'. There Mr Duffy's lonely itinerary at the end of the story takes him to Magazine Hill in Phoenix Park where the 'venal and furtive loves' he chances to see 'filled him with despair' (*D* 130). The location becomes yet more significant in *Finnegans Wake* where the Magazine Wall punningly incorporates the voyeuristic suggestion of a place 'where Maggies seen all' (*FW* 7.31).

None of this need especially suggest Havelock Ellis, though it is striking that one of Ellis's categories of sexual experience is the erotic contemplation of animals or, as he calls it, 'Mixoscopic Zoophilia'. Joyce worked this into *Ulysses*, where Bloom remembers an erotic moment with Molly in Raymond Terrace, 'watching the two dogs at it by the wall of the cease to do evil'. 'Give us a touch, Poldy,' Molly apparently said, 'God I'm dying for it.' And Bloom ruefully ponders on 'How life begins' (*U* 110).

Even more peculiar to Joyce and Havelock Ellis is a perversity which Ellis called 'Pygmalionism', the sexual attraction to statues.[90] Joyce does not use the term but with Lynch's professed admiration for the statue of the Venus of Praxiteles in *A Portrait* (*P* 150), Robert Hand's curious action of kissing a cool stone because it is 'like a woman's temple' in *Exiles* (*E* 54), and Bloom's admiring investigation of the finer anatomical points of the naked female statues in the National Museum,[91] the texts offer quite a strong representation for a rather unusual sexual anomaly.

Where Joyce is not close to Ellis in terminology or detail he is close in spirit, for both of them were prepared to look at sexual anomaly not just as matter for clinical examination but, to some extent, as an aspect of human creativity and imagination. Ellis's idea of sexual 'symbolism' certainly gives this impression, as does Joyce's indefatigably inventive and light-hearted tone when accumulating these details of his characters' psychological life. But Joyce's treatment of sexuality and sexual anomaly owes no conclusive allegiance to any single author or theory, even to such a sprawling and encyclopaedic author as Ellis.

We might take the strong recurrent interest that Joyce's fiction shows in masochism as an example. Masochism is, of course, one of the terms established by Krafft-Ebing (Ellis's

term is 'passive algolagnia'), and Joyce's note for the composition of *Exiles*, calling the play 'a rough and tumble between
the Marquis de Sade and Freiherr v. Sacher Masoch' suggests
the characteristic Krafft-Ebing distinction between two sexual
personalities (*E* 172). The hint is not really exploited in the
play, though Richard is evidently a self-torturing character. He
has that in common with a number of other Joycean figures of
which the most obvious is Bloom, whose admiration for
dominating female presences becomes explicitly masochistic in
'Circe'.

Joyce evidently took this aspect of his work on *Ulysses* very
seriously and there survives considerable evidence of his
reading around the subject. He did not need Krafft-Ebing to
explain Sacher-Masoch, as most modern readers seem to, for
Masoch was a popular author in the later part of the nineteenth
century, particularly in an Austrian corner of Europe, and Joyce
knew his works. Ellmann reports that Joyce and Nora 'shared a
jocular affection' for his writing and indeed a number of titles
appear on the 1920 shelf inventory.[92] These are given by Joyce
as 'Catherine II', 'Liebesgeschichten', 'Grausame Frauen (4
vols)' and 'Scene del Ghetto', apparently four collections of
Masoch's tales, gothic rather than pornographic in the modern
sense.[93]

Joyce allows a title '*Tales of the Ghetto*' in 'Wandering Rocks'
to indicate the kind of books that interest Bloom (*U* 302). The
work *Fair Tyrants* by James Lovebirch appears recurrently too
(*U* 302, 591 and 924–5). The book itself is unknown, though
'Lovebirch' wrote a number of books which survive, including
Les Cinq Fessés de Suzette which achieved a second edition and
was translated into English.[94] Bloom is made to admire *Photo
Bits*, a magazine which Joyce knew in its reincarnated form, *Bits
of Fun*, where masochistic suggestion is common.[95] And
Bloom saves 'a press cutting from an English weekly periodical
Modern Society, subject corporal chastisement in girls' schools'
(*U* 849), a taste he shares with H.G. Wells's *petit bourgeois* hero
Mr Polly who finds *Modern Society* 'a penny paper of infinite
suggestion'.[96]

Joyce's library shows that his interest went further than these
popularly available hints. In Jacques Desroix's *La Gynécocratie*
there is an explicit work of masochistic fiction, prefaced, in
Joyce's edition, with a long essay on the history of masochistic

literature by Laurent Tailhade, and serious looking supplementary essays on the nature of masochistic love.[97] Phrases and situations from the novella may well have been borrowed for 'Circe'. Bloom, like the hero of the novella, suffers the indignity of being forced to wear female clothing and is made to act a female role for a purportedly male guest.[98] Through the introductory material Joyce may have seen a variety of works in his library in a more especially masochistic light. Thailhade discusses Swinburne and Flaubert in these terms and has a long extract from Thomas Otway's play *Venice Preserved* (1681–2), which has two explicitly masochistic scenes. Joyce, as Phillip Herring has discovered, knew this play and made notes from it during the composition of *Ulysses*.[99]

Joyce had an eye for this issue in literature, having Stephen point to Shakespeare's domination by women, Socrates' shrewish wife Xanthippe and the legend of Aristotle's masochism (*U* 505). Joyce might have noticed in Burton's *Anatomy of Melancholy* the idea that love could find such extremes and might have found Petronius on Circe cited as an example.[100] Moreover it is apparent that his interest went beyond the simply literary and consisted in an investigation of this aspect of sexual psychology both in literature and in his life. The 1909 letters to Nora, among a variety of sexual anomalies (such as coprophilia) which they uninhibitedly display, show a definite masochistic inclination. Joyce wishes 'to feel you flog, flog, flog, me viciously on my naked quivering flesh',[101] and perhaps there is a masochistic suggestion in the 'striking furs'[102] he offers to buy for Nora.

We can no more neglect the relevance of these letters to an understanding of the fiction than we can suppose that the fiction dealt with such issues as this in a cold and abstracted way that did not draw on experiences in Joyce's own life. To an extent the confessional Church system from which Joyce grew and the system of psychological analysis which developed alongside his work both drew on life experiences and the extrapolation of hidden desires as key aspects of their mode of knowing the human mind. These were the raw materials from which new scientific and new fictional understandings of humanity were constructed. Yet even in places like this, where Joyce seems most to be investigating the furthest reaches of that raw material, his writing never becomes confessional in the sense of suggesting a spontaneous rendering of raw emotion or thought. Its dominant mode remains parodic: furtive desires suggested in terms of furtive literature and wordy diagnosis overwhelming inarticulated feeling. We do not feel that a defining aspect of Bloom's character has been revealed and still less that Bloom has been interpreted in the light of any one theory of sexuality. Joyce drew on a huge variety of sources for his presentation of Bloomian sexuality and the traces of different, potentially conflicting, kinds of discourses on the question are woven into the book so that we feel that the history and literature, as well as the phenomenon of masochism have been presented to us.

Bloom's sexuality is perverse. When Bella Cohen summons up the 'sins of the past' in 'Circe', they enumerate a catalogue of outrages, from 'clandestine marriage', to onanistic exposures, coprophilia, masochistic willing cuckoldry and voyeurism (*U* 649–50). Evidently an aesthetic of excess is at work here, but it is nonetheless a pointed or measured excess. The list is a calculated outrage to the principles of casuistic legitimacy. Yet Bloom retains his precarious normality throughout. He is, as Joyce's letter explained, saved (even when he has given up his protective potato to Zoe: *U* 599–600) by his 'indifference due to masturbation'.[103] More than any physiological benefits he may derive from his solitary practice, it is the new onanistic concept of sexuality that saves him in the reader's eyes, permitting, even requiring, a degree of 'perversity' in order to guarantee the 'normality' of his deviation from the narrow traditional ideal.

The discursive perversity through which that sexual perversity is articulated offers extravagant condemnations or vindications of his sexual character, draws attention to itself, and even leaves us in a state of uncertainty as to what precisely may be said to be Bloom's sexual character. Yet it never fully obscures the polemical, modern, onanistic idea of sexuality which is implicitly endorsed by our celebration of Circean excessiveness and our sympathy with Bloom's character and actions.

3 Women

Joyce and feminism

Joyce's writing played little part in the upsurge of interest in feminism and feminist literary criticism that took place in the 1960s. Kate Millet in *Sexual Politics* found Joyce worthy of no more than a passing mention. She wrote that he was guilty of naive participation in the 'cult of the primitive' and 'fond of presenting woman as "nature", "unspoiled primaeval under-standing", and the "eternal feminine"'.[1] Critics tended to represent Joyce either as uninterested in such issues or else were led to admit, if reluctantly, that his fictional representation of women seems to fall into many of the faults against which modern feminists complain. 'It seems certain,' wrote Marilyn French, with a disturbing conviction, 'that Joyce had contempt for women'.[2]

Perhaps it is not altogether to be regretted that there has been this kind of neglect, since some feminist critics have been keen to diagnoze characteristic failings in past literature, and with the increasing philosophic and psychological complexity of their arguments, have found failings in most male writers. Yet that neglect has obscured important ways in which Joyce's fiction suggests a continuity of feeling with some of the strongest traditions of nineteenth- and twentieth-century feminist thought.

That continuity of feeling is apparent in the circumstances of Joyce's publication of his work from 1901, when his disdainful, mandarin attack on the Irish National Theatre, 'The Day of the Rabblement', having been rejected by the college magazine, was privately printed along with Francis Sheehy-Skeffington's essay on the admission of women to universities.[3] It would be impossible to overstate the importance of Joyce's 'discovery' by *The Egoist* to the recognition of his literary talent. *Dubliners* had still not appeared in print when the serialization of *A Portrait* began there and that breakthrough was needed to make Grant Richards move.[4] *The Egoist*, as is well known, grew out of the feminist magazines *The Freewoman* (1911–13) and *The New Freewoman* (1913),[5] and Joyce highlighted the feminist connection in *Finnegans Wake*, compressing the chronology of *A Portrait*'s appearance to commemorate 'that New Free Woman with novel inside' (*FW* 145.29). Harriet Shaw Weaver, who was closely involved with *The Egoist* (and for that matter, was a keen supporter of the WSPU), furthered Joyce's literary career for the rest of her life, in the most generous and dedicated spirit.[6]

Most influential criticism has played down the feminist aspect of this connection.[7] It was Pound who acted between Joyce and *The New Freewoman*. His first approach suggested little enthusiasm for the feminist cause, apologizing for the name of the paper '*guère que d'hommes y contribuent*',[8] and many critics have felt that Pound's increased involvement constituted a break with its feminist past. Yet the situation at *The Egoist* was parallel to that of *The Little Review* in Chicago where *Ulysses* was first serialized. There too Pound found a niche for Joyce among forward-looking literary women whose position on feminism was made clear in their opening editorial: 'Feminism? A clear-thinking magazine can have only one attitude: the degree of ours is ardent!'[9]

To some extent Joyce's popularity amongst influential literary women declined on the appearance of *Ulysses*. Virginia Woolf, who had written favourably of its early episodes in *The Times Literary Supplement*, began to find Joyce 'underbred'; Rebecca West, a contributor to *The New Freewoman* before 1914, attacked him in *The Strange Necessity*; and Katherine Mansfield objected strongly to his 'peculiar male arrogance'.[10] But that was a Bloomsbury reaction more than a general one. In Paris Joyce enjoyed the continued friendship and support of Sylvia Beach and Adrienne Monnier through the 1920s and 30s and Harriet Weaver remained loyal to the end. Few of Joyce's recorded comments in these later years offer much evidence of an enlightened interest in feminism. Sylvia Beach describes Joyce's peculiar, old-fashioned politeness in the company of ladies and his 'puritanical ideas';[11] Frank Budgen records an outburst when Joyce declared the inability of women to compose philosophical systems;[12] and Mary Colum was the

victim of an apparently unequivocal attack, recorded in Ellmann's biography, when Joyce said 'I hate intellectual
women'.[13] It is comments like this that have coloured the
popular image of Joyce and obscured the relationship between
contemporary feminism and his success. But Joyce did not
forget that relationship. When Bloom is riding high in a
hallucination on Bella Cohen's doorstep in 'Circe', praised as
'the world's greatest reformer', 'A feminist' quite appropriately
joins the accolade (*U* 604).

Is there, then, more interest in these issues in the fiction than
has been recognized? Skeffington himself appears as a character
in both *Stephen Hero* and *A Portrait* and that might be the first
place to look. He is introduced into the surviving chapters of
Stephen Hero as 'a serious young feminist named McCann' (*SH*
43), who attends the literary and musical evenings of the
Sheehy family (the Daniels, as they are called in *Stephen Hero*)
that provided Joyce with much material for his epiphanies, for
Stephen Hero, Dubliners and *A Portrait*. He is potentially a
friend and ally, though also a rival to Stephen. McCann is the
only one of Stephen's peers who knows anything of Ibsen (*SH*
46 and 51); it is to his debating society that Stephen reads his
controversial paper and McCann is one of its few defenders (*SH*
104–10). It is true that Stephen expresses little overt sympathy
with McCann's liberal schemes. He loves 'to riddle these theories with agile bullets' (*SH* 54) and is critical of McCann's
society and his student newspaper 'The Tablet' (no doubt thus
named to suggest its decalogic orthodoxy or its anodyne
effect). He refuses to sign McCann's petition for universal
peace (*SH* 117–20). Yet McCann's is the only figure whose
intellectual stature is allowed to rival Stephen's.

Elsewhere the book seems to display kinds of feminist sympathy, in its sympathetic portrayal of the hopeless death of
Stephen's sister Isabel, for instance, who was always 'an after-
thought' in the family (*SH* 170). The misery of Isabel
is contrasted in *Stephen Hero* to the life and vigour of
Emma Clery. Stephen meets Emma at the Daniel's and she is
introduced precisely as a forward, self-possessed, modern
woman:

A dark full-figured girl was standing before him and, without waiting
for Miss Daniel's introduction, she said:
– I think we know each other already.   (*SH* 51)

It is this quality he admires in her and when their relationship is at its strongest the feminist implications are clear. She accuses him of misogyny. He denies it. She asks him if he is 'a believer in the emancipation of women'. 'To be sure', is his reply (*SH* 158). He tries to shock her, talking of the sins he would like her to confess to him, and is pleasantly surprised by the quickness of her reply (*SH* 159).

What Stephen dislikes in Emma is her coyness and the root of this is quite explicitly declared to be social convention and not some inherent quality of the female sex: 'he suspected that by her code of honour she was obliged to insist on the forbearance of the male and to despise him for forebearing' (*SH* 73). In the end, when he proposes directly to her that they abandon convention and make love, his suspicions about the power of her obligations to society arc confirmed. Despite her feministic admiration of a skit called '*The Female Fellow*' in the College magazine, she is not emancipated enough, as he sees it, to go to bed with him (*SH* 192, 202–3).

Emma's brightness and nationalism were traits that Joyce worked into the character of Molly Ivors in 'The Dead'. She is 'a frank-mannered talkative young lady' who teases Gabriel effortlessly and cheerfully about his reviewing for *The Daily Express*. There is no doubt that she is portrayed as an Ibsenite new woman among the quiet Dublin set, arguing for nationalism and refusing to be shepherded home by Gabriel when she can quite easily fend for herself.[14] Gabriel is 'lame' by comparison with her, yet such is the close narrative sympathy of Joyce's technique that many readers agree with his sensitive reaction to her 'propagandism' and feel well pleased with the gibe he makes in his speech at her '*very serious and hypereducated generation*' (*D* 219).

We might be on unsteady ground looking for an expression of Joyce's feminism in his presentation of Molly Ivors's character, for she is the object of that mild satire of which *Dubliners* is full. But the story of Gabriel Conroy seems tailor-made for feminist interpretation. Gabriel's evening consists in a succession of significant encounters with women. He slightly misjudges his opening remarks to Lily, thinking of her as a girl with a rag doll and patronizingly commenting, 'I suppose we'll be going to your wedding one of these fine days' (*D* 202). He is taken aback by the forwardness and self-possession of her manner. His speech is calculated to please the three middle-aged women that are his hostesses, but his complacent enjoyment of that success is built up only to be deflated by the climax of the story when he recognizes, despite his pride in her 'wifely' manner and his desire to 'master' or 'overmaster' Gretta, that the most important parts of her life are the parts that are hers alone. He is a Torvald Helmer, only gradually recognizing that his kindly meant comments may not be so sympathetically received.

Many features of Gabriel's character, not least his reviewing work and fascination with his wife's infidelities, are features Joyce drew from his own life, but we should not be taken in by that. Gabriel is a sympathetic character in two important respects. We see with an astonishing clarity what it is like to feel as he does; moreover, technically, the narrative, in its idiom and point of view, conveys attitudes that we might suppose to be those of Gabriel himself.[15] But the larger sympathy that the story invites from us is neither for Gabriel's rather prim and largely deferential sensibility, nor for his success in flattering the 'Three Graces', nor his denigration of Molly Ivors. It is for Gabriel's great recognition, at the end of the story, of the separateness and individuality of Gretta, and of the fact that she is no mere instrument of his desires, that we are asked to feel most strongly.

Whilst the spirit of *A Doll's House* evidently informs the story (and sharp-eyed readers may feel that the talk of a superstition of seeing a white horse on O'Connell Bridge recalls the horses of *Rosmersholme*[16]), it is characteristic of the subtlety of Joyce's allusive strategy that there is no overt recognition of the central articulations of feminism. There is no reference to what Joyce calls, in *Finnegans Wake*, 'Mill (J) *On Woman* with Ditto on the Floss' (*FW* 213.2), but rather an angry reference which Aunt Kate makes to a papal decree made in 1903 excluding women from Church choirs.[17] The story articulates its feminist critique by examination of anti-feminism, whether that be the well-intentioned but patronizing attitudes of Gabriel or the reactionary authority of the Church. In that it is rather typical of the *Dubliners* stories, many of which share a broadly feministic understanding of social and sexual relationships, but none of which articulate that in a directly polemical way.

There are no 'new women' besides Molly Ivors. The women

may be self-seeking, materialistic mothers looking to exploit the commercial potential of their daughters, like Mrs Mooney in 'A Boarding House' or Mrs Kearney in 'A Mother'. The girls are deluded and incapable like Eveline, unable to break out of their inhibitions like Maria in 'Clay', or cynically exploited by men like the servant girl in 'Two Gallants'. Hélène Cixous in her psychobiographical account finds them so unsympathetically portrayed as to suggest that, in them, Joyce was expressing his own misogynistic fears of women and of the 'marriage trap'.[18] Downtrodden they are, but the manner of their constraint, misled by vain, romantic longings and forced to sell themselves to the highest matrimonial bidder, suggests a kind of complaint against the social institutions governing the lives of women similar to that which many feminists have made.

Critics have noticed the stereotyping of the women; but the male characters in *Dubliners* are just as constrained by their sexual identity, whether that be the childish longings of the boy in 'Araby', the self-destructive competitiveness of Jimmy in 'After the Race', or Little Chandler in 'A Little Cloud', or the blind, self-centred isolation of James Duffy in 'A Painful Case' which brings about the suicide of the only woman to whom he can get at all close. Joyce drew on details of his own life to create these characters and the sensitivity and understanding of his portrayal of them has suggested to some critics an almost complete identification. Even so they remain portrayals of limited understandings, ironic depictions of victims of the social expectations demanded of them because of their sex.

There is no difficulty in identifying the source of this 'structure of feeling' which binds Joyce's stories to feminism. It is to be found in his reading of Ibsen at university. Joyce is reported to have said to a journalist in 1936 that Ibsen 'was no more a feminist than I am an archbishop',[19] but that clearly contradicts what he said to Arthur Power: 'You ignore the spirit which animated him. The purpose of *The Doll's House*, for instance, was the emancipation of women, which has caused the greatest revolution in our time in the most important relationship there is – that between men and women; the revolt of women against the idea that they are the mere instruments of men.'[20] Joyce said in his famous review of *When We Dead Awaken* that 'Ibsen's knowledge of humanity is nowhere more obvious than in his portrayal of women', choosing to admire Irena, who 'holds our gaze for the sheer force of her intellectual capacity', forgetting that she makes such a point of her subservience to Arnold Rubeck.[21] The view of Ibsen is endorsed by Havelock Ellis in his book *The New Spirit*, which Joyce owned in Trieste. Shaw's better known *Quintessence of Ibsenism* valued the 'discussions' in Ibsen, but Ellis finds 'the rise of women to supreme power in the near future' as 'an unfailing source of hope'. His account praises not just Ibsen's overt feminist polemics but his creation of 'a strong and passionate woman, instinct with suppressed energy to which the natural outlets have been closed, and which is transformed into volcanic outbreaks of disaster'.[22]

According to Ellis, 'the women – Selma, Iona, Nora, Mrs Alving, Rebecca – are full of unconquerable energy', and Joyce may well have been remembering the list when he sets out in the *Exiles* notes to go one step beyond Ibsen: 'Europe is weary even of the Scandinavian women (Hedda Gabler, Rebecca Rosmer, Asta Allmers) who the poetic genius of Ibsen created when the Slav heroines of Dostoievsky and Turgenev were growing stale. On what women will the light of the poet's mind now shine?'[23]

By the time he was preparing to write *Exiles* Joyce's views on women had developed from the Ibsenite model, to the extent that in his notes towards the characterization of Richard Rowan he says, 'Richard must not appear as a champion of woman's rights. His language at times must be nearer to that of Schopenhauer against women and must show at times a deep contempt for the long-haired, short-legged sex' (*E* 169). Joyce wanted Richard to seem, as indeed he does seem, a self-enclosed, highly principled kind of rebel, commenting, as his note continues, that Christ was just such a figure who (if Catholicism 'with its infallible practical instinct' had not invented the figure of the Madonna) would have had nothing to do with women. Schopenhauer's essay 'On Women', from which the two epithets are drawn, is listed among the Trieste books and its superior, knowing tone served Joyce's purpose well.[24] The misogynistic isolation of Gabriel Conroy and James Duffy is put to work in Richard Rowan in the cause of a wider kind of emancipation, for, though Richard is not to appear 'a champion of woman's rights', the whole drift of his moral stance is to insist that Bertha make her sexual and emotional choices by herself. That much he has in common with feminism; the main bone of contention is the same as Joyce's central characters have had with feminists all along. When Stephen and McCann are discussing *Ghosts* in *Stephen Hero*, Stephen's exasperation reaches a high point when McCann claims that '*Ghosts* teaches self-repression' (*SH* 57). For Stephen, part of the problem may be that plays don't really 'teach' anything but, more to the point, he cannot accept that Ibsen's spirit argues for anything other than liberation. It is not the feminism but the refusal to be fully emancipated, in Emma Clery's residual coyness and in Molly Ivors's high neckline and narrow nationalism that is the indication of the limitedness of their views.

Sexual dimorphism

In Simone de Beauvoir's memorable account, the root of the difficulty in sexual attitudes is the dominant male habit of thinking of women as separate beings: 'He is the Subject, he is the Absolute – she is the Other.'[25] It is a habit of thought which is utterly pervasive in writings on sexuality, from Darwin who averred that 'Man is more courageous, pugnacious and energetic than woman, and has a more inventive genius'[26] as far as Freud, whose habit of talking of women's 'genital deficiency' has been much attacked by recent feminist critics.[27] Post-Darwinist writers particularly reckoned that there was a host of 'secondary sexual characteristics' that determined and justified the divisions of social role between the sexes; these included avowedly feministic writers like Havelock Ellis, whose *Man and Woman* deals with the theme.[28]

Belief in dimorphism of secondary sexual characteristics was very widespread and had some impact on avant-garde literary circles in the form of Rémy de Gourmont's mystically Darwinist *Physique de l'amour*, which was translated by Ezra Pound and admired by, for instance, Guillaume Apollinaire.[29] De Gourmont depicts evolution as a development from primitive asexuality to the enormous differences between the sexes among the 'higher' races of mankind. Sexuality is entirely determined by reproduction and he extols the virtues of the human couple whose sole aim, as he sees it, is to 'free the female from all care that is not purely sexual, to permit her the most perfect accomplishment of her most important function'.[30] Men alone, he says, are capable of abstract and inventive thinking; the brain is mysteriously related to the male sperm. Nature is feministic inasmuch as the male of the species is merely accidental to the all-important reproductive function of the female. The 'factitious equality' which modern feminists claim (he says) would only ensure their prolonged slavery.[31]

Sexual difference was in the air, then, and Joyce was among those whose imagination was exercised by it. Conventionally he wrote to Stanislaus, suggesting that women were a group apart about whom one needed specialist knowledge: 'As a matter of fact I know very little about women and you, probably, know less and I think you ought to submit this part of the case to Aunt Josephine who knows more than either of us.'[32] According to Ellmann, Joyce 'was always labouring to isolate female characteristics' and some of the results of this labour survive in the *Scribbledehobble* notebook, where Joyce collected a number of remarks beginning with the letter 'w' that refer to supposed special characteristics of women, from 'W go in twos' to 'W not know her serv's name'.[33] Ellmann records, and Joyce's notebooks confirm, that Joyce knew the work of Otto Weininger, who wrote an extreme work of sexual metaphysics, *Sex and Character*.[34] He argues that women are essentially irrational and consequently unable to participate in intellectual or moral disciplines: a theory whose credibility is severely limited by the fact that Weininger includes all Jews of either sex along with women in his classification. Yet from such books Joyce gathered enough material on the observed or presumed differences between the sexes that Jung famously praised his expertise on the subject: 'I suppose the devil's grandmother knows so much about the real psychology of a woman. I didn't.'[35]

Some of the material Joyce collected went into Bloom's day-long cogitations, which return with a high degree of psychological verisimilitude to this theme. Women are fickle, he thinks, 'They believe in chance because like themselves' (*U* 480), and vain, 'Best place for an ad to catch a woman's eye on a mirror' (*U* 484). There is a neat division between the sexes which Bloom looks to pin down: 'Woman and Man that is. Fork and Steel. Molly, he' (*U* 487). The world is full of analogies to sexual difference: 'Man and woman, love, what is it? A cork and bottle' (*U* 619). When Bloom unlocks the yard gate at 7 Eccles Street to let Stephen go home he puts 'an arruginated male key in the hole of an unstable female lock' (*U* 826). Ultimately superstitions may be rationalized in its terms, like Bloom's theory of the aphrodisiac effect of 'bivalve' oysters given in 'Circe': 'Always open sesame. The cloven sex. Why they fear vermin, creeping things' (*U* 633). 'Three holes all women' (*U* 368), he reductively concludes.

The Schopenhauer essay that Joyce used in the notes for *Exiles* begins with a quotation from Jouy, placing women's role as a threefold one, ministering to men's needs in birth, reproduction and then in laying out their bodies.[36] Bloom, in 'Hades', makes just this kind of statement, commenting that it is 'Extraordinary the interest they take in a corpse. Glad to see us go we give them such trouble coming' (*U* 108). Stephen, when asked to supply details of the life of Anne Hathaway in 'Scylla and Charybdis', makes just the same association. 'She saw him into and out of the world,' he says. 'She took his first embraces. She bore his children and she laid pennies on his eyes to keep his eyelids closed when he lay on his deathbed' (*U* 243).

Stephen is critical of the naivety or anti-feminism of others. He remembers Patrice Egan, whom he met in Paris, with his 'plump bunny's face'. 'About the nature of women he read in Michelet' (*U* 51) is his comment and Michelet, in *La Femme*, *L'Amour* and *Priests, Women and Families*, does indeed describe the nature of women: their weakness and unsuitability for work; the tragedy that results if they are separated from domestic and maternal duties; the fact that men should marry even though the prospect seems so unappealing.[37] Stephen can observe the anti-feminism of Best and Eglinton: 'Unwed, unfancied, ware of wiles, they fingerponder nightly each his variorum edition of *The Taming of the Shrew*' (*U* 274). Yet it is undoubtedly the case that his own thinking and that of Bloom are based on notions of sexual difference.

Joyce's fictional world is one which clearly depends upon a strong sense of difference between the sexes. 'Penelope,' he wrote, 'begins and ends with the female word yes.' He constructed a special 'female' language for it. It is a chapter whose impact and success is built on the idea of a separate female character which it newly reveals: an abstracted female identity of 'perfectly sane full amoral fertilisable untrustworthy engaging shrewd limited prudent indifferent *Weib*'.[38] This list of female qualities, we might note, is a far cry from the English Victorian sentimentalization of female domesticity, from 'The Angel in the House' and from Acton, who wrote that 'love of home, of children and of domestic duties are the only passions [women] feel'.[39] It contains some rather Weiningerian elements (like 'untrustworthy' and 'amoral'), but it is evidently designed to be a celebratory characterization. It contains intellectual and moral, as well as physical qualities and in its suggestion, for instance, that women are 'perfectly sane' it goes some way toward mitigating the suggestion, in many such lists, that women are 'inferior' or 'other'.

Joyce was by no means innocent in his attempt at constructing a separate female identity. The pitfalls of such thinking are well communicated in 'Nausicaa', where Gerty sentimentalizes her relationship with Reggy Wylie, feeling that Reggy cares for her because she is 'a womanly woman', 'not like other flighty girls, unfeminine, he had known, those cyclists showing off what they hadn't got' (U 466). Gerty feels sure that Father Conroy will indulge any amount of the coy drivel she confesses to him as coming 'from the nature of woman instituted by God' (U 466–7). In Joyce's writing such assumptions about male and female identity are made self-consciously apparent; in Gerty their shallow self-deceit is evident and in 'Ithaca' the full weight of catechistic rationalization is applied to the 'special affinities' that exist between the moon and woman, under which weight any potentially mystifying effect of such conventional analogies is crushed (U 823–4).

The self-consciousness with which Joyce exploited such attitudes is surely one of the means by which A Portrait is so psychologically convincing in its portrayal of Stephen's adolescent relationships with women. Criticism has been confused on this point, seeming to think Joyce a naive example of that male tendency of seeing women either as virgins or as whores, against which feminists understandably complain.[40] It is, however, apparent that the distinction between 'virgins' and 'whores', between Emma and the woman in the black straw hat, begins in Stephen Hero as a form of sociological critique more than as a projection of Stephen's desires. It was during the process of revision that the division became a part of Stephen's psychology; Joyce's reading contains three novels from which he might have been able to gain a conscious and detached

understanding of this aspect of adolescent thinking. In Jacobsen's *Siren Voices* the young bride Fennimore scoffs at Niels
Lyhnne's defence of female purity: 'why will you exalt us to the
stars with the one hand when, with the other, you must drag us
down? Can you not let us walk with you on earth as fellow-
mortals and nothing else?'[41] In Marcelle Tinayre's *The House of
Sin*, which Joyce reviewed in 1903, there is a contrast between a
modern materialistic attitude to sex and that of a traditional,
religious young man who thinks of women as 'Sin, Damnation,
the Scarlet Woman' and Joyce commented on this 'double
temperament' in his review.[42] The hero of Dujardin's *L'Initiation au péché*, which Joyce bought as *A Portrait* was under-
going its revision, is also torn between idealization of the
Catholic Virgin Mother and desire for prostitutes.[43] Joyce
apparently used these books to reshape Stephen into an adolescent idealizer of women with the same conscious distance
that he used when he made Gabriel into a Torvald Helmer.

Men's half-conscious attitudes to women were quite well
recognized by Joyce before recent attention was focussed onto
them by feminist writers. Characteristic sexual identifications
were also recognized by him. In *Finnegans Wake*, we might
want to say that there is a degree of conventionality in the
consistent identifications between girls and the days of the
month, girls and flowers, women and rivers, men and build-
ings, and so on. The world is pressed into gender. Yet there is a
considerable amount of intentional disruption of sexual
identifications. ALP has a 'female' Lord's Prayer, 'haloed be her
eve, her singtime sung, her rill be run, unhemmed as it is
uneven' (*FW* 104.2–3). In a particularly sexually confused part
of Book II Chapter 4 there appear the Irish liberators 'Mrs
Dana O'Connell' (*FW* 386.22) and 'Lady Jales Casemate' (*FW*
387.22–3), as well as 'Her Grace the Bishop' (*FW* 387.25). We
need look no further than the first line of the *Wake*, where
Adam and Eve is changed to 'Eve and Adam's' (*FW* 3.01), to
observe this quasi-feministic inversion: one that is only to be
expected in what Joyce once called his 'mistresspiece'.[44] Gerty
thinks she is a 'womanly woman' and the preening Miss
Kennedy in 'Sirens' is 'like lady, lady like' (*U* 340); but in 'Oxen'
the identifications are turned over when we are told of Miss
Purefoy's birth that the 'brave woman had manfully helped' (*U*
550). The exclamation 'how like a woman' (*FW* 454.20) is far

from stereotyping when, as here in *Finnegans Wake*, it is used
to describe a man.

Though Joyce's women have characters which are determined by their sex to an extraordinary degree, this can hardly be
called a misogynistic approach since many of his men suffer the
same fate, when seen through women's eyes, like Gabriel and
Michael Furey in 'The Dead', Richard and Robert in *Exiles*, or
Bloom and Boylan in *Ulysses*. Bloom himself, we might argue,
has to undergo a distinct split in his personality between the
uxorious 'Poldy' and the spurious gallant Henry Flower (as he
appears in 'Circe': *U* 634–8) because of the sexual oppression
he suffers.

We can hardly object to the characterization of Molly Bloom
on the grounds that she is given little abstract or philosophic
intelligence, when Joyce does his best to create for Leopold,
too, a down-to-earth, pragmatic, everyday curiosity and when
he evidently values Bloom's mentality as highly as the more conventionally impressive intelligence of Stephen Dedalus. Joyce,
when composing *Exiles*, was trying to think of a way of repre-
senting women which, far from rejecting the feministic
advances of Ibsen, envisaged a new tradition, continuing from
the 'Slav heroines' of Dostoievsky, through Ibsen's spirited,
self-discovering women, to some new, as-yet-undiscovered
figure. Bertha in *Exiles* achieves little stature and hardly fulfilled
Joyce's hope, but Molly Bloom surely does represent a new
kind of fictional woman: massive, potent and self-possessed.
Though few modern feminists have wished to avail themselves
of that image of femininity, it was evidently one which Joyce
constructed out of his own version of feminist literary tradition
and its obtrusive sexual dimorphism is conceived as a vindication of, rather than an attack on, femininity.

Joyce's interest in a work like that by Weininger needs to be
put into context. It is the impossible identification of Jews and
women that most offends reason in Weininger's argument and
reveals that he is describing the effects of (more than a justification for) the oppression of these groups. Joyce retains the
twinned prejudice in the views of Deasy in 'Nestor', who is
both anti-feminist and anti-semitic, but more importantly he
inverts the value system of Weininger's book, making womanliness and Jewishness positive features of these new figures
for modern literature. In that sense he uses sexual dimorphism

in a radical and progressive way. One of the most common arguments of the Darwinist analysts of primitive societies was that man was archetypally the hunter and woman the domestic.[45] We know that *Ulysses* in its first conception was to be a short story for *Dubliners* about a man named Hunter.[46] Some authors might have found it appropriate to have portrayed a philandering Byronic Odysseus truly representative of 'man the hunter'. Joyce's joke was to imagine a 'hunter' who was also a cuckold, passive as well as active and the victim of his sexual role.

Ulysses, as much as *Finnegans Wake*, purports to be a 'mistresspiece' and Joyce found the Homeric authority for such a view in Samuel Butler's theory that *The Odyssey* was written by a woman.[47] Butler's scholarship, identifying the Homeric locations in places around the coast of Sicily, is deliberately perverse. But there is a sense in which his argument that the militaristic, bloody *Iliad* is 'masculine' and the domestic, travelogic *Odyssey* 'feminine', holds true to the 'feel' of the two books. Butler identifies 'love of a small lie' and the concern for the blood on 'the dining room carpet', when Penelope's suitors are killed, as feminine qualities. Of course this upholds traditional distinctions between male and female characters, and ones that may be offensive to many modern ears, yet the fact that Joyce emphasizes the female and domestic in creating his modern *Odyssey* has obvious importance here.

The sense that *Ulysses* is a 'female' book and that a radical reinterpretation of masculinity and femininity is taking place is confirmed by Stephen's theory of Shakespeare articulated in 'Scylla and Charybdis'. Stephen may talk of women in Schopenhauerian terms but the larger import of his theory is to give women a central position in Shakespeare's plays and in his life. It is 'female' theory, elevating the figure of Anne Hathaway from her traditional position of obscurity to a central role, a theory which depends on a new characterization of, as Best calls her, 'Mrs S' (*U* 258). 'Till now we had thought of her, if at all, as a patient Griselda, a Penelope stay at home' (*U* 258). Stephen makes her into a powerful, sexually aggressive, deceitful woman, just as Joyce redefines the classic image of a faithful 'Penelope' to present a self-possessed, adulterous Molly Bloom.

The third sex

While a sense of sexual dimorphism was strong in Joyce's fiction and he was able both to disrupt its naive assumptions, to exploit them for psychological verisimilitude and to convert them into the creation of a new kind of woman, Joyce also experimented with ideas of intermediate or androgynous sexual identity. The first surviving incident is in the 'epiphany', re-worked into *A Portrait*, in which an older woman (presumably one of Joyce's great aunts in the house on Usher's Island) mistakes Stephen's sex.[48] Oblique as are many of the epiphanic moments, we may presume that this is the important and revealing element since in the reworking many of the other elements are modified.

In *Stephen Hero* Stephen observes the students in the Christian Brothers' school 'holding their soutanes up as women do with their skirts when they cross a muddy street' (*SH* 77), and when he is defending his paper to the College President he once more notices the 'slow hermaphroditic gesture' made with the long robe (*SH* 103). In *A Portrait* the clergy get the same treatment. The dean of studies at the university is 'womanish' (*P* 203) and 'the Capuchin dress', according to the director at Belvedere, 'is rather too ...', leading on to an epiphany-like exchange whose transsexual implications are clear:

–*Les jupes* they call them in Belgium.
The vowel was so modified as to be indistinct.
–What do they call them?
–*Les jupes*.
–O.   (*P* 158)

Stephen's schoolfriends are implicated, like the Clongowes student Boyle, who 'was called Tusker Boyle but some fellows called him Lady Boyle because he was always at his nails, paring them' (*P* 44). Bertie Tallon has to play a female part in the Whitsuntide play at Belvedere and the incident is not allowed to pass without a teasing little exchange (*P* 76).

Clergy and school are lightly satirized here, not just in the suggestion of effeminacy but in the recognition that purportedly chaste institutions can nevertheless be seen to have strong sexual undercurrents. Feminine traits, in themselves, are hardly to be condemned in Joyce since Stephen himself has, as we are told in *Stephen Hero*, 'a small feminine mouth' and since his father in *A Portrait* calls him a 'lazy bitch', much to his grammatical indignation (*P* 178–9). In 'Circe', Zoe notices his 'woman's hand' (*U* 667).

Bloom too has feminine characteristics. He is able to be sympathetic to women, in his visit to Mina Purefoy, and in smaller details such as in 'Hades' where he thinks of John O'Connell, the joking graveyard caretaker: 'Fancy being his wife' (*U* 136). Bloom has a 'firm full masculine feminine passive active hand' in 'Ithaca' (*U* 788). On Howth Head among the wild ferns with Molly he is on the receiving end of a sexually inverted kind of insemination: 'Softly she gave me in my mouth the seedcake warm and chewed' (*U* 224). In 'Circe' he is diagnozed by Mulligan as 'bisexually abnormal' and by Dr Dixon as 'the new womanly man' and 'about to have a baby'. He is showered with generosity and instantly, like the story-book goose, gives birth to eight golden and silver children (*U* 613–14). The number, presumably, recalls the eight children of John O'Connell's wife with whom he felt sympathy in 'Hades'.

Bloom's confinement and delivery in 'Circe' are apparently an exaggerated recapitulation of the joke Mulligan makes in 'Scylla and Charybdis' (though how it finds its way into Bloom's unconscious is not clear). The joke begins with Stephen's theory of Shakespeare. The idea is that Shakespeare is to be identified with the ghost of the old king in *Hamlet*, not with the young prince. Stephen argues that Shakespeare's own father died as he was writing the play and that he was therefore no longer likely to represent himself as a son but as a father figure. Fatherhood, Stephen explains, is not to be thought of as a biological relationship. He dismisses the 'instant of blind rut' that connects son and father biologically and says that, since Boccaccio's Calandrino, no man has 'felt himself with child' the way a woman does. Mulligan's response is immediately to play-act at giving birth: 'Wait. I am big with child. I have an unborn child in my brain. Pallas Athena! A Play! The play's the thing! Let me parturiate!' (*U* 267). It is a joke repeated in the 'Oxen of the Sun', where Mulligan's beer paunch is described as a 'male womb' (*U* 528): a serious point in Stephen's argument, since Stephen thinks that Shakespeare, no longer a son to his father, could become, through the creation of his plays, the 'father of all his race' (*U* 267).[49]

It is from one's mother, Stephen claims, that one learns 'how to bring thoughts into the world' (*U* 243); the imagination is in this sense androgynous. But sexual indeterminacy is important to literature in another way since, on a more practical level, men must be able to identify with women to construct convincing female characters and vice versa. This is the point Joyce made in his college review of *When We Dead Awaken*, where he complimented Ibsen on his female characters:

he seems to know them better than they know themselves. Indeed, if one may say so of an eminently virile man, there is a curious admixture of the woman in his nature. His marvellous accuracy, his faint traces of femininity, his delicacy of swift touch, are perhaps attributable to this admixture.   (*CW* 64)

It is this quality in Ibsen that Joyce tried to emulate when, twenty years later, he was completing his 'female' *Odyssey*. Fascinated by such ideas, Joyce could not resist working into *Ulysses* the theory of Edward Vining that Hamlet was, in fact, a woman and the production of *Hamlet* that did indeed take place on 15 June 1904 in Dublin, with an American woman actress in the role of the prince. Both Bloom and John Eglinton mention these things (*U* 93 and 254). It is through *Hamlet* that Stephen prophesies that in heaven sexual distinctions will be removed. There will be 'no more marriages, glorified man, an androgynous angel, being a wife unto himself' (*U* 274).

There are a number of works which Joyce had in his library which confirm this interest in androgyny. In his copy of Allan Kardec's spiritualist interpretation of the Bible, Joyce marked off a passage which argued that the story of the creation of Eve from Adam's rib has a concealed moral. It shows that women are made of the same substance as men and are not therefore separate or subservient creatures.[50] The idea that originally there were no sexual divisions but a common sex is a surprisingly widespread one. It is expressed, for instance, by Birkin in Lawrence's *Women in Love*.[51] Blake, on whom Joyce lectured in Trieste, subscribed to a similar view: the sexual divisions between Los and Enitharmon are an aspect of a cosmic fall into division while the apocalyptic future holds out a promise of sexual unity. Ultimately the theory derives from the contribution of Aristophanes to Plato's *Symposium*, explaining the myth of Otis and Ephialtes, whose ambition caused the gods to create sexual difference. Joyce had translations of the *Symposium* in his library and refers to this myth in *Finnegans Wake* on at least two occasions.[52] 'Early bisectualism' (*FW* 524.12 and 36) and 'the old middlesex party' (*FW* 532.28) are mentioned in *Finnegans Wake*, and one of the titles of ALP's 'Mamafesta' weaves together Abraham and Sarah and Isaac Newton in an apparently relevant way: '*Abe to Sare Stood Icyk Neuter till Brahm Taulked Him Common Sex*' (*FW* 106.28). Joyce's 'Oxen' notesheets show him noting the presexual beginnings of the embryo in a modern scientific confirmation of this mythic history of sex: 'embryo 1st asexual'.[53]

However, there were other contemporary works in which the idea that sexual divisions were not absolute but originated at some point in history, and might be eradicated at some time in the future, took on a distinctly radical character. Joyce, as has recently become better known, was greatly interested by the sociological theories of Guglielmo Ferrero, whose works he read in 1906 in Rome.[54] Ferrero, besides his interest in antimilitarism and nationalism, was interested in the relations between the sexes. He was, as Dominic Manganiello points out, the son-in-law of the famous contemporary criminologist Cesare Lombroso and collaborated with him on a study of *La Donna delinquente* in 1893, a book which attempts to explore the criminality of women as an intrinsic quality which can be observed in physical features, the size and shape of the head and of the facial features.[55] Ferrero, Joyce acknowledged, inspired 'Two Gallants'. It was this work, rather than more conventional feministic sources, which suggested to Joyce the sexual exploitation of Corley's relationship with his servant girl; the absence of genuine 'gallantry', in Ferrero's argument, being a symptom of the militarism and decline of modern societies. In *L'Europa giovane* Ferrero elaborates a notion of 'il terzo sesso': of the 'third sex', of women who are kept apart from maternal responsibilities. Nuns and spinsters seem to him to form a separate social class which may achieve a similar rationality and power in the social world to that of men.[56]

A better-known exponent in England was Edward Carpenter, known to Lawrence and a contributor to *The New Freewoman*.[57] Carpenter's idea, argued in *Love's Coming of Age* and *The Intermediate Sex*, was that the homosexual enjoys an inherent superiority over other individuals in that he or she is not limited by sex but can sympathize with people of both sexes.

These androgynes, whom Carpenter calls 'homogenic', thus hold the key to a utopian future.[58] Carpenter's term seems to be remembered in *Finnegans Wake* where HCE is described as 'that homogenius man' (*FW* 34.14) and where 'modes coalescing proliferate homogenuine homogeneity' (*FW* 279, left margin 1–7).

It is ideas like those of Ferrero and Carpenter that Joyce draws on when he has Dixon celebrate Bloom as the 'new womanly man'. Such writers do not appear in the works explicitly but their theories evidently informed Joyce's fictional conceptions in highly important ways. Bloom might be a comic figure in his great civic fantasy in 'Circe', but the elements of 'womanliness' in his character, his passivity, domesticity, sympathy and frugality, stand at the core of his morality and significance as the credible everyman of modern fiction. Hints at this interest in transcending the barriers of sexual division can be seen in Bloom's thoughts on gelded horses ('Might be happy all the same that way': *U* 94) and the use of castrati in eighteenth-century choral music: 'Eunuch. One way out of it', he thinks (*U* 101). Yet more suggestively, Joyce confirmed the intermediate sexual identity of his leading character by giving him a grandfather whose personality might be conventionally male but whose name, Virag, has a strong flavour of the virago: a manly woman who is ancestor to a womanly man.[59]

The dominant sex

In one of the notebooks Joyce kept during the 1920s he noted down the title of a book written by Matthias and Mathilde Vaerting entitled *The Dominant Sex*.[60] It is a striking book which offers a radical revision of the theory of sexual difference proposed by writers like Otto Weininger. The Vaertings observe that, in Weininger, sexual differences are abstracted, impersonal entities more than the observed characteristics of individuals of either sex, and they argue that such abstracted qualities may not necessarily result from sexual difference at all but from the relative political dominance of either sex in any given society. They draw from such available studies of primitive matriarchy as those by Bachofen, Westermarck and Lewis Morgan to prove what they call 'the principle of monosexual dominance', that in matriarchal societies men may have what we might consider to be 'womanly' qualities and women may have 'manly' ones. They record such customs as the prostitution of women in male-dominated societies and, like Joyce, note the 'womanly' dress of priests. Indeed the whole study, though it did not appear until 1921, has much in common with the radical reading of Weininger that Joyce apparently made and with his own presentation of the relations between the sexes.

Joyce had been interested in the relative strengths of the two sexes for more than twenty years. The view that women are the 'weaker sex', fawningly obedient or else fatally mistaken like Milton's Eve, 'soft and weak and smooth', as Katherine says at the end of *The Taming of the Shrew*, formed no part of his thinking. He was much more attracted to the views expressed in Hauptmann's *Vor Sonnenaufgang* ('Before dawn') which he translated in 1901, where the social idealist Alfred Loth expresses his amazement that women are called the weaker sex since the pains they face in childbirth can be so acute.[61] Loth's comment is made at the start of Act 5 of the play, an act during which the men discuss and smoke and drink, and a doctor comes in and out from a room where a birth is taking place, rather like Joyce's scene in 'Oxen of the Sun', where Mina Purefoy acts so 'manfully' in her three-day labour.

Alfred Loth who is, in a way, the first prototype of Joyce's self-portraiture, takes the opportunity to explain the kind of woman that attracts him. He is determinedly anti-alcoholic and highly conscious of the dangers of hereditary disease, so his ideal partner will be of sound body, mind and parentage. She must be prepared to make certain renunciations but not those a conventional husband might require.

On the contrary she must act of her own free will and may ask 'everything that has been denied her sex for so many years.'[62] He is rewarded by the affection of Helen Krause, daughter of his drunken host, who is impressed by his modern ideals and faints into his arms. This may not be the most modern sexual approach but it is one that identifies her as an advanced, forward woman. In *Stephen Hero* Emma promises a similar modernity when she leans on Stephen's arm, but she denies it at last. Far from making a sexual advance, she is not even able to respond to Stephen's proposition in any other than what he sees as a passively conventional way.

Joyce admired strength and self-possession in women. His brother records his admiration for the full-figured Music Hall actresses who played in Dublin at the turn of the century,[63] and Ellmann notes that, in particular, he conceived an enthusiasm for the famous Eleanora Duse, whom he saw in London in 1900.[64] His admiration for the female figure celebrated in *Giacomo Joyce* leaves no doubt that the imperious demeanour of the woman is part of her attraction. She apparently likes horse-riding (*GJ* 4 and 8). Her furs and quizzing glasses (*GJ* 13) are reused in the characterization of Mrs Bellingham in 'Circe' (*U* 591). The implication that this strength is a kind of sexual modernity is present when Joyce breathlessly exclaims 'Hedda Gabler! Hedda Gabler!' (*GJ* 8). Another of Joyce's flirtations, revealed in the new edition of Ellmann's biography, was with a woman of the new professional class, a doctor, Getrude Kaempffer.[65]

That women should be in some part active in their sexual desire was as deeply important to Joyce as to Stephen. In his letters to Nora written in 1909 his desire to be dominated in this way is frequently apparent. He particularly enjoys recounting those incidents where Nora took the active part. 'It was you who slid your hand down inside my trousers and pulled my shorts slightly aside and touched my prick,' he insists. 'It was your lips too which first uttered an obscene word.'[66] Stephen in 'Proteus' longs to be touched by a woman's soft hand (*U* 61).

Bloom has a preference for strong women which is never far from the surface of his consciousness. He may not (as he tells Josie Breen in 'Circe' and Molly in 'Ithaca') actually have been to see Mrs Bandman Palmer in *Leah* but he has seen the advertisement hoardings and commented approvingly on her male impersonations and trenchancy.[67] The 'amours of actresses' fascinated him in 'Nausicaa' too: 'Nell Gwynn, Mrs Bracegirdle, Maud Branscombe' (*U* 482). Bloom's own amours during the day indicate the same taste. The girl next door is admired for her vigorous carpet-beating: 'strong pair of arms', he thinks (*U* 70). The tone of Martha Clifford's letter is flirtatiously authoritative; Josie Breen appears in 'Circe' wearing a man's overcoat (*U* 572); and even Mary Driscoll, the apparently exploitable servant girl, Bloom says 'counter-assaulted' him (*U* 587).

This aspect of Bloom is most apparent in his admiration for high-society women: for the 'haughty creature' he glimpses in 'Lotus-Eaters' (*U* 89–90); for Lady Mountcashel in the social pages of *The Irish Times* about whom he fantasizes; and for Miriam Dandrade with whom he associates her (*U* 203). It becomes explicitly sexual in 'Circe', where three fantasy high-society ladies (Mrs Yelverton Barry, Mrs Bellingham and The Honourable Mrs Mervyn Talboys) rebuke him for supposed sexual advances and threaten to flog and humiliate him (*U* 594). Finally Bella Cohen, the brothel madam, subjects him to a full range of masochistic humiliations. These have already been discussed as kinds of sexual aberration that Joyce built into the texture of Bloom's mind to expose the narrowness of traditional definitions of sexual normality. But masochism is a kind of aberration whose relevance to the discussion of the balance of power between the sexes is clear.

It was at one time thought (by Freud and Krafft-Ebing) that all women had an element of masochism in their sexual personalities and enjoyed a degree of subjection to the male, a suggestion quite properly rejected by feminists like Kate Millet.[68] But this idea of female masochism is partly misconceived, since masochistic feeling (as it appears in Masoch or Joyce, or in any of the immediate sources) is characteristically a feeling experienced by men, and one whose novelty and peculiar excitement is brought on by the experience of degradation before a supposedly inferior woman. As Gilles Deleuze pointed out, the kind of woman who is masochistically admired is typically not just a ruffian but has strong, rational views: 'she believes in the independence of women and the fleeting nature of love'.[69] Joyce's authority on the subject, Desroix's *Gynécocratie*, and the essays which are printed with it, is not, like Krafft-Ebing, anxious to present female domination as a psycho-sexual aberration at all but as a 'gynecocracy' or female rule, the implications of which are social and economic as well as erotic. Gynecocracy was not altogether a spurious notion, since one of the best-known anthropological studies of the century, Bachofen's *Das Mutterrecht*, was subtitled *Eine Untersuchung Über die Gynaikokratie der Alten Welt*, and the term appeared in Joyce's 'Ithaca' notesheets and in *Finnegans Wake*.[70] In Desroix's story the young Vicomte is forced to recognize (however ironically) *'Quels êtres horribles égoistes et méprisables sont les hommes*' and, in Laurent Tailhade's introduction and the concluding essays, consistent links are made between the female dominance of the story and the coming threat (since most of the essays are decidedly anti-feministic) of female rule.[71]

Bloom's encounter with Bella Cohen in 'Circe' is one which emphasizes these aspects of masochism. It is one which borrows from Desroix and, unlike Sacher-Masoch, emphasizes the exchange of sexual roles in the masochistic relationship: Bloom becomes a woman and Bella becomes a man as the conventional power-relationship is overturned. Part of Bloom's humiliation is to be forced into female clothing: 'laced with cruel force into vicelike corsets' (*U* 647). His duties are spelled out in a kind of inverted marriage ceremony, which becomes most explicit in its sense of the comparative injustice of marriage to the female partner when 'Bella' declares, 'With this ring I thee own' (*U* 650) and when Bloom is abused and sold as a mare by the whoremistress's vet.

The sexual institutions of the Arab world are introduced through Bloom's dream and further explored when, in 'Circe', Bloom is sold into the harem of Haroun Al Raschid (*U* 652). 'Bella' gives him instruction in all the coquettish wiles he will need as a woman to sell himself to the highest bidder (*U* 652) and he is ultimately condemned to the flames of a 'suttee' pyre (*U* 655).

That female domination turns Bloom into a woman and reflects the atrocities of man's domination over women is a clear indication of the closeness of Joyce's view to that of Mathilde and Matthias Vaerting. That Bloom is forced to become a male prostitute makes this section a cleverly inverted microcosm of the whole episode where, in a male-dominated world, it is implied, the women of nighttown are permanently so oppressed. It is not just that Bloom dislikes his treatment because he is 'naturally' a man but that the sexual relationship is shown to be a form of exploitation. That is the point which was made in 'Two Gallants'. Continuing his interest in Ferrero's theory of the sexual imperialism of soldiers, Joyce has Bloom think with disgust of soldiers 'courting slaveys': 'Square-pushing up against a backdoor. Maul her a bit. Then the next thing on the menu' (*U* 207). When Boylan and Lenehan appear in 'Circe' they are identified as two more gallants, joking about the conquest of Molly (*U* 669), but the point about sexual exploitation is made much more alarmingly clear when it is Bloom that is on the receiving end.

In 'Circe', Molly encourages Bloom's degradation, threatening to write to 'Bartholomona, the bearded woman' to have him beaten (*U* 670), but this is not the most important way in which she is a dominant female personality. She makes her own point about gynecocracy. It would, she says, 'be much better for the world to be governed by the women in it you wouldnt see women going and killing one another' (*U* 926). Joyce's choice of a partly masochistic temperament for his leading male character is a confirmation of this view, especially since Stephen insists on the value of female domination when expanding his Shakespeare theory in 'Circe', connecting 'shrewridden Shakespeare', 'henpecked Socrates' and the 'all-wisest stagyrite' who was 'bitted, bridled and mounted by a light of love' (*U* 565).

It is significant that it should have been in the preparation for a marital drama like *Exiles* that Joyce noted down his plans for a new direction in the presentation of women in literature. For it is not in the macrocosm of public life so much as in the microcosm of sexual relationships that the impact of his interest is felt. The character of Molly Bloom is, as I have argued, one which Joyce saw as a development from the 'slav heroines' which fascinated contemporary enquirers into matriarchal society and the Ibsenite women who did much to inspire the feminism of the early twentieth century. Molly's character also responds to the problems set up by the dramatic conflict in *Exiles* and only partially resolved by the character of Bertha Rowan. What motivates Richard is not his fear of being deceived by Bertha as much as his desire to act on the principle of honouring her free will in all things. And part of his fear is that her will is not strong enough to be able to sustain the difficulty of choosing. Bloom has no such worries with Molly since she is a much stronger woman. He can see the fallacy, as it is put in 'Ithaca', of the 'fallaciously inferred debility of the female, the muscularity of the male' (*U* 866) and this feministic recognition of female strength allows him to think his way out of a jealous reaction to Molly's infidelity.

Joyce's feminism articulates itself not only in his characters and situations but in relation to other literature. It is an

attitude which is most clearly expressed in Stephen's theory of
Shakespeare, his way of reading the plays. That theory has its
closest analogues in the two lectures Joyce gave in Trieste on
Blake and Defoe. In both lectures his approach is biographical
and deals prominently with the writers' married lives. In the
Defoe lecture, particularly, this becomes a way of reading the
work, looking at its female characters and, in this case, explicitly
relating their strength to more familiar kinds of feminism. He
inevitably praises 'the adventuress Roxana and the unforgettable
harlot Moll Flanders'. Defoe's women have the 'indecency and
continence of beasts' and in that there is a prophecy, he says: 'Mrs
Christian Davies is the presumptive great-great-grandmother of
Mrs Pankhurst'.[72]

Part of the difficulty of recognizing these views in Joyce is
that his feminism might easily be mistaken for other things.
Paul Léon wrote to Frank Budgen on the 'Nausicaa' episode of
Ulysses: 'you will receive a ponderous volume of some six
hundred pages on the origin and history of what he chooses to
call "Le Manteau de Tanit". He believes that this subject should
be treated by you with immense seriousness, respect, circum-
spection, historical sense, critical acumen, documentary accuracy, citational erudition and sweet reasonableness' (L III 280).
Budgen's treatment of the subject in his book had few of these
qualities as it transpired and a sense of frivolous eccentricity has
gathered around Joyce's interest in women's drawers. The issue
does, of course, have its serious side and one that Joyce may
well have wished to alert Budgen's attention to. He did read
about the origin and history of 'draped virginity' in the book by
Adrian Beverland (in the Buffalo library), which enquires
minutely into the clothing of Roman prostitutes. The Vaertings discuss the current masculinization of women's clothing
as an indication of a change in the power relationships between
the sexes. Indeed women's underclothing took on a distinctly
political air in the 1850s when Amelia Bloomer caused a
scandal by wearing 'bloomers', whose main offence was that
they seemed to resemble male trousers. Such a connection
between women's underclothing and their assumption of male
responsibilities was clearly felt by Joyce. He has Bloom's grandfather Virag taunt Bloom by asking: 'have you made up your
mind whether you like or dislike women in male habiliments?'
(U 631). Molly recognizes the similarity between Mrs Bloomer's

name and her own: 'girls now riding the bicycle and wearing peak caps and the new woman bloomers God send him more sense and me more money I suppose they're called after him I never thought that would be my name' (*U* 903). Women's drawers were a sociopolitical as well as a psychosexual symbol for Joyce.

One of the books whose critique of bourgeois marriage helped Joyce to develop his views, Charles Albert's *L'Amour libre*, also has a full appendix entitled *La Femme et sa libération*.[73] Albert was a socialist but one whose mind was deeply shaped by Darwinist modes of thought. Consequently, though Albert found much to admire in contemporary feminist agitation, he has to face Darwin's central notion of sexual difference. He believes that there may be kinds of difference between the sexes but that there is no inferiority: '*si la femme est plus agissante que pensante, plus spontanée et plus intuitive, plus pratique en un mot, nous ne voyons pas là preuve d'infériorité le moins du monde*'.[74]

Many modern feminists might find such an attempt to reconcile traditional ideas of sexual differentiation with an imperative of sexual equality deeply unsatisfactory, but not all have done. Germaine Greer, for instance, discussing women's so-called 'undifferentiated perceptions', commented that it was all the more unfortunate 'for men to have feeling and thought in opposition'.[75] Albert's solution is satisfactory to him since the drive of his argument is socialist as well as feminist. Economic exploitation is the evil that must be eradicated and, whilst that remains, purely sexual equality will be only what he calls '*la concurrence intersexuelle sous le fouet du despotisme capitaliste*' (intersexual concurrence under the whip of capitalist despotism).[76] This is a position which is echoed in a number of the Fabian Tracts on 'women's questions' which Joyce had in Trieste. 'No sane person', writes Mrs B.L. Hutchins in Tract 129, 'can argue that adaptability to the conditions of profit making industry can afford any test of woman's merit *qua* woman'.[77]

In Joyce's fiction the sense of the exploitation of women, either in modern 'gallantry' or in conventional marriage, is strong. He recognized, through the Vaertings' revision of Weininger and through his own fascination with kinds of androgyny, that sexual differences were as much indications of a power relationship as of pure biological differentiation. Yet the sense of sexual difference remains strong in his work. Here we might see the closeness of his thought to writers like Albert, and a genuine desire to effect a *rapprochement* between feministic and other kinds of forward-looking, liberal thought. In the masochistic sequences in 'Circe' the implication may be that sexual differences contribute to sexual exploitation, but the more characteristic impression of his fiction is that Joyce valued women characters whose sexual difference was strong. The drama of Richard Rowan in *Exiles* is one which requires, and the story of Bloom in *Ulysses* one which supplies, a new kind of woman among whose qualities self-generating free will and self-determination are high. Of that self-determination and strength, her 'shrewdness' and 'indifference', her independence, her sexual infidelity, and to an extent her sexual difference, combine to provide a full guarantee.

Joyce liked to present female characters with strong sexual desires. These sexual desires may be exposed satirically, like the self-deluding romantic aspirations of Gertie Macdowell for her Reggy Wylie in 'Nausicaa', but when they are explicitly recognized and put into words in Molly's soliloquy they are among the most strongly-endorsed feelings that an ironized Joycean character may express. Such a stance placed Joyce's work in a controversial relation to trends in contemporary thought on the subject. One of the forms of sexual differentiation common in England in the nineteenth century was the view, now frequently attributed to William Acton, that women 'are not very much troubled with sexual feeling of any kind'.[78] Joyce's fiction clearly gives the lie to that. Suzette Henke has noted that Joyce's presentation of sexuality has little in common with that of Krafft-Ebing in this respect.[79]

Contemporary feminists did not, it is true, complain much against this kind of characterization of women. Though they did not present themselves as the victims of erotic exploitation and abuse quite as vociferously as some more recent feminists, there was often an apparent distaste for sexuality among women like Josephine Butler who, along with W.T. Stead, campaigned against prostitution, and among the Pankhursts and leading suffragettes. It is this aspect of contemporary feminism that Stephen most dislikes in *Stephen Hero*. McCann, a keen reader of Stead's *Review of Reviews*, is a feminist; but for

Joyce the depth of his sexual radicalism is unimpressive since he bows to the censorship of the papers to be given to his debating society and prints such lame, timid stuff in his student paper. Emma's feminism is applauded inasmuch as it enables her to be intelligent and lively but condemned inasmuch as it cannot liberate her sufficiently to accept Stephen's sexual proposition. Stephen wants a situation where women's sexual desires are recognized as legitimate and can be gratified in a straight-forward way. Joyce evidently felt in some ways the same, insisting on the sexuality of women according to his brother's disapproving diary record of 1904. 'Jim says he has an instinct for women,' he writes. 'He scarcely ever talks decently of them even those he likes. He talks as of warm, soft-skinned animals. 'That one'd give you a great push!' 'She's very warm between the thighs, I fancy.' 'She has a great action, I'm sure'.[80]

Such ideas may, no doubt, have been culled from adolescent talk amongst his friends and from anti-feminist writings, like that of Beverland which traditionally complained against Eve as the authoress of all evil and of 'woman's sovereignty in lust'.[81] Yet the mature Joyce, writing the early episodes of *Ulysses*, deliberately distances Stephen from the conventional anti-feminism of Garrett Deasy. Deasy drones self-congratulatingly:

A woman brought sin into the world. For a woman who was no better than she should be, Helen, the wife of Menelaus, ten years the Greeks made war on Troy. A faithless wife first brought the strangers to our shore here, MacMurrough's wife and her leman O'Rourke, prince of Breffni. A woman too brought Parnell low.   (*U* 43)

His anti-feminism is identified with his anti-semitism as an equivalent kind of prejudice. Stephen's memory of himself 'on the top of the Howth tram alone crying to the rain: *naked women!*' (*U* 50) is, by contrast, a partially vindicated outburst against the enforced hypocritical chastity of the Irish women he knew.

Joyce can be seen puzzling over the question of female sexual desire in his letters of 1906, talking of men's 'cerebral sexualism and bodily fervour (from which women are normally free)' whilst women have 'maternal' and 'egoistic' love.[82] Evidently sexual difference was important to him but so was sexual desire in women. By the time he wrote 'Ithaca' the idea was of 'a constant but not acute concupiscence resident in a bodily and mental female organism' (*U* 864). The kind of liberation he valued was what he identifies in his work by quoting or misquoting the title of Grant Allen's popular novel *The Woman Who Did*. It is a version of sexual revolution cheerfully identified in *Finnegans Wake* as a time 'when all us romance catholeens shall have ones for all amanseprated. And the world is maidfree' (*FW* 239.21–2).

Whilst the suffragists thought little about the problem of rehabilitating female sexual desire, such contemporaries as Marie Stopes did their best to reject the idea that sexual instincts were abnormal in women.[83] Female sexual desire posed problems for Freudian psychoanalysis too. In founding a theory of the psychological life on sexual desire, Freud was consistently thwarted by his difficulties in placing the exact nature of female sexual desires, as several recent feminist critics of Freud have explained.[84] It is no wonder that Jung found Molly Bloom's soliloquy such an impressive piece of psychology. For Molly's desires are clearly articulated and secure and seem to answer the question that psychoanalysis could not.

In this fiction which celebrates the personal strength and sexual desires of women, and which recognizes the depth of sexual and economic exploitation, Joyce was arguably offering a kind of feminism which was as far reaching as that of the English suffragists or of such of his contemporaries as Skeffington and the Sheehy sisters. He was, moreover, presenting a kind of feminism that was compatible with his interests in socialism and with the other kinds of sexual liberalism which informed his ideas.

The woman in the black straw hat

Joyce's sense of the intrusion of mercantilism into the sexual life is a strong one. He presents marriage as an economic or legalistic institution but, rather than contrasting it with affective relationships in the romantic mode, he chooses to expose such of its manifestations as the greed of Mrs Mooney in 'A Boarding House'. Of the great catalogue of corruptions experienced by the unfortunate Krause family in Hauptmann's *Vor Sonnenaufgang*, Joyce took care to preserve the snatch of dialogue in Act 4 where Mrs Spiller hints to the obnoxious Kahl that he might trap Helen into marriage by seduction.[85] Marriage is trade and sexual attraction just one of its tricks. As Bloom learns in 'Circe', the 'daringly short skirt' is 'a potent weapon' (*U* 652). Chastity is no virtue but sexual avarice ('Guard that gem', commands Jaun in his sermon: *FW* 441.18). The naivety of Maria in 'Clay' is seen sympathetically by Joyce but not indulged since he exposes her and ironically lodges her in a house for reformed prostitutes, as if to suggest that her restraint is as much the cause as the cure of sexual exploitation. He kept to his view of chastity, expressing it in a striking reading of *Othello*, which appears as a brief note in the *Scribbledehobble* notebook: 'cruelty of sexual idiocy (Desdemona)'.[86] The idea seems to be that neither Othello's jealousy nor Iago's malignity cause the tragedy so much as Desdemona's sexual innocence. Virginity is not innocence but coyness and flirtation, whether conscious or unconscious. That is the point of transporting Gerty MacDowell's friend, Cissy Caffrey, from the sickly atmosphere of 'Nausicaa' to 'Circe' where she appears as a 'shilling whore'. Even the Church's use of the virgin as a religious symbol, Bloom thinks, is a kind of sexual bait: 'All comely virgins. That brings those rakes of fellows in' (*U* 334).

The effect of this keenly materialistic view is to blur the distinction between respectable marriage and prostitution: to see them both as forms of sexual contract that are analogous or interdependent. Such was the view of the historian W.E.H. Lecky, whose *History of European Morals* Joyce knew.[87] 'Herself the supreme type of vice,' Lecky argued,' 'she is ultimately the most efficient guardian of virtue'. Many contemporary feminists objected to what they saw as the complacency of this view but Joyce may well have been attracted to the implication that the present order of social and sexual relationships depends so much and so hypocritically upon prostitution. Of the available contemporary attitudes, Lecky's materialism seems closer to Joyce than the theory of psychological types which Lombroso and Ferrero brought to their study of *La Donna delinquente*, or the moral reformism of a W.T. Stead.

Prostitution had figured as a theme in fiction throughout the eighteenth century and, though English fiction turns its attention from such things, in the nineteenth century, in France, Balzac and Zola developed the subject still further. There was a precedent for Joyce, then, in writing on the theme and one of the surviving epiphanies shows that this interest was among the earliest he had.[88] In *Stephen Hero* it provides the basis for one of the most significant threads which runs through the surviving chapters. Stephen takes his leave of Emma in Chapter 24 and wandering on the Grand Canal bank thinking about love he runs into a woman in a black straw hat whose greeting, 'Good-night, love', sets up a contrast in his mind (*SH* 194–7). He works out his thoughts in conversation with Lynch, coming to argue, paradoxically, that it is the 'virgin' Emma who is greedy and materialistic in her sexual behaviour and the prostitute who is generous and loving (*SH* 206–8). Marriage, he argues, is a 'simoniacal' exchange in that it proposes to sell spiritual things like love, honour and obedience and 'revolts our notion of what is humanly possible' (*SH* 207). The contrast echoes that in 'Counterparts' between the sexual generosity of the prostitute and the 'little, sharp-faced woman' that is Farrington's wife at home. Prostitution is at least a more explicit exchange.

Stephen calls girls 'marsupials' and, since all women are obliged to sell their bodies in one way or another, in his scheme Emma is 'the most deceptive and cowardly of marsupials' (*SH* 215). His sympathy for whores is not all Lecky, Balzac and nineteenth-century urbane materialism, however. Typically Stephen's interest is posed as a subversive, Blakean reading of the Bible. The early notes which Joyce made for *Stephen Hero* include a reference to 'Christ's unique relations with prosti-tutes'.[89] That note explains the surprising association Stephen makes on seeing the 'Woman in the Black Straw Hat' in *Stephen Hero*, thinking immediately of Renan's narrative of the life of Christ. Renan does not stress this aspect of Christ's life (though he does mention Christ's popularity with his women followers in general and Mary Magdalen in particular), but he evidently represented for both Stephen and Joyce a key by which the scriptures might be read as a polyvalent historical document rather than as predetermined doctrine. And Joyce, here as elsewhere, gets a special pleasure from expressing a radical, materialistic point of view in terms of the life of Christ.

In *A Portrait* Stephen's wanderings take him to Dublin's red-light district and we are given a vivid scene of the young woman in the pink gown to whose charms he is only too willing to succumb. She is described as 'proud and conscious' in her sexuality, qualities which Stephen evidently values highly. Yet the starkly reasoned contrast between whore and virgin is not retained in *A Portrait*. Here Stephen's mind is the focus of attention and the situation of the girl herself obscured (*P* 103–4). It comes back into focus, though, at the end of the 'Sirens' episode of *Ulysses*, where Bloom, leaving the Ormond Hotel, encounters the 'whore from the lane'. She also wears a 'black straw sailor hat' and causes Bloom some embarrassment since she has apparently stopped him in the lane to beg his washing. Bloom does not miss the opportunity for a little well-intentioned cogitation: 'O, well, she has to live like all the rest' (*U* 375). She turns up again beside the cabman's shelter in 'Eumaeus', giving Bloom the opportunity for some pious, paternalistic observations to Stephen about the 'crying scandal that ought to be put a stop to *instanter*', tempered with a typically Bloomian qualification: 'I suppose some man is ultimately responsible for her condition' (*U* 731). Stephen, continuing in the *Stephen Hero* vein, theorizes that she is not the most culpable of merchants, since she sells only the body not the soul and he too sympathizes that 'she is a bad merchant. She buys dear and sells cheap' (*U* 731). Bloom has already warned Stephen '*re* the dangers of nighttown' (*U* 706), though he is rather too late and hardly in a position to moralize, since his own sexual initiation took place at the hands of the whore Bridie Kelly (*U* 540–1).

Stephen and Bloom have had some experience of prostitutes and Stephen claims that they share this with Christ. Joyce reinforces the sense that it is a common experience for men in Stephen's narrative of a Shakespeare who enjoys the 'foul pleasures' of 'scortatory love' with the 'punks of the bankside' (*U* 258). The thought makes Stephen remember his own indulgences in Paris: 'Cours-la-Reine. *Encore vingt sous. Nous ferons de petites cochonneries. Minette? Tu veux?*' Paris, in fact or by repute, was a familiar territory for such encounters. Stephen in nighttown offers a range of brothel *franglais* in response to Zoe's request for some 'parleyvoo' (*U* 672–3), just as Gallaher in 'A Little Cloud' has tantalized Chandler with tales of the Parisian life (*D* 83–4). Joyce fills his fictional Dublin with prostitutes, expanding the spare incident in *Stephen Hero* where the students visit the 'kips' after their exam results to the full 'Circe' episode in *Ulysses*. In 'Circe' Stephen, Lynch and Bloom are entertained by Bella Cohen, Zoe Higgins, Florry Talbot and Kitty Ricketts: whores modelled closely on the celebrated women of Dublin's 'Monto' district, as Ellmann explains in his account of the 'Backgrounds of *Ulysses*'.[90] In 'Scylla and Charybdis' we learn of earlier encounters between Stephen and Georgina Johnson, as well as Mulligan's 'two gonorrheal ladies', Fresh Nellie and Rosalie, the Coalquay whore.[91]

In *Finnegans Wake* Joyce consistently weaves the vocabulary of prostitution into his description of all his female characters to reinforce his point about the mercantilism of sexual relationships. Most familiarly he calls his girls 'maggies'. The process can be observed thanks to Danis Rose's edition of the Buffalo notebook VI.B 46, the so-called *Index Manuscript*.[92] Under the heading, 'white slave', Rose identifies a string of words and phrases which Joyce noted down from a book, *The White Slave Market*, by A. Mackirdy and W.N. Willis. They have been harvested from the notebook and used: some to add spice to the list of titles of ALP's 'Mamafesta' in Book I Chapter 5 and some to implicate Buckley in his account of shooting the Russian general in Book II Chapter 3 (*FW* 351–2).

From Beverland's *Law Concerning Draped Virginity* Joyce would have learned that the word 'fornicate' derives from the latin 'fornex' or arch under which the Roman prostitutes used to ply their trade. He worked the knowledge into *Giacomo Joyce*, where 'under the arches in the dark streets near the river the whores' eyes spy out for fornicators' (*GJ* 3). In *Finnegans Wake* a prostitute is described as an 'arch girl' (*FW* 186.18), or defined as 'whoso stands before a door and winks or parks herself in the fornix near a makeussin wall' (*FW* 116.17–18).

Dublin was a city where prostitution was rife, largely because of the presence of a garrison of English soldiers. 'Monto' was arguably one of the clearest indications of Ireland's imperial subordination and that is an aspect Joyce brings to the surface by staging Stephen's fight with the absurdly patriotic English soldiers in that area in 'Circe', even bringing Edward VII, in freemasonic trowel and apron, to back his representatives up (*U* 688–9).

Prostitution seemed an extreme of capitalism for Charles Albert in *L'Amour libre*. 'Les prostituées sont les amoureuses types du régime capitaliste', Albert says.[93] Joyce's 'Circe' episode seems to endorse this, since commercialism is the 'sordid reality' to which, as Joyce said of his episode, all things return (*L* I 144). This is the case when Bloom's dreams are burst after his onanistic vision of the nymph. As soon as he retrieves his protective potato from Zoe, Bella starts demanding payment. When Stephen's sight of his mother's ghost provokes his outburst and flight, money quickly becomes the issue again. 'Circe' gives a very materialistic account of the world, especially when Stephen declares, 'we are all in the same sweepstake' and in typically allusive style, *Dans ce bordel ou tenons nostre état* (*U* 664).

At first sight Albert's prostitute might seem to typify capitalism because she puts profit before other considerations to an exceptional extent, but that is not quite the point that Albert or other contemporary socialists made. It is, rather, that the prostitute herself is exploited by the economic system, much as are the wage-earning classes. Bloom makes the analogy in his alderman's speech in 'Circe', declaiming against the 'hideous hobgoblins produced by the horde of capitalistic lusts upon our prostituted labour' (*U* 602). Another vigorous critic of prostitution, Tolstoy, writes in his 'Afterword' to *The Kreutzer Sonata* that it is 'Governments' who 'organise debauchery by regulating an entire class of women destined to perish physically and morally'.[94] Tolstoy has particularly in mind those countries, like France under Napoleon, where some degree of prostitution was regulated by the state. For other writers, like Albert or the utopian socialist August Bebel, prostitution was sanctioned by society because it was 'a necessary institution of the bourgeois world'.[95] For such writers any kind of reformist campaign to improve the morals of the streetwoman was doomed to failure. Bebel argued that prostitution was a much deeper problem, that 'for modern society the prostitution question is a sphinx, whose riddle it cannot read'.[96] Prostitution could not be eradicated without a major revolution in society.

Bloom in 'Eumaeus', echoing Alfred Loth's judgement on Emile Zola in *Vor Sonnenaufgang* and Stephen's comments on King and money in 'Circe', says that prostitutes are 'a necessary evil'.[97] It seems an unexceptionable comment, deliberately vague and bland, but, in relation to those radical apocalyptic attitudes, it may take on more energetic connotations. An evil that is 'necessary' within the contemporary social order might argue for a break with that order which makes such evil so necessary. Apocalypticism of this kind is often suggested in

'Circe'. On entering nighttown, Bloom sees a fire and thinks (not inappropriately if we understand Dublin's brothels to be a far from stable part of the English empire), 'London's burning, London's burning!'[98] It is the memory of J. Alexander 'Antichrist' Dowie that brings about a hallucinatory 'end of the world' and a New Jerusalem. But the gramophone scratches out suggestively that it is a whore's Jerusalem, a 'Whorusalam' that is coming about (*U* 625).

If utopian socialism provided a contemporary tradition of thought by which Joyce could present a vision of the revolutionary or apocalyptic potentiality of prostitution, then the writer through whom he most clearly articulates his vision is Blake. Though the authors Joyce chose for his lecture in Trieste, Blake and Defoe, have little in common (and his stated justification for pairing them was that they represented opposing strains of idealism and realism in English literature), Joyce did show an interest in a theme both writers share, that of prostitution. In the Defoe lecture Moll Flanders's spirit is praised. In the Blake lecture the issue is more complex: Joyce sees in Blake the potential for an art and a philosophy 'flowering in the more or less distant future in the union of the two social forces felt more strongly in the market place every day – women and the proletariat' (*CW* 220). This, like the 'generous idea' in the Wilde article or the 'confederate will' that closes the early 'Portrait of the Artist' essay, is one of Joyce's rather high-flown and perphrastic articulations of a socialistic philosophy. The role of prostitutes is brought out in 'Nestor', where Stephen thinks 'old England' is dying and, quoting a couplet from Blake's 'Auguries of Innocence', thinks its decay will come about through the harlot':

> The harlot's cry from street to street
> Shall weave old England's winding sheet.   (*U* 41)

The phrase returns to Stephen's mind in 'Circe', where it is slightly altered to include 'Old Ireland's' winding sheet as well.

A new world-order, coming about through the exposed scandal of prostitution, seems promised by Bloom's elevation in 'Circe' and by the confrontation between Stephen and the soldiers: an order whose relation to socialism is suggested by the proletarians, the 'blacksmith', the 'paviour and flagger' and the 'chapel of freeman typesetters', who assist (*U* 604–6). It is a socialistic, feministic apocalypse anticipated in *Stephen Hero*, again not directly but through reference to another piece of writing. Stephen's bookish appetites lead him to discover on a bookstall by the river a copy of Yeats's stories *The Tables of the Law* and *The Adoration of the Magi*. The first, of which he remembers every word, leads him to researches in the heretical philosophy of Joachim, Abbot of Flora, whose idea, curiously appealing to the revolutionary visions of Yeats and to Joyce's aesthetic socialism, is that the Old Testament age of the 'father' has been replaced by the New Testament age of the 'son' and is now about to be replaced by a new age of the 'spirit'.

The second story is also luxuriously Yeatsian, breathing a gothic atmosphere of mysterious revelation, 'heavy with incense and omens' as Joyce puts it (*SH* 183). In the story three wise men of the new age tell how they have been sent by Michael Robartes to witness the symbolic birth of a new order. The story is set in Paris, a suitable location for spiritualist exoticism. For Joyce, though, much more aware of the popular reputation of Paris for the bohemian life, a striking part of the story must have been that the three old men are led to 'narrow and shabby streets' beside the Seine, to a house that is evidently a brothel'.[99]

Stephen's thoughts in *Stephen Hero* return to the story, during his conversation with Lynch about prostitution, and he quotes it at length:

> – You remember in *The Adoration of the Magi* – 'When the immortals wish to overthrow the things that are today and to bring the things that were yesterday they have no-one to help them except one whom the things that are today have cast out?'   (*SH* 197)

Renan's version of Church history, that Joyce admired, argued that Christianity was a new religion which attracted the poor and the outcast and built its power-base among them. The religion of the modern age, in Stephen's reading of Yeats, is apparently to do something similar, and the subtle purpose of the introduction of the story is to suggest that Stephen, like Christ, looks to prostitutes as his allies in exposing the exploitations of the old order and heralding the universal 'generous' love of the new.

This seems to be the difficult focus of Stephen's (and to a considerable extent Joyce's) thinking on the question of women's exploitation and social reform. In the beginning of the 'Circe' episode, Bloom assumes an interest in the 'rescue of fallen women' as a cover for his presence in the red-light district, and all such interests, by implication, are held at a low estimation (U 573). Bloom's moral frailty is part of the point here, of course, but the 'rescue of fallen women' in Joyce's feminist, socialist apocalypticism is irrelevant for the further reason that 'fallen women' hold the key to the 'rescue' of the whole world.

4 Sexual reality

A sexual aesthetic

Joyce's abandonment of the Church consisted, as we have seen, in a shift of ideas that both he and his brother described as a shift from belief in a God to a belief in the sexual instincts that make up the human spirit. It was a shift from the traditional authority of the Church account of humanity to the modern materialistic authorities of medicine and of rationalist morality. Wherever Joyce's reading took him (to Blake and Defoe; to the mystical fictions of W.B. Yeats; to his earliest and strongest authority, Ibsen; to the Bible, Aquinas and esoteric theology; or to Shakespeare and Homer in whom he invested the full imaginative energy of his mature years) he found a confirmation of his interest in sexuality and he shows his own preoccupation with each author's treatment of sex.

There is no better example than his reading of *The Divine Comedy*. His imagination flew straight to the Inferno and to the second circle where those who have died because of their erotic passions are forever whirled. It is from this section of the poem and in particular from the famous story of Francesca da Rimini that the piece of *terza rima* quoted in 'Aeolus' is drawn and, as Mary Reynolds's book estimates, it is this section of the Inferno that Joyce most often quoted or used in his work.[1]

In the momentous letter which he wrote to his brother in November 1906, in which he enquires into the 'Jewish divorce case' in Dublin that was ultimately to provide the plot for *Ulysses*, Joyce railed against *Sinn Fein*'s idea that Ireland suffered from 'venereal excess'. He had explained in an earlier letter that venereal disease was not the result of excess but of 'ill-luck',[2] and the problem of the Irish was venereal negligence rather than excess and the hypocrisy that disabled them from realizing it. If 'I put down a bucket into my soul's well, sexual department,' he wrote (with a Christian-sounding metaphor but clear

Ibsenite-materialistic intent), 'I draw up Griffith's and Ibsen's and Skeffington's and Bernard Vaughan's and St Aloysius' and Shelley's and Renan's water along with my own.'[3] At the bottom of the soul was its 'sexual department' and the universality of its working proved its significance. No doubt part of Joyce's attraction toward divorce cases was that they represented an unusually public recognition of this concealed 'sexual department' and its ubiquity. Whatever else Joyce's scepticism caused him to doubt, he retained his faith in the importance of this 'sexual department' in the soul. Even the 'living wounding doubt' which closed *Exiles* was one whose disbelief in moral convention may be seen to rest on a deeper belief in the incontrovertible reality of sexual desires.

Joyce's writing presses towards the revelation of this sexual heart of things which he especially strives to make evident in persons, phenomena and institutions that are normally supposed to be chaste. Many of the *Dubliners* stories share this motive, more subtle than the study of 'the venereal condition of the Irish' that he says he wishes to see in another letter of 1906, but similar in intent. It is the sexual situation of the negligent clerk Farrington that is exposed in 'Counterparts' by the emphatic, structuring contrast between the 'woman in the big hat' he sees in Mulligan's bar and his 'sharp-faced' wife at home. A sexual situation lies behind the suicide of Mrs Sinico in 'A Painful Case'. The secret sexual longings of adolescence in 'Araby' and 'Eveline', and the sexual secrets of the Conroys in 'The Dead' constitute the hinges on which the stories' actions turn. It is no wonder that certain readers have wished to see in 'The Sisters' a priest whose mysterious 'paralysis' is none other than syphilis.[4] Whatever extra secrets of this kind we may wish to discover in the stories, it should be evident that, on the surface of a story like 'Clay', the celibate state of Maria and the radical sociological belief that it was celibacy that caused prostitution (Maria pointedly lives her narrow life in a house for reformed prostitutes[5]), provides the focal point for Joyce's conception of her character.

It has rarely been noted that in 1904 Joyce translated into Italian the first pages of George Moore's story 'Mildred Lawson' (from the 1895 volume *Celibates*), though students of Joyce's linguistic modernity might well have found interest in the poetic reverie or interior monologue that they offer. Such impressionism contributed to Joyce's evolution of a poetic and psychologically suggestive style, but it was Moore's identification of the sexual problem of celibacy and his firm disapproval of the superficial chastity of Mildred (shown to be nothing more virtuous than an egotistic frigidity) which constitutes the most striking continuity of feeling between his stories and Joyce's portraits of such 'celibate' Dubliners as Duffy and Maria.

The avowed sexual purity of the Church came continually under fire from Joyce's imagination. Bloom wanders into All Hallow's Church in 'Lotus-Eaters' and his train of thought defines its function as a 'Nice discreet place to be next some girl' (*U* 98). Sexual undercurrents seemed strongest in the practice of confession and Joyce played frequently on its suggestive potential, such as when Stephen says to Emma with seductive intent that he would like to hear her sins (*SH* 159). Gerty MacDowell is coyly conscious of the intimacy of the confessional, 'crimsoning up to the roots of her hair' (*U* 466). Molly Bloom gets her confessor into an embarrassing situation too, when he asks where 'on her person' her young man has dared kiss her and she answers 'on the canal bank like a fool' (*U* 875): an ambiguity Joyce had earlier exploited in *Exiles* when Bertha asks where she is to come to meet Robert and his reply says where he would like to kiss her: 'Your eyes: Your lips. All your divine body' (*E* 46). Much of the tension of the play arises from the sexual inquisition to which Richard subjects Bertha.

The most extravagant version of Joyce's portrayal of the confessional as a sexually intimate rather than a chaste institution occurs in the 'Oxen of the Sun' episode where Stephen, Lenehan and Dixon all contribute to an account of the Church as a great spermacetically oiled bull whose sexual contact through the confessional is more attractive to the Irish 'maid, wife, abbess and widow' than any contact with the Irish male (*U* 522–3). Such outrageousness is different in the degree of its exaggeration, rather than in the balance of its sympathies, from that rejection of the priesthood which accompanies Stephen's choice of a life of literary art.

The Stephen of *Stephen Hero* is 'indignant' that his old schoolfriend Wells should be entrusted with 'spiritual difficulties' as a confessor, but by the time *A Portrait* was written it was more than the generalized materiality of the priestly training that constituted the difficulty. Stephen in *A Portrait* aspires to become a priest partly in reaction to his experience of sexual sin. He hopes to attain a perfection which will nullify any erotic component in the confessional exchange of secrets:

He would know obscure things, hidden from others, from those who were conceived and born children of wrath. He would know the sins, the sinful longings and sinful thoughts and sinful acts, of others, hearing them murmured into his ears in the confessional under the shame of a darkened chapel by the lips of women and of girls: but rendered immune mysteriously at his ordination by the imposition of hands . . .   (*P* 162)

Stephen hopes to become a priest of 'the order of Melchisedec' (*P* 163), a reference to the mysterious status of the Christian priest according to Paul's letter to the Hebrews, lacking father and mother and inheriting through mystical apostolic succession in a way that Joyce used for his Shakespeare theory in 'Scylla and Charybdis'. Yet Joyce's working note for the *Portrait* scene, 'Not a eunuch priest. Melchisedec',[6] makes his own attitude and the likelihood of Stephen ever attaining this mystical estate of priestly chastity quite plain. Joyce stayed with this theme when he was writing *Finnegans Wake*, constructing in Book III Chapter 2 a priestlike valedictory address from Jaun to Issy and the girls where, on the surface, chastity is recommended but, as we have seen, that chastity is only a cover for avaricious sexual bartering: it is not brotherly but 'brokerly advice' (*FW* 439.25). It is not only the content but the manner of Jaun's advising that reveals a strong sexual undercurrent since Jaun begins to bray like an organ ('his voixehumanar swelled') with an obtrusive virility. After relishing the catalogue of sanctions he will inflict on anyone who tries to seduce his sister and her friends, he turns to the punishments he will inflict on the girls themselves: 'I'll be all over you myselx horizontally,' he promises (*FW* 444.18–19). While they are out walking by the railway lines he will 'beat behind the bush', suggesting masturbation, flagellation and the kind of implicit sexual cruelty Joyce saw in sexual dishonesty or 'beating around the bush' (*FW* 445.1–3). In his final demand for 'plenary sadisfaction' (*FW* 445.8) the hidden sexual import of this sermon is least concealed.

Joyce's treatment of the Catholic Church in this way, his subjection of its mystical apparatuses to irreverent enquiry, shows the richness of his debt to nineteenth-century rationalist approaches to the Bible. Such approaches, including Strauss's *Leben Jesu*, translated by George Eliot, Swinburne's paganized 'pale Galilean' that Mulligan quotes (*U* 257), and certain of the poems of Robert Browning, were prominent in the literature of the generation which preceded Joyce; while Joyce was especially struck by the contribution of Ernest Renan, whose life of Christ is mentioned in *Stephen Hero* and in the letters of the period.[7] Renan gave Joyce the freedom to write about Biblical situations in humanistic terms and there is an unmistakable atheistic frisson in the comparison of Renan's account of the death of Christ and that of the evangelist 'from the literary point of view' (*SH* 194) and in the reverie on 'the narrative of the life of Jesus' (*SH* 116) which occupies Stephen intermittently throughout *Stephen Hero*. Renan's distance from Catholic orthodoxy is that of the historian and literary man but Joyce's sense of the life of Christ – its recognition of adultery and association with prostitutes – is one which, like his sense of the confessional, brings the sexual element to the fore.

The reader's attention is drawn to this cast of thought by Stephen's consideration of authors like Renan but also by his thoughts about such works as Leo Taxil's blasphemous *Vie de Jésus* in 'Proteus', where among the irreverences sexual imputations figure prominently. Bloom notices such anti-Catholic productions as the scandal-mongering *Awful Disclosures of Maria Monk* on the bookstand in 'Wandering Rocks' (*U* 302) and the proselytizing pamphlets *The Priest, The Woman and the Confessional* and *Why I left the Church of Rome* appear in 'Lestrygonians' and 'Circe'.[8] Such writings, scurrilous though they may be, share with Joyce's own literary project the desire to reveal a hidden sexual reality in the Catholic Church's chaste stand. Their presence in *Ulysses* helps identify that aim.

More notice might have been taken of the implications of this attempt to base a view of life and art on the importance of sexuality had not the most apparently reliable indication of a theory of art in Joyce's writings – Stephen's discussions with Lynch in Chapter 5 of *A Portrait* – seemed explicitly to frustrate any such investigations. A primary part of Stephen's theory is the distinction he makes between static and kinetic art: art which transcends as opposed to that which provokes 'desire' and 'loathing'. 'Pornographic' and 'didactic' arts are dismissed as 'improper'. It should, perhaps, be emphasized that Stephen is questioning their pertinence rather than their decency in this choice of word 'improper'. Yet this term, his avowed reliance on Aquinas, his priestly and liturgical metaphors and the austere style of his aestheticism have all contributed to the presumption that his theory of art is one where sexuality plays a very small part.

In one way the desire to distance art from sexual desire in this theory is merely superficial. If we trace back Joyce's aestheticism to its origin in the debating society paper 'Art and Life' dramatized in *Stephen Hero*, it is clear that the idea that art should be independent arises not in opposition to political or to erotic art but in direct opposition to those arts pressed into the service of the Catholic church or patriotism. This is apparent in Stephen's confrontations in *A Portrait* with his peer group over the respective literary excellences of Byron and Tennyson, where they refuse to accept the 'heretic and immoral' Byron (*P* 82–3). It is an underlying thread in Stephen's discussion with the Dean of Studies in *A Portrait*, but the issue is much clearer in *Stephen Hero* where Stephen discusses the censorship of his paper with the College President. There Stephen's aesthetic is most evidently a desire to recognize certain 'subjects' (not to avoid all 'subjects' in art), notably sexual subjects. The President's objections are exclusively based on his determination to subordinate literary to prudential Catholic considerations.

The original role of the 'Aquinatian' philosophy in Stephen's theorizing is apparent here. Far from suggesting that Stephen's mind is basically in sympathy with Catholic church orthodoxy on aesthetic questions, or even suggesting (as William Noon has helped to show[9]) that Stephen is especially well versed in Aquinas, the purpose of his reliance on these few tags is to insinuate his thoroughly heterodox intellectual position into the mind of an orthodox listener, and to reveal possible supports for his position in the orthodox view. Stephen finds no trace of the Puritanism of his scholastic teachers in Aquinas' writing, nor indeed does he take much notice of Aquinas' ultimate theological aims. He picks out a phrase which most suggests an aestheticist freedom from moral constraints: '*Pulchrae sunt quae visa placent*'. Seen in its full context, what Stephen means by 'pornography', in the final version of this theory in *A Portrait*, is not so much the treatment of sexual or erotic subjects in art, but the intrusion into art of non-aesthetic considerations, and the threat of intrusion comes more from the censorious than from the libertine party.

There is the possibility that Joyce was being consciously ironic in his choice of the term 'pornography' for the kinds of art Stephen rejects in *A Portrait*. The word 'pornography' is a nineteenth-century one deriving from Greek words meaning writing about prostitutes. The term was coined to deal with the realistic kind of fiction that was becoming familiar to Europe with such authors as Balzac often treating prostitutes as part of their subject-matter. The trend increased throughout the century and besides Balzac's own *Splendeurs et misères des courtisanes* (from which Joyce drew Stephen's famous catch-phrase 'silence, exile and cunning'[10]) such writers as George Moore, who closely influenced Joyce, form part of the tradition. Prostitution is, as we have seen, one of the main themes of Joyce's fiction and we get a further hint of Joyce's consciousness of the potential ironies in his choice of subject for Stephen and Lynch to discuss. The only work of art they discuss as an example of this 'anti-pornographic' theory is the copy of the Venus of Praxiteles in the Dublin Museum, and that statue (as accounts in Pliny and Athenaeus and standard classical dictionaries confirm) is said to have been modelled on the well-known Greek courtesan Phryne. Stanislaus, in *My Brother's Keeper*, shows how close these issues were to Joyce's mind, commenting that the love poetry of *Chamber Music* was not love poetry but 'prostitute poetry', to which Joyce replied that 'a great part of all lyric poetry correspond[s] to that description'.[11]

To take too literally the apparently anti-sexual streak in Stephen's theory of art would be to misrepresent Joyce's own aesthetic achievement, since Joyce's fiction is quite evidently not one which seeks to reinforce the conventional distinction between serious art and sexual explicitness but one which deliberately and systematically offends that distinction. Our knowledge of Joyce's reading suggests that he had quite a lively interest in writing which is not only pornographic in the above sense but in any other sense of the word. He owned an English translation of *Le Rideau levé*, attributed to the Comte de Mirabeau, which parades its erotic intentions under the outrageous publisher's imprint 'Putitin, Rogers & Co. Nineinch Street'.[12] The narrative consists of nothing more than a series of sexual encounters (mainly heterosexual though including buggery and incest) which are enjoyed under the familiar pretext of providing an 'education' for the heroine Laura and a life history of her companion in pleasure, Rose. On the same shelf-inventory are listed titles of books now unrecoverable, *History of Excess* and *Lustful Acts*, the character of which is no doubt similar. Of French libertine literature Joyce would, of course, have known de Sade, but the 'shadow of the Divine Marquis' seems not to have been cast so strongly over his work or in his reading as over that of the romantic and decadent writers listed in Mario Praz's famous study, nor is it so strong as that of Sacher-Masoch. It was, at any rate, the substance as much as the shadow of pornography that Joyce employed. He used such material freely in *Ulysses* and *Finnegans Wake*. It had a role in fleshing out the details of personal psychology in the former book. Joyce, in 1921, wrote to Budgen requesting a copy of 'Fanny Hill's Memoirs (unexpurgated)',[13] and seems to have worked one detail from it into Molly Bloom's memoir of her sexual life: the passage 'they always want to see a stain on the bed to know you're a virgin' (*U* 914), recalling the deception practised by Fanny and Mrs Cole upon Mr Norbert in Cleland's story. Joyce used erotic or mildy erotic magazines which he knew to assist in the characterization of Stephen – who returns home from Paris to his mother's funeral with the 'rich booty' of '*Le Tutu*' and '*Pantalon Blanc et Culotte Rouge*' (*U* 52). Bloom's characterization is similarly extended by his knowledge of and interest in the magazine *Photo Bits* (whose suggestive, sometimes masochistic flavour I have noted and from which the 'Bath of the Nymph' picture above the Blooms' bed is said to be taken), and by the books on the bookstall in 'Wandering Rocks'.[14] Bloom comments that '*Sweets of Sin*' is Molly's kind of taste, 'more in her line' (*U* 302), but we are left in no doubt by his response to the other books and indeed by certain revelations in 'Ithaca' that his own taste extends to work of this kind. In the idyllic 'Bloom Cottage', about which he dreams, among the 'lighter recreations' he reserves a place for the 'lecture of unexpurgated exotic erotic masterpieces' (*U* 841). He has photographs too: 'erotic photocards showing a) buccal coition between nude senorita (rere presentation, superior position) and nude torero (fore presentation, inferior position): b) anal violation by male religious (fully clothed, eyes abject) of female religious (partly clothed, eyes direct)' (*U* 850). Such material functions to insist on Bloom's normality: on the distance of the reality of his character from any dignifying or prescriptive ideals.

Pornographic writing also has its own distinctive linguistic flavour and this Joyce incorporated into his own rich blend, such as the title that appears in the spurious list of the 'World's Worst Books' in 'Circe', 'Love-letters of Mother Assistant (erotic)' (*U* 607), or the list of titles for ALP's 'mamafesta' at the start of the Book I Chapter 5, which includes '*I Ask You to Believe I was his Mistress*' (*FW* 105.13), '*In My Lord's Bed by One Whore Went Through It*' (*FW* 105.34–5) and '*First and Last Only True Account all about the Honorary Mirsu Earwicker, L.S.D., and the Snake (Nuggets!) by a Woman of the World who only can Tell Naked Truths . . .*' (*FW* 107.1–6).

In *Finnegans Wake* the excessiveness and outrageousness of such linguistic echoes seems the main aesthetic justification of their use. But there is a more specifically intended and substantial shock imparted to readers of *Ulysses*. Bloom's mental fabric is a network of interrelated strands and his erotic photocard of the senorita comes more firmly into focus when we remember that he has photographs of Molly too, which he shows to Stephen in 'Eumaeus' in such a way that at least one reader of *Ulysses* sees a specific sexual offer,[15] and any perceptive reader might notice the overtones of the suggestion that she is a 'Spanish type' (*U* 758). The connection between Bloom's erotic pictures and those of his wife are made explicit in 'Circe', where the hallucinatory image of Mrs Mervyn Talboys objects that Bloom has shown her a picture of 'a partially nude senorita, frail and lovely (his wife as he solemnly assured me, taken by him from nature), practising illicit intercourse with a muscular torero, evidently a blackguard' (*U* 593).

This detail might remind us that, throughout the day (though Joyce casts them as Odysseus and Penelope or as Shakespeare and Anne Hathaway), Bloom and Molly see their relationship through the eyes of 'a volume of peccaminous pornographical tendency': *Sweets of Sin* (*U* 865). *Sweets of Sin* seems to be the creation of Joyce's imagination rather than an actual book. Grant Allen, whose work Joyce knew, wrote *A Splendid Sin*, Henry Johnson (the author of *The Pride of the Ring* on which at least part of the title of Joyce's '*Ruby: the Pride of the Ring*' is based[16]) wrote *The World of Sin* and Hume Nisbet, another popular contemporary author, wrote *A Sweet Sinner*; but none of these is the book. The point, unusually here, seems not to trace the actual title but to recognize the depth to which the erotic psychology of the Blooms is based on this genre of writing as we see in the repetition of 'for him! For Raoul!' (*U* 303) and 'Perfumed for him' (*U* 353) throughout. Milly Bloom, too, is characterized both by the popular music-hall song 'Seaside Girls' and by reference to the magazine *Photo Bits*. She says in her letter that she is 'getting on swimming in the photo business now' (*U* 80) and her talk of picnics and seaside is strongly reminiscent of the teasing photo captions in the publication.

Part of the reason for this reliance on pornographic or erotically suggestive material is, evidently, to add a note of grotesquery to the portrait of the Blooms, to place them socially and to explode pretension and hypocrisy. There is also the more subtle and interesting suggestion that Joyce makes, drawing our attention to the fact that the world of the erotic imagination is governed by or transacted through the language and ideology of such kinds of literature. Psychological realism and a new kind of psychology, highly aware of the role of language, are at work here but evidently, also, this feature of Joyce's writing deliberately disrupts any kind of aesthetic designed to exclude sexual subjects, eroticism, or even vulgarly pornographic art. Far from remaining aloof from a sexual art Joyce increasingly identified himself as the Shem-like author of a 'usylessly unreadable Blue Book of Eccles, *édition de ténèbres*, (even yet sighs the Most Different, Dr Poindejenk, authorized bowdler and censor, it can't be repeated!)' (*FW* 179.26–9).

The new spirit

What kind of theory was it, then, that animated Joyce's literary ambitions and which took account of his belief in the irreducible significance of sexuality? In some ways it was the artistic attitude which was most easily available to him during his formative years as a writer. When Joyce writes about the books he was reading in the years after his move to Europe the sense of values is clear. The listings of new books in the *Daily Mail* are his prime source of information. Joyce seeks out realistic fiction and his notion of what constitutes its realism is apparent: 'I saw a review in the heel of a D.M. column of a book by E. Temple Thurston, called "The Realist". It was very daring and unpleasant, D.M. said, but showed unmistakable talent. I have ordered it from England.'[17] With characteristic irritation he exposes the Italians as preoccupied by their *'coglioni'*, berates James as a 'tea-slop' for romanticizing them and talks in detail of a Hardy short story, 'On the Western Circuit', from *Life's Little Ironies* (1894). He recounts the love interest of the plot but complains 'Is this as near as T.H. can get to life, I wonder?' Compared to his own stories, he says that 'What is wrong with these English writers is that they always keep beating about the bush'.[18]

Such artistic values derived from the materialist indignation of the Ibsen of *An Enemy of the People* and from Gerhardt Hauptmann, the sexual focus of whose indignation (if not the ultimate achievement of his dramatic art) was that much more remarkable. Joyce valued Hauptmann in these terms as his comparison between the two writers makes clear. Hauptmann 'deals with life quite differently, more frankly in certain parts (this play opens with Rosa and her lover emerging one after the other from opposite sides of a bush)'.[19] That 'third minister', anticipated in Joyce's 'The Day of the Rabblement', who will supersede Ibsen and Hauptmann, and who is usually identified as Joyce himself, will clearly have to 'beat around the bush' still less (*CW* 72). Many interesting pieces of subsequent criticism covering the period have blurred the outlines of these feelings. For Raymond Williams the contemporary attack on sexual revolt in Ibsen by Clement Scott and others was a 'mistake of emphasis'.[20] There has been a consistent movement away from the idea centrally expounded in Shaw's *Quintessence of Ibsenism* (which Joyce knew and used in his criticism[21]) that the heart of Ibsen's achievement was to introduce 'discussion', and especially the discussion of marital morality, into the drama. Perhaps now we need to re-emphasize the real, felt association between literary novelty and modern sexual morality at this time.

More critics than Shaw took pains to document it and several of these critics were well-known to Joyce. Havelock Ellis is a clear case. His *The New Spirit*, in Joyce's library, consists of an

identification of the literary spirit of the modern age as he sees it
in Diderot, Heine, Whitman, Ibsen, and Tolstoy. Ellis talks
enthusiastically of a 'quickening pulse of life' and he provides a
Blakean, or inverted, reading of Genesis to sum up his humanistic vision of modernity: 'For it all comes of that primitive
manifestation of the new spirit, the "Fall", which raised us
onto our hind legs and enabled us to drink the cider of
paradise.' The argument hinges on a strong conception of
reality and has a distinctly positivistic and rationalistic flavour
in its desire to 'search out the facts of things, and to found life
upon them broadly and simply, rather than to shape it to the
form of unreasoned and traditional ideals.' These 'facts of
things' are noticeably conceived in a way which is resistant
rather than sympathetic to the accepted moral order and they
frequently emerge as facts about sexuality. Thus Diderot is
praised for his recognition that there would be prostitution and
adultery whatever the legislation against them. Heine was able
to harmonize flesh and spirit and was sexually unconventional
in his personal life in a way that Joyce, as we have seen, found
relevant to his own situation. Walt Whitman is praised by Ellis
for his 'mood of sane and cheerful sensuality' and for the 'kernel'
of his philosophy that 'for the lover there is nothing in the loved
one's body impure or unclean'.[22] Joyce was an admirer of
Whitman from early on, cheerfully quoting 'The Song of
Myself' to Stanislaus in 1903 and working the incident into
Ulysses.[23]

Ellis's view of Ibsen is clearly relevant to Joyce's own. He
emphasizes Ibsen's proud isolation and defiance, basing his
notion of the author's personality on that of Stockmann in *An
Enemy of the People*. Ellis refers to Ibsen's unfulfilled ambition to
study medicine, his exile and his aristocratic brand of socialism,
all characteristics that Joyce was to pick up. *A Doll's House* is
treated prominently as a 'tragedy of marriage' and a play written
in the cause of women. Ellis's Tolstoy is a social and sexual
radical too. According to Ellis, his view was that 'Every healthy
man and woman should have sexual relationships; and Tolstoy
makes no distinction between those that are called by the name
of marriage and those that are not so called.'[24]

Another well-known contemporary critic who tried to
identify a characteristically modern spirit in a selected group
of writers was Georg Brandes. In his studies *Det Moderne*

Gjennembruds Maend and *Moderne Geister* Brandes takes such writers as Ibsen, Bjornsen, Jacobsen, Drachman, Flaubert, Renan and J.S. Mill to be especially representative of modernity. Joyce may not have known either book but these writers evidently were among his own favoured few. Brandes was one of the strongest champions of Ibsen, and so closely did Joyce identify with his critical programme that he hoped to translate *Stephen Hero* into Danish to send it to him.[25]

That Joyce had 'Ibsenite' ideas in his youth but grew away from them as his art matured is, or used to be, a commonplace of Joyce criticism. It is characteristic of Tysdahl's full-length study of the relationship between the two writers[26] and, perhaps more significantly, typical of those critics whose evaluation of Joyce depends upon a comparison between him and other high-modernist authors. Hugh Kenner in *Dublin's Joyce*, for example, dealt with the problem of *Exiles* by claiming that it was of little interest in itself other than that it 'frees Joyce from Ibsen the undernourished doctrinaire whose "wayward, boyish" pseudo-rigours of revolt had for some years compromised a portion of his spirit'.[27] Yet it is by no means clear that Joyce's allegiances changed so dramatically nor, still more importantly, that he would ever have felt the need to exclude from his definition of modernity these subject-oriented terms. The Dublin journalist Arthur Power visited Joyce in the 1920s and his account of their conversation over books and issues consistently suggests a naturalistic sense of literary value. According to Power, Joyce expressed preference for naturalistic Ibsen over the more lyrical or poetic Synge, and preference for argumentative Chekhov and Tolstoy over romantic Pushkin. 'Circe' is described as realistic and the 'imagination' criticized throughout. The following passage, which Power recounts, might almost have been written by Havelock Ellis:

For you must be caught up in the spirit of your time, and you admit that the best authors of any period have always been the prophets; the Tolstoys, the Dostoievskis, the Ibsens – those who brought something new into literature. As for the romantic classicism you admire so much, *Ulysses* has changed all that; for in it I have opened the new way, and you will find that it will be followed more and more. In fact from it you may date a new orientation in literature – the new realism ... the modern theme is the subterranean forces, those hidden tides which govern everything and run humanity counter to the apparent flood: those poisonous subtleties which envelop the soul, the ascending fumes of sex.[28]

In the Buffalo library there remains another literary critical book, this one dating from the 1930s: Janko Lavrin's *Aspects of Modernism from Wilde to Pirandello*. Lavrin was able to include later authors than Havelock Ellis or Brandes in this survey and though he uses the term 'modernism' he still does not emphasize the identification of modernity with formal experimentation that has been taken for granted in so much literary history written since the Second World War. Lavrin's modern writers are modern because of a new shared view of life, one that has its roots in the 1890s rather than in the First World War. The main trends he observes in his selected literary works are 'utter atomisation of the individual, and parallel with this, a passionate though impotent will to achieve at least some balance and harmony in spite of all'. He takes Wilde to be typical of many authors who 'thought that they would find salvation in a new return to the "fundamentals" of life, or in the mystery of sex.' And he says that Knut Hamsun shows 'the erotic libido as the vital sap and fountain head of life'.[29] The survival of such ideas may help to explain Joyce's problematic relation to his modernistic contemporaries. Despite his obvious contacts with Eliot and Pound during and after the First World War, his recorded commentary on their work is sparse to the extent that Ellmann credibly concludes that 'Joyce had no interest in Pound's later work, which he probably had not read'.[30] The most striking instance of literary sympathy between Joyce and Pound arises in relation to Pound's poem, 'L'homme moyen sensuel'. Joyce politely, if unenthusiastically, approved of these 'amusing and high-spirited lines' in a letter of 1917.[31] Pound's poem values the sexual honesty of literary realism, despite its modern parodic tone, bewailing the condition of America 'sans song, sans home-grown wine, sans realist!' The hero of the poem, Radway, is celebrated as normal for his hypocritical denial of sex as well as his indulgence in it, but the idea behind it all is clearly that sex is a universal and fixed point of human experience and, in that way, the poem posits a sexual basis for the definition of reality:

> When last I met him he was a pillar in
> An organisation for the suppression of sin ...

Not that he'd changed his tastes, nor yet his habits
(Such changes don't occur in men or rabbits).[32]

Pound was himself quite able to see that the movement away
from certain kinds of realism did not preclude, indeed might
often exaggerate, the interest in sexual psychology which
realism took as one of its central preoccupations. Writing in
1920 on Rémy de Gourmont he makes the highly suggestive
remark that 'Sex, in so far as it is not a purely physiological
reproductive mechanism, lies in the domain of aesthetics',[33] a
remark as true to the feeling of the 1920s as to that of the
1890s. Even in 1934, when Joyce's writing had taken on its
most extravagantly experimental character, sexual subjects
were not abandoned. He wrote a verse 'epilogue' to Ibsen's
Ghosts which, in the voice of Captain Alving, clearly identifies
the purpose of the play as a sexual one and shows the survival of
this aspect of Joyce's view of life and literature:

Nay, more, were I not all I was,
Weak, wanton, waster out and out,
There would have been no world's applause
And damn all to write home about.[34]

One of the most characteristic pieces of Joycean literary
criticism is the background article he wrote on Oscar Wilde for
Il Piccolo della Sera in March 1909. It was written on the
occasion of the first performance in Trieste of Strauss's opera
Salomé based on Wilde's play. Though neither opera nor play are
mentioned by Joyce, he is happy to cast Wilde in this mould,
entitling his piece '*Oscar Wilde: il poeta di "Salomé"*'.[35] This
article falls into three sections. The first and longest gives an
account of Wilde's life, especially his early life and ultimate
collapse, drawn in part from Sherard's biography. The second
section deals most explicitly with the work, placing it securely
in the context of his life, situation, and sexual tastes. In Joyce's
account the 'pulse' of Wilde's art is 'sin'. Wilde thought himself
'the bearer of good news of neo-paganism to an enslaved
people' and his characteristic qualities – claimed by Joyce for
the Irish race – are 'keenness' (wit), 'generosity' (the Italian
original is '*l'impulso generoso*', a Joycean periphrasis for socialism) and 'a sexless intellect'. The art is one generated by
blasphemy and sexual transgression, what Joyce calls the 'truth
inherent in the soul of Catholicism: that man cannot reach the

divine heart except through that sense of separation and loss called sin . . . '[36]

The copy of *Salomé* which remains in the Trieste library, among the full list of Joyce's books by or about Wilde, is a Tauchnitz edition of 1909, but the most celebrated edition was that translated from the original French by Wilde's friend Alfred Douglas and luxuriously illustrated by Aubrey Beardsley. This seems to be the book mentioned by the innkeeper in *Finnegans Wake* Book II Chapter 3 when, after the dialogue between Butt and Taff, he comments that their story is 'too true enough' and gives an example of 'a (suppressed) book' he has just been reading where the fall of his own 'distend relations' seems to be depicted. The 'expurgative plates' are described, particularly those which depict two women, Joyce's 'raven' and 'dove' and, presumably, Beardsley's Herodias and Salome. The elfin figures that decorate Beardsley's illustrations are suggested in the phrases 'liggen gobelimned theirs before me' and 'blossomly emblushing themselves'. Though there is a suspicion in the reference to the 'wordcraft of this early woodcutter' that some writing by Beardsley (such as his erotic narrative vignette *Under the Hill*) is meant, the general idea of *Salomé* as a type of aesthetic work based on sexual sin seems repeated here.[37]

Sexual sin is no less held to be the key to Shakespeare's art, according to the theory that Stephen Dedalus offers in the 'Scylla and Charybdis' episode of *Ulysses*. Joyce, we know, gave ten lectures on *Hamlet* in Trieste, beginning on 5 November 1913. He refers to them in *Giacomo Joyce* and, though the full texts have not survived, we may presume them to have been the basis of the Shakespeare theory in *Ulysses*. Stephen, at any rate, has a similar critical strategy to that adopted by Joyce in his Wilde article and his Defoe and Blake lectures. He begins not with aesthetic precept but the biographical summary, even to the extent of conjuring a 'day in the life' of his subject. The best known and most often discussed part of the theory is that which identifies Shakespeare himself with Hamlet's father's ghost, rather than with the young prince, and the issues of fatherhood which it raises. But there are also issues of literary theory here. Evidently Stephen no longer feels the artist to be 'like the God of Creation, within or behind or beyond or above his handiwork, invisible, refined out of existence, indifferent, paring his fingernails' (*P* 214–15). Shakespeare-the-man is the point to which the work is related.

Stephen constructs a psychobiography for Shakespeare out of the characters and relationships in the plays and it is a biography – and consequently a reading of the plays – which stresses sexual themes. *Venus and Adonis*, Shakespeare's most fluently Ovidian and first published (if not first written) work, is used to argue that the young Shakespeare, like the young Adonis in the poem, was seduced by an older, sexually dominating woman, Anne Hathaway. Anne is remembered as Katherine in *The Taming of the Shrew*, Gertrude in *Hamlet*, Cleopatra and Cressida in *Troilus and Cressida*. She is not only strong but deceitful since, after Shakespeare went to London, in Stephen's view she deceived him with his brothers Edmund and Richard, whose treachery forms the basis of the theme of the 'usurping or adulterous brother' which is 'what the poor is not, always with him' (*U* 272).

Shakespeare, meanwhile, tries to live the life of a rake, having affairs with a burgher's wife, Mary Fitton, Lady Penelope Rich, the mother of William D'Avenant (who according to Aubrey's *Brief Lives* was proud to claim himself Shakespeare's bastard) and the 'punks of the bankside' (*U* 288). Stephen happily gathers all such material from the apocryphal biographical literature to present a Shakespeare torn between his two roles as London rake and Stratford cuckold, able to invest his imaginative energy in both 'bawd' and 'cuckold': in Iago and Othello; in Adonis in *Venus and Adonis* and Tarquin in *The Rape of Lucrece*; and in the ravisher Iachimo and the abused Posthumus in *Cymbeline*. The black mood of the tragedies is connected to the period of Shakespeare's marital estrangement, and the spirit of reconciliation in the late plays to a reconciliation with Anne and return to his Stratford home.

The Shakespeare theory can be held to occupy as significant a place in *Ulysses* as does the aesthetic in *A Portrait* yet, whereas Stephen's youthful thoughts have frequently been used in subsequent criticism as a way of accounting for the work, the later theory has been examined and interpreted but never accepted or applied as an equally valid approach (though it might be observed that the fact that the most successful work on Joyce has been an outstanding biography itself goes some way to vindicating the Shakespeare theory of art). The criticism of as distinguished a figure as Eliot shows the tendency to adopt the aesthetic theorizing of *A Portrait* but to neglect that of *Ulysses*. His essay *The Three Voices of Poetry*, delivered as a lecture in 1953, seems to echo Stephen's threefold distinction between lyric, epic and dramatic kinds of artistic mediation; and 'Ulysses, order and myth' seems to define a means by which the later work can be accommodated to the demands for order and limitation required by the earlier one. Yet to seek to find stasis in *Ulysses* seems a curious project when so many of its pleasures are those of variety and inclusiveness rather than order and exclusion. As soon as ask *Ulysses* to conform to the aesthetic theory of *A Portrait*, we may note how conveniently *A Portrait* fits the aesthetic values of 'Scylla and Charybdis', providing a biography of the artist as well as a theory of art, stressing those parts of the life where sexual matters seem most important and showing, when Stephen does produce a poem, a poem arising specifically out of a sexual situation.

It need hardly be an anachronism to read the earlier book in terms of the later one in this way. Joyce's *Hamlet* theory was delivered in outline if not in detail in 1913 when *A Portrait* was still some months from its first serial appearance in *The Egoist*. By that time his biographical method of criticism and his attention to the treatment of sexual subjects by authors who fell under his critical eye was well established and, for that matter, the intense, aphoristic fragments of the aesthetic theory which had been first set down in the so-called Paris and Pola Notebooks were ten years out of date (*CW* 141–8).

The wind in the sails

No one would deny the importance of Eliot's 'Ulysses, Order and Myth' essay in raising questions about the aesthetic significance of Joyce's use of the *Odyssey* and, indeed, in presenting an account of *Ulysses* which provided the conditions for its acceptance by a generation of readers at the highest level of intellectual sophistication. Stephen's theory of aesthetic *stasis* has a similarly unavoidable importance. Both documents have their place in shaping that modern situation where modern fictions, as Iris Murdoch suggested in her essay, 'Against Dryness', seem either 'crystalline' or 'journalistic'.[38] Eliot's argument that Joyce

used Homer to maintain 'a continuous parallel between contemporaneity and antiquity'[39] has a strong general appeal but it
also has less appealing implications. It tends to lift *Ulysses* out of
its immediate literary context and place it in an other-worldly
atmosphere of timelessly applicable narrative forms. It seems to
depend upon a sense of mythic archetype but such a sense –
associated with the psychology of Jung or the literary theory of
Northrop Frye – can only ever account for a part of an author's
use of past narrative forms. It can be highly misleading to
neglect the conscious or half-conscious ways in which the
choice and manipulation of such forms consists in a contemporary 'reading' which responds to contemporary concerns.

Joyce was, no doubt, aware that the antiquity of the Homeric
scaffold conferred a certain timeless status on his work but he
was also aware of the subtle shifts of interest and attitude that
made up the contemporary scene. Many of his critical comments show that he knew literary history to be as much a matter
of succession and supersession as of timeless parallels and that,
in some ways, we could say that he adhered to a 'dynamic'
rather than to a 'static' theory of art. His idea of realism, drawn
from his reading of the realist fiction of the time, was one of
superseding or extending the achievement of earlier authors
and that, in its way, implies a complex sense of the past, not as
fixed and dead but as (in the words of the early *Portrait* essay) a
'fluid succession of presents'.

Joyce's fluid sense of history and its importance for the
shaping of his own works can be seen in the working notes for
Exiles. Joyce writes about cuckolding, the subject-matter of his
play, and the 'changed point of view' towards it which he
perceives in French literature, comparing the brilliance of Molière's *Georges Dandin* and *Le Cocu imaginaire* with the later
treatment of the theme in Paul de Kock's *Le Cocu*. He feels that
the 'spring is broken somewhere' and his understanding of this
change in taste is the subject of a note on *Madame Bovary*. The
publication of the 'lost pages' of the novel, Joyce says, shows
that the 'centre of sympathy appears to have been aesthetically
shifted from the lover or fancy man to the husband or cuckold'
and he evidently thinks of this shift not just as new light on
Flaubert's novel but as an indication of a larger movement in
the history of aesthetics, arguing that 'this displacement is also
rendered more stable by the gradual growth of a collective

practical realism due to the changed economic conditions of the mass of the people who are called upon to hear and feel a work of art relating to their lives' (*E* 165).[40]

Modernity, here again, is understood as an advance on realism rather than a rejection of it in favour of experimentation. Literature does aspire towards timelessness, but hopes to gain momentum from changes in popular taste that are closely tied to social and economic circumstances. This sense of literary momentum is nowhere more evident than in Joyce's comment to Budgen, complaining that *Le Cocu magnifique* by the Belgian playwright Crommelynck 'took the wind out of the sails of *Exiles*'.[41] The author of these comments seems closer in spirit to the theory of literary *engagement* in Sartre, or to the complex sense of a relationship between social circumstances and realism developed by a Marxist critic like Georg Lukács, than to the Aristotelian aestheticism of Stephen's theory of *stasis* or to the 'archetypal' reading of *Ulysses*.

Rather than from any theoretical source, Joyce's 'dynamic' theory of art is most likely to have developed from (and is certainly most forcefully expressed in terms of) his relationship with the institutions of literary censorship. Along with that of Lawrence, the history of Joyce's engagement with the censor is one of the best known of all such histories but, under the shadow of Ellmann's biography, the tendency of Joyce critics has been to emphasize the personal psychology of Joyce's artistic stance rather than to investigate the censorship issue as an engagement in the contentions of the contemporary scene. The censorship of Joyce's works had been an issue in publishing history and biography but its relevance to the sense of art that motivated the fiction has been ignored.

Joyce's conflict with literary censorship began with his ambitious attempt to contribute an autobiographical essay to the new journal called *Dana* that was to be produced by John Eglinton and Fred Ryan at the beginning of 1904. Ellmann gives a fine account of Joyce's attempt to terrorize the literary editors of Dublin in those years and of the rejection of this essay (which Joyce commemorated in the rejection of Stephen's Shakespeare theory by the same John Eglinton in 'Scylla and Charybdis'). Eglinton's reason for rejecting the essay was, no doubt, as he later admitted, 'I can't print what I can't understand', but Stanislaus, according to his diary, had the impression that the rejection was a result of the 'sexual experiences narrated in it'.[42] The sixth of the seven paragraphs in the surviving text of this essay does indeed celebrate a sexual encounter and a movement from the 'yellow gaslamps' and 'groups gathered at the doorways' of Dublin prostitution to some semi-mystical encounter with a 'dearest of mortals'. It is hard to imagine that such opaque writing could ever be considered obscene but nevertheless the sense of a battle with censorship is established. Sexual impropriety more genuinely provoked Joyce's disagreement with a succession of publishers over the *Dubliners* stories (though other kinds of impropriety exacerbated the problems). Were it not for the sexual liberality born of feminism shown by the *Egoist*, *Dubliners* might never have found its way into print. Joyce's correspondence with Grant Richards gives some indication of his attitude to this question, claiming that he finds it 'extraordinary' that the issue of censorship should arise and unbelievable that 'any civilised tribunal could listen for two minutes to such an accusation against my book'. He goes on to claim:

I care little or nothing, whether what I write is indecent or not, but, if I understand the meaning of words, I have written nothing whatever indecent in *Dubliners*.[43]

Joyce's argument is a sensible one, allying his work with high literary disinterestedness and complaining against an uncivilized and ignorant Puritanism. He claims to be travelling in the artistic mainstream and that English prudishness is a provincial aberration. Such is the implication of his complaint to Stanislaus in a letter of 1908 that 'what I write with the most lugubrious intentions would probably be prosecuted in England as pornographical.'[44] But Joyce, however serious he was about his art, never had a 'lugubrious' intention in his life and, inasmuch as these comments suggest that the conflict between his work and the censorship was some kind of unforeseen accident, they are deliberately colouring the truth. Later in the letter to Richards, Joyce cannot resist an explanation of the polemical drive of the stories and their role of exposing the 'venereal condition' of the Irish. 'I seriously believe,' he maintains, 'that you will retard the course of civilisation in Ireland by preventing the Irish people from having one good look at themselves in my nicely polished looking-glass.'[45] Like the rationalist historian Lecky he believed that 'had the Irish peasants been less chaste, they would have been more prosperous' and in his fiction he tried to provide a diagnosis of that illness.[46] Of course behind his high-minded stance he was aware of the radical character of his stories, aware enough to tone down the unacceptably detailed account of the girl in Mulligan's Bar in 'Counterparts' to which Richards had objected.[47] He says that authors like Hardy or George Moore or Arthur Wing Pinero might well have provoked objections from 'a manager of the middle Victorian period' and implies that, since change is taking place, it is important to be up-to-date. His resolution to keep abreast of such changes became more and more evident. Moving to Paris in the 1920s he comments on the contemporary activities of writers like Guillaume Apollinaire, whose *Mamelles de Tirésias* must have made the Zurich literary scene, with all its wartime flourishing, seem rather tame and provincial. It was during the 1920s that Joyce's most extravagantly sexualized piece of writing, 'Circe', was produced.

As events developed Joyce took less part in the battles fought over the publication of his books. It is hard to imagine that the author of a work so dependent upon a delight in linguistic and physical eroticism as *Giacomo Joyce*, could have found much to commend in the famous 1933 judgement which allowed *Ulysses* to be published in America on the grounds that it was 'emetic' not 'aphrodisiac'. That seems a defensive estimation of the book's worth, whilst Joyce's own campaigns (like the 'curious history' he wrote for *The Egoist* and the letter he sent to the press including his correspondence with King Edward VII over 'Ivy Day in the Committee Room'[48]) show a more active, rational, offensive spirit.

Joyce must have become quite knowledgeable about the changing laws of censorship. He has Bloom notice in 'Lestrygonians' the sudden disappearance of advertisements for cures for venereal disease ('used to be stuck up in all the greenhouses. Never see it now.' *U* 193): a pointed memory, since an Act of 1889, repeated in 1918, specifically outlawed such displays. Where possible Joyce took the opportunity to write openly about the censorship question. His trip to Dublin gave him the chance to write on what seemed to him to be the big news event of August 1909 (almost overshadowing the Dublin Horse

Show, he ironically opens his essay): the performance of Bernard Shaw's banned play *The Shewing-Up of Blanco Posnet* at the Abbey Theatre. His article perfunctorily recounts the plot of Shaw's play and shows little or no enthusiasm for it. What attracts his interest is the farcical comedy of the 'Dublin clause' which allowed the play to be performed exempt from the English censor's opposition. The condemnation of the play links it, in Joyce's review, with Ibsen's *Ghosts*, Wilde's *Salomé* and Tolstoy, but Joyce turns away from this opportunity for critical praise, suggesting that Shaw's play is all the more bland since it contains nothing much for the censor to get upset about (*CW* 206–8).

After Yeats's rejection of his translation of Hauptmann, it took some such scandal to get Joyce interested in the Abbey Theatre and, of course, he had been provided with such a spur two years earlier during the riots that accompanied the production of Synge's *Playboy of the Western World*. Joyce, reading of the riots in his *Daily Mail*, and in the *Freeman's Journal*, wrote enthusiastically to Stanislaus, pouring scorn on the supposed liberalism of Dublin's literary men and finding much to commend in the defence of the play proposed by an old schoolfriend, Daniel Sheehan, who claimed that Synge's main drift was not to write about parricide so much as matrimonial manners and to show that Irish women would rush to greet any man who 'was not afraid of life, and his nature'. Joyce warmly recounts the 'great phrase' that started the riots: 'if all the girls in Mayo were standing before me in their shifts'. He notes down that Synge uses the word 'bloody': an indication of sympathy with his own cause since Richards was complaining about the occurrence of that word in *Dubliners* too.[49]

The article on Wilde's *Salomé* throws more important light on Joyce's attitude to literary censorship. Joyce refers approvingly to an argument Wilde made in his own defence to the *Scots Observer* in 1890, claiming that everyone 'sees his own sin in Dorian Gray' and that in some strange way, 'anyone who recognizes it has committed it'. The clever Wildean idea seems to be that a reader's own knowledge is necessarily complicit in any literary indecency: an idea that Joyce took up and used in 'Circe', where the nymph accuses Bloom of using indecent words. Bloom's question 'You understood them?' shows up the element of hypocrisy and the nearby Yew trees murmur 'shh'

(*U* 657). Joyce showed obscenity to be as much the reader's responsibility as the author's in his attack on those 'plain blunt' printers who objected to the superficial indecency of the word 'bloody' but failed even to notice the greater sexual enormities of 'An Encounter'. His sexual subjects were shrouded in difficulty from the *Dana* essay onwards and, no doubt, he was fully aware that the difficulty of parts of *Ulysses* and of *Finnegans Wake*, the fact that readers have to contribute so much conscious effort to understand their language, itself vindicates the author from the 'plain blunt' charges of corruption that may be brought against him. Difficulty provided a means for evading the censor whilst continuing to pursue the literary and intellectual goals which censoriousness threatened to frustrate.

The idea that Wilde's art is a kind of 'sin' provides another link in the chain of these ideas, since the word 'sin' clearly implies something rather different from mere sexual 'explicitness' or 'honesty'. It is, first of all, another example of that habit of Joyce's and Stephen's thought which I have described as the habit of linguistic duplicity or of 'using the language of people whose opinions I don't share.' To call art 'sin' without wishing to endorse the suggestion that there is any wrong in it is to set up a meaningful tension in the word itself, and ultimately to bring a whole system of values that stands behind it into question. It carries the further suggestion that writers or artists, as much as seeking to create a 'static' abstracted artefact, may be held to transgress or offend deliberately as an essential condition of their creativity. Writers, at least those like Wilde, must make their art out of that which orthodox opinion would count as 'sin'.

This was the idea of art which Joyce presented in his literary critical articles and it is confirmed by the tastes he cultivated for those authors whose works were embattled with authority on grounds of sexual radicalism. There was, of course, no shortage of such authors at this time but Joyce's reading seems especially to favour them. The Trieste library listings confirm his interest in authors like D'Annunzio and Maeterlinck, who suffered at the hands of English stage censorship.[50] Wedekind's *Die Büchse der Pandora* appears along with his *Die Zensur*, which tells the story of its conflict with the censor.[51] Arthur Schnitzler's *Lieutenant Gustl* is another work which interested Joyce, in part because of its experiments with interior monologue, but no doubt also because of its offence to Austrian officialdom caused by Schnitzler's opposition to anti-semitism and because of his concentrated and disillusioned erotic drama *Reigen* (better known as *La Ronde*) which provoked one of the best-known theatre scandals of the age.[52]

In trying to recount the history of Joyce's clash with censoriousness we are, in part, acting out a drama whose plot was written by Joyce himself. When we talk about censorship, it is to this partly prefabricated fiction we refer and it is to Joyce's own conclusions about the necessarily alienated and condemned position of the artist that we are drawn. Joyce's earliest artistic self-portraits were an attempt to define a role of this kind for himself, casting him as the champion of dangerously modern or sexually explicit authors. In the dramatic 'epiphanies' he appears as the member of his social group who knows about Ibsen and as someone who is likely to know about a risqué book with a title like *The Escaped Nun*.[53] The early *Portrait* essay shows a seething contempt for those fellow students who found the death of Zola in 1902 a proof of 'the hand of Emmanuel God with us' and for their submission to authority: 'if a student were forbidden to go to *Othello* ("There are some coarse expressions in it" he was told) what a little cross was that?'[54]

In *Stephen Hero* much of the discussion of art takes place in these terms. The dispute over Stephen's paper and the arguments he puts forward are, as I have suggested, best seen in this context. All writers seem, by Stephen's interlocutors, to be categorized alongside sexual sinfulness and one of the most fully achieved aspects of the book is its author's ability to characterize such half-conscious habits of literary critical thought. Books like George du Maurier's sensational novel *Trilby* described by the trainee priest as 'a bit blue', set the tone of the debate (*SH* 76). With the coldness of observation that went into the 'Hades' episode of *Ulysses*, Joyce sets another Dublin critical discussion at the funeral of Stephen's sister Isabel. One of Mr Daedalus' friends complains about the prohibited books he has to handle as a clerk in the Police Courts and Uncle John weighs in against the 'Scandalous' Boucicault; on the grounds that 'children should be kept in their places' (*SH* 171). The character Moynihan, who is 'auditor' of the Literary and Historical Society, is introduced as another example of this level of literary taste. He wishes he could read Italian since the *Decameron* 'took the biscuit for "smut"' and 'must be ten times as bad in the original' (*SH* 155). Characters who have never read Ibsen (like the College President) complain about his revolutionary theories (*SH* 97–8) and those who have little real interest in art accuse Stephen of contempt for classicism. The discussion of Stephen's paper reaches its climax in the student Hughes's claim that 'the moral welfare of the Irish people was menaced by such theories' (*SH* 107).

Stephen's reaction to this boorishness might have consisted in an attempt to deny that literature had anything to do with sexuality but he does not do so. Joyce allowed Stephen's tastes to confirm the identification between sexual and linguistic luxury that Dublin society condemned, making the issue not just one of a difference in literary taste but one of a conflict in a whole system of values. His tastes seem not evasions from but explicit responses to this central issue, not just in the obvious case of Ibsen but in the 'elegant songs of the Elizabethans' that please him despite, almost because of, their 'dubious' moral (*SH* 48). In these self-portraits Joyce is only half able to present himself as a 'disinterested' aesthete who suffers some unforeseen disapproval from his peers. The situation seems rather to be an equivocal one where that very disapproval helps to direct and define the aesthetic revolt. And whilst the situations and responses described may have their roots in Joyce's own experience, the universalizing character of the fictions extends them into a metaphorical commentary on art itself.

'The young men at the college,' we are told, 'regarded art as a continental vice' (*SH* 38) and Joyce indeed embraced both vice and the continent on his way to literary art. Such seems to be the implication of the theory of artistic exile developed in *A Portrait* as one of the three watchwords for the aspiring writer and as the condition to which Richard is damned in *Exiles*. Robert Hand tries to represent Richard, in his deceitfully journalistic editorial article, as a kind of prodigal son returning to the new nationalist Ireland at last. But Richard's position is one of permanent, willed sexual and literary exile, consciously resisting the possessiveness, deceit and self-interest that passes for conventional morality in his view. Joyce's decision to be an exiled author was surely part of the same way of seeing the world as his position as reader and writer of censored or censorable books. His exile made it practically possible for him to read and write what may not have been possible in Ireland: that is, it made possible his conscious determination to transgress and to offend those moral values which the censorship was designed to enforce. Notions of exile and censorship were closely tied in his mind, as appears from his puzzlement over an active or passive title (*esuli* or *esigliati*) for the Italian translation of *Exiles*, and his memory of the German title *Verbannte* in talking of censored books ('they should quite rightly verbanned be') in *Finnegans Wake*.[55] It is almost a revolt by self-condemnation that begins in the characterization of Stephen's puritanical interlocutors in *Stephen Hero* and ends in the portrayal of Shem in *Finnegans Wake* as an oppressed, forbidden figure described by his enemies as 'self-exiled', 'the worst, it is hoped, even in our western playboyish world for pure mousefarm filth', and 'every day in everyone's way more exceeding in violent abuse of self and others' (*FW* 184.6, 183.3–4, and 183.2–3).

The exile in these passages has become a process of exceeding everyone and in every way, but it began as a more single-handed need to supersede realist writers in writing about sexuality. As for many of the Elizabethan writers Joyce admired, the author who was most readily identifiable with sexual writings, sexual transgressions and sexual exile was Ovid, whose erotic activities earned him the displeasure of the Emperor Augustus. Joyce forged a definitive identification with Ovid in taking the name of his fictional self-portrait and his epigraph from *The Metamorphoses*. The implications of the Daedalus story, particularly the relevance of the relationship of Daedalus and his son Icarus to the reading of *A Portrait* have been much discussed, but there has been a tendency to neglect the whole of the story in favour of the suggestive last part. Presumably Joyce's first inkling was that this story of an inventive designer served the Roman poet as something of a self-portrait and was therefore an appropriate choice for his own self-portraiture. The myth is strongly relevant to Joyce's sexual subjects too. Daedalus's first task was to construct a wooden cow by means of which Pasiphaë was able to commit the most notorious sexual transgression in classical mythology and his next job was, at the commission of King Minos, to construct a labyrinth at whose heart the product of that transgression, the

Minotaur, could be concealed.[56] It is only then that the third part of the myth, on which Joyce critics have dwelt, takes place and Daedalus builds wings to escape the labyrinth in which he too has been imprisoned. If repressive Ireland is the labyrinth from which Stephen flies then we may read the earlier part of the myth with the aid of that indecorously Swiftian passage in the 'Oxen of the Sun' episode of *Ulysses*. That passage offers a history of Ireland as a kind of bestial sexual congress between pious Irish women and the 'bulls' of both Papal authority and the John Bull type of English imperialism.[57] Later in the conversation Ovid's story is mentioned in a reference to 'the elegant Latin poet' and his story of 'copulation between women and the males of the beasts'.[58] The drinkers at the maternity hospital are the close neighbours of the students at the end of *A Portrait* (if not in the chronology of Joyce's writing then in that constricted temporal and geographical space that Joyce chose to fictionalize in his writings) and it is highly suggestive to think of *A Portrait* as a concealed political allegory of this kind. Furthermore Joyce's art, I have argued, is one whose motivations begin with a desire to go beyond realistic writers in their attempt to base a portrayal of human relationships on a belief in the importance of sexuality; to transgress, and to offend those agencies who would perceive such a view to be sin. No less than that of Daedalus, it is an art based on sexual transgression and, like that of Daedalus, its work develops as a labyrinthine concealment more than as an explicit statement of that transgression. May not this be the 'reading' of Ovid that Joyce offers in *A Portrait* and *Ulysses* and whose implications conditioned Joyce's choice of this story as the central metaphor for the artistic situation?

The Irish word for love

Joyce's idea of art, even his idea of modernity, emerged in relation to the realistic writers of the turn of the century and, far from opposing their doctrines, his writings strove to supersede their achievements at least to the extent that they offer a view of humanity based on the determining significance of sex. Any simple contrast between realism and modernity (even that of such a distinguished critic as Edmund Wilson in *Axel's Castle* between Flaubert's 'Naturalism' and Joyce's 'Symbolism'[59]) runs the risk of obscuring these important continuities. But to say that Joyce's writing shared certain priorities with those of the realists is not to suggest that it was by writing more explicitly about sex that he chose to proceed.

Alongside the desire to recognize this kind of reality, Joyce's writing showed from the first a wish to be highly-wrought and periphrastic in its literariness. Literary pleasure was as 'real' as sexual pleasure and also needed to be recognized, or so we may infer from the indulgence in phrase-making that clogged the early *Portrait* essay. Its locutions are consciously worked, whether they be disdainfully satiric (describing footballing schoolfellows as 'the grunting booted apparition'), pre-Raphaelite ('the secret fall of leaves, the fragrant rain, the mesh of vapours moon-transpierced'), socialistic ('the vision ... of congenital lives shuffling onwards between yawn and howl, starvelings in mind and body'), blasphemously erotic ('A Litany must honour thee; Lady of the Apple Trees, Kind Wisdom, Sweet Flower of Dusk') or just downright pompous ('use of reason is by popular judgement antedated by some seven years').[60] There was little chance that a writer who played on an organ with this variety of stops would ever be explicit: either in the sense that pornography is explicit or even in the sense that an emotionally sensitive, intelligent and fully articulate author like the Lawrence of *Lady Chatterley's Lover* is explicit. This early piece of Joyce promises a development towards further indirections, the coining of ever more elaborate and resonant (if often dangerously opaque) phrases. It holds out the possibility of an art of sexual secrecy or indirection rather than the discovery of the confident and consistent authorial tone and register that 'explicitness' would seem to require.

The desire to be literary in this way was not by any means an unusual one. Some degree of elaboration in language may be a necessary part of a literary style, as the rhetorical arts of the Elizabethans recognized, and as, more recently, the formalist notion of the 'defamiliarization' which characterizes literary language seems to confirm. Viktor Shklovsky in his famous essay on 'Art as Technique' argues that it is wrong to think that artistic images and metaphors allow us to perceive more economically; their purpose is to create new or special perceptions to add, not to remove, an element of indirection. Significantly Shklovsky chooses examples from erotic art where riddles, metaphors and circumlocutions serve to disguise the organs and acts described.[61] For Shklovsky, of course, the nature of the object described is a matter of complete irrelevance but it is only a short step from noticing the frequency with which erotic art furnishes examples of these phenomena to the suggestion that for some writers the relationship between sexual subjects and literariness may be a profoundly important one.

Stephen's fellows in the Irish language class in *Stephen Hero* giggle over the word 'gradh', the Irish word for love, because of their sexual naivety and, no doubt, also, because of a perceived incongruity of that word in the language.[62] This is one among many 'translations' of the word that recur in Joyce's work. Later on in *Stephen Hero* Lynch, we are told, objects to 'trite and meaningless execrations, to the facile iniquities of the lips' and this objection brings about what Joyce's narrator calls two 'moments of inspiration'. First, instead of saying 'bloody', he 'execrated in yellow' and second, he describes the 'hymeneal tract' and everything pertaining to it as 'oracle' (*SH* 141). In his discussion with Stephen about adultery he bases his judgement on whether or not the woman concerned is 'inclined for oracle' (*SH* 196). Stephen has his own private language of circumlocution for sexual matters, whose most striking element is the term 'marsupial' for prostitute and the circumlocutions run deeper than these aesthetically half-digested, boyish jokes. The narrator's phrase 'hymeneal tract' is itself an awkward one, perhaps remembering some phrase of Lynch's own, or perhaps attempting to gain seriousness and distance by employing a pseudo-medical vocabulary. There is, it seems, no sure resting-place for authoritative narratorial vocabulary on a sensitive subject like this. Direct vernacular seems to be avoided for its obvious offensiveness (not to mention the printing difficulty); medical Latin would seem flat and dry and too anatomically precise for Lynch's vaguely suggestive intention. For the self-conscious stylist there is no 'neutral' choice. Connotations are rife and it is to avoid or at least to control them that both Lynch and the narrator are driven to indirection.

Like Shklovsky's folk tales and riddles, Joyce's fiction is full of memorable periphrases for sexual acts and organs. Those Bloomian thoughts about cork and bottle and knife and fork that I listed in an earlier chapter include an awareness of the potential sexual analogy in lock and key that Shklovsky also observes. The ghastly description of the sexual act in the *Portrait* essay as 'bodies sounding with the triumph of harps' matures into the 'dark pressure of softly parting lips' in *A Portrait* and ultimately into the genuine, if not obviously poetical, delicacy of Bloom's 'How life begins', or, for that matter, Molly's saying 'yes'. If explicitness, as I have suggested, requires a consistent manner and vocabulary, then even Joyce's obscenities are not describable as explicit but are themselves self-conscious periphrases, deliberate exploitations of a grotesque register made in 'Oxen' and 'Circe' in a way that is comparable to the exploitations of the popular sentimental and curt Bloomian modes in 'Nausicaa'.

How, among the welter of possibilities, is the sexual act to be described? From which linguistic register should the definitive vocabulary be drawn? That is the problem that faces Richard Rowan in *Exiles* when he surprises Robert Hand just about to seduce his wife and his solution is a remarkable one. He refers to 'what some old theologian, Duns Scotus I think, calls a death of the spirit' (*E* 95). Robert objects to the phrase, which is hardly calculated to enhance his amorous ambitions, but he too, when later in the play he recounts what took place that night with a girl from a night club in the back of a cab, resorts to describing it as 'what the subtle Duns Scotus calls a death of the spirit' (*E* 155). On one level Robert's naive belief that sex is an 'affirmation' is discountenanced by this reversal but that does not account for the full interest of the phrase. It is a periphrasis whose effect is that it describes the sexual act in the language of an intellectual tradition which is the least apparently likely to be positive or enthusiastic about the act it describes. Here 'indirection' has become pointedly direct. Richard's choice of circumlocution has made apparent the whole intellectual tradition of which he disapproves.

There is no implied endorsement of scholastic morality in the phrase. On the contrary his morality of absolute sexual freedom could not be further from the medieval theologian he chooses to quote. It may be that his sensitivity leads to a linguistic indirection, but it is his bitter and satiric temperament which ensures that it is an indirection with a polemical sting.

Here, in miniature, there seems to be an example of that larger tendency in Joyce's work, on which I have based much of my sense of his sexual attitudes. Like Richard Rowan, Joyce, I have argued, articulates those terms of reference which his views, if expressed more explicitly, would resist. This is the force behind the parody of traditional teachings on birth control in 'The Oxen of the Sun', the voicing of the narrow Jesuitical formula for sexual legitimacy, *emissio seminis inter vas naturale*, that the sexual experiences of the characters in the books serve to disprove, and the anarchically self-revealing parody of orthodox attitudes to sexuality in Shaun's valedictory address to the girls in *Finnegans Wake* Book III Chapter 2, to which I have repeatedly turned. In this latter passage something beyond parody has been achieved: the imitation of an alien mode of thinking and talking, whose inadequacies and self-contradictions are deliberately revealed through punning neologism and heightened ambiguity. It may, to be sure, not always have been obvious that such polemical intentions are to be found in *Finnegans Wake*, but there is a logic of development which leads from Lynch's moments of 'inspiration' or from the awkward literariness of Joyce's early style towards first parody (with its curiously divided logic of imitating the very arguments it hopes to defeat) and then to the intentional self-contradictoriness of Joyce's last work.

Indirection may be characteristic of Joyce's literariness. If so, at the heart of the indirection there seems to be a recognition of the difficulties (we might say the poetically productive difficulties) of writing on sensitive sexual subjects. But does not indirection necessarily detract from the ability of an author to make statements about such subjects or, indeed, about any subjects? Once the literary habit of inexplicitness has been adopted such apparently self-defeating devices as parody and punning self-contradiction may be the best ways of making a polemical point. Parody, at any rate, was the means by which works like Swift's *Modest Proposal* or Defoe's *Shortest Way with Dissenters* made their points, imitating the arguments that (if they had adopted a more explicit mode) they would have had to attack.

Another aspect of his literariness that Joyce turned to discreet polemical advantage was his allusiveness. T.S. Eliot in his essay 'Tradition and the Individual Talent' reminds critics of what the poet instinctively already knows: 'that not only the best, but the most individual parts of his work may be those in which the

dead poets, his ancestors, assert their immortality most vigor-
ously'.[63] Poetry may become poetic by the depth of its absorp-
tion of the literary tradition, by the pattern of hidden echoes
and allusions which make up its strongest effects. Modernist
writing in particular, I argued in my introduction, can be
characterized by its dependence on the allusion as a literary
device and Eliot himself provides the most obvious example of
a modernist poet whose 'Waste Land' is so built of allusion that
it comes with its own notes. Joyce was highly aware of the
literary importance of allusion and he incorporates that
awareness into his self-portraiture. 'For the artist', he explained
in the early *Portrait* essay, 'the symbols of words and allusion
were paramount things.'[64] Stephen's mind is crammed with
literary memories and he is half-aware that he makes his poetry
out of them, a fact that Joyce makes fully clear in his depiction
of Stephen at the end of Chapter 4 of *A Portrait*. Stephen draws
a poetic phrase from his 'treasury' and repeats it: 'A day of
dappled seaborne clouds' (*P* 170). The phrase and the scene in
front of him 'harmonised in a chord' but that chord, when
investigated from a reader's point of view, represents a curious
semantic knot which can only be unravelled by means of a
side-step to a book by Hugh Miller called *The Testimony of the
Rocks*, where the phrase of which it is a partial memory is to be
found.[65] Miller's immediately comprehensible phrase is 'a day
of dappled breeze-borne clouds', but Stephen has made it
meteorologically unsound by a poetic transference that both
veils and yet acknowledges the debt to Miller. That small initial
transference leads Stephen into a longer metaphorical elaboration on clouds as 'greyfringed fleece' and as 'a host of nomads
on the march' (*P* 170–1). It is a fine example of what Michael
Riffaterre in a recent examination of the language of poetry
calls intertextuality: the semantic dependence of literary texts
on past literary texts, which has a role in generating their
literary sophistications.[66]

Joyce's portrayal of Stephen's creativity shows up this aspect
strongly and it is an aspect of Joyce's own creativity which is
never far from the surface. His writing is, as I said in my
introduction, characteristically bookish, allusive and full of
quotation. In a work like *Ulysses* the sources of Joyce's material
are unprecedentedly wide and unprecedentedly demand the
reader's investigative attention. The influences which lead

Joyce to write as he does need scrutiny and leave their traces in the furthest corners of his work. However it is not the unconscious ways in which *Ulysses* may be said to derive aspects of its theme or structure from earlier achievements that thrusts itself on our attention, so much as its conscious manipulations of previously written material. The importance of allusions and quotations is not merely secondary to the main intention or aesthetic statement of the work; as often as not they themselves constitute that statement.

Take the parallel incidents in 'Wandering Rocks' where Bloom and Stephen are observed. Both characters are seen in the act of contemplating books, and characterization is effected by the books they choose. Bloom indulges his weakness for *Aristotle's Masterpiece*, Sacher-Masoch, James Lovebirch and *Sweets of Sin*; Stephen is more interested in the apocryphal 'Eighth and Ninth books of Moses' with their mysterious magical charms and in the French grammar his sister has acquired. Bloom relates to his family as a borrower of books for Molly; Stephen as an 'expert' but one whose books have once more, we are told, been sold. The atmosphere of each episode depends heavily on the character of the books mentioned and quoted (some real books, some partly fictionalized titles with a strong basis in fact). Stephen's interior monologue has an obvious literary dependence: his poetic and philosophic thoughts are built of truncated memories of such authors as Homer, Shakespeare, Milton, Matthew Arnold and the Bible, in whose words during these few pages he thinks. Less obtrusively, some kinds of popular literature provide the elements of Bloom's consciousness. The structure of the episode derives, of course, from Joyce's reading of Homer (though in this case the episode is only tenuously Homeric) and its 'day in the life' feel, in part, from Joyce's reading of popular biographies of Shakespeare and reconstructions of his daily life. At least in the depiction of Dublin, we might think, we have unmediated geographical detail. Not so. The bookstalls may be a memory of the same Dublin bookstalls depicted in *Stephen Hero*, where Stephen picks up a copy of Yeats's stories, *The Tables of The Law* and *The Adoration of the Magi*, which he knew by heart (*SH* 182). In the first of these stories the narrator is by the Dublin Quays 'stopping from time to time to turn over the works upon an old bookstall', when he recognizes Owen Aherne whose Faustian tragedy is the subject of the story.[67]

For Eliot, the poet's immersion in 'tradition' is an 'escape from personality', a guarantee of disinterestedness and of transcending the merely subjective. Riffaterre also suggests that the value of a poetic memory resides in that it is a memory, more than in any extra-poetic significance in the work it may be a memory of. But if such veiled debts are indeed characteristic of poetic language, then an obvious way forward for a writer poetically responsive to contentious issues is to exploit the potential significance of such memories. In Stephen's case, poised between clerical vocation and secular artistry, the relevance of a resonating echo of Hugh Miller's book is clear, since it was one of the many nineteenth-century responses to the discovery of the inadequacies of the Genesis account of creation. An intertextuality may be the trace of a contentious issue in this way and, in a fiction where authorial attitudes are inexplicit, such traces may be among the most reliable indicators of these issues that we can find. The memory of the bookstalls has a similar importance, reinforcing Joyce's allegiance to the spirit of the Yeats story; its narrative of heretical mysticism that supplants the Catholic orthodoxy being an endorsement and justification of both Stephen's and Joyce's own.

This story, which so penetrated Joyce's literary consciousness, was one at the heart of which was the notion of heresy. And heresy is the final and definitive form of literary relationship which can help explain the blend of contention and allusiveness in Joyce's work. For Eliot, writers are immersed in tradition in a particular way. They may not take in the past as 'an indiscriminate bolus', nor may they restrict their admiration to certain authors or periods. 'Blind or timid adherence' to tradition is discouraged but it seems presumed by Eliot's essay that the continuity of interest between writers of the past and of the present will be strong. The relationship between the writer and tradition is one between members of the same community. But for Joyce one of the most fascinating kinds of writerly response was the response of the heretic.

One of Joyce's first critics was a lay teacher of English composition at Clongowes, George Dempsey. According to Stanislaus, he was impressed by Joyce's essays, but when it came to *A Portrait* Joyce chose to present an incident where Dempsey, as Mr Tate, comments on the 'heresy' in Stephen's essay. This 'heresy' is passed off as a slip of the pen but is later explained as the influence of Stephen's leisure spent in the 'company of subversive writers'. Stephen's cowardly and ignorant schoolfellows taunt him for his error in theology but the point of the incident (particularly since Tate is a lay teacher, not a Jesuit) seems to be to identify heresy as a fundamental characteristic of Stephen's literary creativity. Heresy returns as a key term in *Exiles*, where Robert's superficial irreverence is called blasphemy and Richard's 'much worse' principled unorthodoxy is heresy. In 'Telemachus' Stephen's thoughts turn to the spiritual tyranny of the Roman church, imagining a scene where a group of heretics is driven away by the Archangel Michael and his host. The heresies mentioned bear on his situation since they all deal with the question of Christ's divinity which Stephen (with his interest in Renan and his heretical readings of the gospels) also seems to challenge (*U* 24–5). They bear on Stephen's psychological need to deny his 'consubstantiality' with his own father and on the Shakespeare theory which Mulligan first voices as a version of the heresy of Sabellius. Stephen fears the undignified end of Arius, who died in a watercloset (*U* 47), but his allegiance to the 'heresy' of his Shakespeare theory and to his 'heretical' atheist and anarchist views is undimmed.

In *Ulysses* heretics are called 'mockers': a term which links them to Mulligan, since his 'mockery' of Sabellius introduces both the Shakespeare theory and the theme of heresy into the book. It might also remind us of Mulligan's first 'mockery': his mock mass that opens the book and sets a jokey, impersonative and, of course, heretical mood. Critics have pondered on the theology and the symbolism of this and have argued for an opposition between Stephen and Mulligan in these terms. But it is the semi-autobiographical Stephen who delights in heresy, from the fascination with the 'heresiarchs of initiation' in the early *Portrait* essay to the 'wave of speech' which introduces them to the young lady in *Giacomo Joyce*. And heresy has obviously literary as well as theological implications.

Conscious heresy is a curiously hybrid mode of rebellion: not an ignorance nor a rejection of orthodoxy but, like Joyce's idea of Wilde's art, a deliberate kind of sinning. It is a mode of thinking which, rather than presuming to forge new ground from first principles, offers a deliberately perverse or provocative revision of an established view or system: its rebellion couched in the very terms to which it objects. Even the great heresies, like that of Luther mentioned as such in 'Circe', are not rejections so much as revisions and re-readings of orthodox belief. In that way they seem especially emblematic of a fiction built out of revisions and re-readings of earlier fictions, one whose attitudes are expressed as a 'reading' of past literature such as Joyce's seems to be. They are also emblematic of the kind of fiction whose notion of modernity arises out of a desire to extend and supersede the achievements of past literary work. Sophisticated theoretical criticism has, in the figure of Harold Bloom, come up with a theory of poetry as misprision or intentional misreading of past poetry[68] but Joyce's artistic self-portraiture anticipated this theory with its final vision of Shem's 'piously forged palimpsests', his 'blasphematory spits': its vision of a Shem who is an artistic 'hiresiarch'.[69]

Byron is the heterodox poet on whose behalf Stephen runs into trouble in *A Portrait* but it was Blake (on whom Joyce lectured in 1912) whose heresy was more significant from an artistic point of view. It is as a heretic that Joyce describes him, comparing his principled but conscientious and humane unorthodoxy to the morality of the Jesuits Suarez and Mariano de Talavera y Garces (worked into *A Portrait* too) who, despite their orthodoxy, could justify tyrannicide.[70] Joyce's lecture touches on Blake's visionary abilities but, once again, stresses their heterodoxy, their dependence on the humanistic Michaelangelo and Swedenborg and the 'glorified humanity with which all of Blake's work is stamped' (*CW* 221).

It was more than just a form of humanism that Joyce learnt from Blake. It was that essentially heretical cast of thought which gave Blake's work its angrily revisionist manner: Blake the annotator of Reynolds; Blake the composer of prophecies to ape and outdo those of Isaiah or Ezekiel; Blake the proponent of a radical reading of *Paradise Lost* with Satan as hero and Blake the putative author of a 'Bible of Hell'.[71] Though his lecture does not deal explicitly with this aspect of Blake, it was most likely from Blake that Joyce learnt to read radically and to make his own works an expression of that radical re-reading. Here he learnt the freedom to read the Bible in an atheistic way, seeing Christ as a Defender of adultery and prostitution, and perceiving a feminist allegory in the creation of Eve. Here he learnt to see Paolo and Francesca as hero and heroine of Dante's *Divine Comedy*; here he learnt to turn Ovid into the subtle vehicle of self-portraiture and art theory that is *A Portrait*. Here he learnt that Thomas Aquinas was potentially a sexually liberal aesthete and that the casuists offered the key to sexology. Here he learnt that views drawn from modern sociologists like Charles Albert, Ferrero, the Vaertings, or Havelock Ellis might be expressed by means of literary or even ecclesiastical tradition. Here he was inspired to compose a heretical theory of Shakespeare (one that, since Shakespeare's Christianity is hardly obtrusive enough to be exploded, had to be 'heretical' in that one of its arguments was derived from Sabellian heresy and another overturned an 'orthodoxy' in the interpretation of *Hamlet*). According to Harry Levin, and most subsequent critics, Joyce admired Defoe 'as the most matter of fact' and Blake 'as the most visionary' of authors.[72] But it was Defoe the parodist and Blake the heretic and deliberate misreader who most interestingly anticipated his own advances in fictional technique. Stephen's debt to the 'revisionist' Blake is made explicit at the start of 'Scylla and Charybdis'. He has apparently planned a Blakean *Paradise Lost* to be called 'The Sorrows of Satan' (*U* 235). It was by the same energetic turn of mind that Joyce was enabled to read Homer as a modern fiction of bourgeois marriage, as a book which could be read in terms of a discussion on birth control or feminism and as a modern Dublin day.

This practice of radical re-reading may be best understood as Blake's legacy but it may have first suggested itself to Joyce through Yeats. For Joyce, Yeats's mysticism was not seen in reaction to a materialist world so much as in resistance to the orthodox mysticism of the Catholic Church. Stephen is shown to reject the 'passive' Christ of the gospels for the 'disdainful' Christ of Renan's narrative account and for the 'infrahuman or superhuman' Nietzschean attraction of Aherne and Robartes in Yeats's stories.[73] Stephen (and we may infer Joyce) absorbed these stories as a kind of luxurious heresy. Joachim of Flora, whose secret prophecies of a third age of the Holy Spirit are discovered by Owen Aherne in *The Tables of The Law*, appealed to Stephen as a symbol of his conversion to a literary career and as an indication of a new humanistic or heterodox age, spelled out by Havelock Ellis in his literary criticism, to which such a career seemed to point.

The *Divine Comedy*, in its persistent commentary on and disposition of the intellectual figures of the classical and pre-medieval Christian world, might itself be considered a form of imaginative literary criticism, or at least a work whose ideas and attitudes express themselves as ideas on and attitudes to writers and past works. One of its curiosities in this respect, as Yeats's narrator points out, is that Joachim of Flora, despite his heresy, is accorded a place in Paradise.[74] Such unorthodoxy, read into Dante's no doubt innocent text, is used to justify Joachim's heterodoxy and is typical of this 'heretical' habit of mind. The phrase from Yeats's story that most sticks in Stephen's imagination is one where the spirit communicators of the new vision ask, 'Why do you fly from our torches which were made out of the wood of the trees under which Christ wept in the gardens of Gethsemane?' (*SH* 184).[75] It is as a defence of their heretical vision that the 'spirits' in the story speak these lines and their argument is indeed a suggestive one, or must have been to Stephen and to a Joyce whose art was new but one whose novelty consisted in the fact that it was built out of heretical revision and re-reading of the orthodoxy it hoped to supplant.

Notes

Introduction

1 'Aramis', 'The Scandal of *Ulysses*', *Sporting Times*, no.34 (1 April 1922), 4. Reprinted in *James Joyce: The Critical Heritage*, ed. Robert H. Deming (London: Routledge, 1970), 192–4.

2 G.B. Shaw, letter to Sylvia Beach, 6 November 1921, *The Letters of James Joyce*, vols. II and III, ed. Richard Ellmann (London: Faber, 1966), vol. III, p.50. Vol.I, ed. Stuart Gilbert (London: Faber, 1957) and *Selected Letters*, ed. Richard Ellmann (London: Faber, 1975). Hereafter cited as *L* I, II and III and *SL*. Virginia Woolf, 'Modern Novels', unsigned review in *The Times Literary Supplement* (10 April 1919), 189–90. Arnold Bennett, 'James Joyce's *Ulysses*', *Outlook* (29 April 1922), 337–9. H.G. Wells, 'James Joyce', *Nation* (24 February 1917), 710–12. Rebecca West, 'The Strange Case of James Joyce', *Bookman* (New York) (Sept. 1928), 9–23. The writings above are all reprinted in Deming, *Critical Heritage*, 189–90, 125–6, 219–22, 86–8 and 430–6 respectively.

3 Stuart Gilbert, *James Joyce's 'Ulysses': a Study* (London: Faber, 1930), 31–2.

4 T.S. Eliot, '*Ulysses*, Order and Myth', *Dial* 75 (Nov. 1923), 480–3, reprinted in Deming, *Critical Heritage*, 268–71.

5 Morris L. Ernst, *United States Circuit Court of Appeals for the Second Circuit. USA vs. 'Ulysses' by James Joyce. Brief for Claimant Appellee* (New York: Bakou Press, 1934), 4, 8 and 51.

6 William M. Schutte, *Joyce and Shakespeare* (New Haven: Yale University Press, 1957), 1–17. Wayne C. Booth, *The Rhetoric of Fiction* (Chicago: Chicago University Press, 1961), 327–35. Richard Ellmann, *James Joyce* (London: OUP, 1959, revised 1982). The term 'epiphany' has been given its widest application in Morris Beja, *Epiphany in the Modern Novel* (London: Peter Owen, 1971), but perhaps the best account of it is that given by a non-Joycean, M.H. Abrams, in *Natural Supernaturalism* (New York: Norton, 1973), 421–2, where Abrams explains its kinship with romantic aesthetic notions, that the energy of the term in Joyce derives from the fact that it is a *secularization* of a religious term, and that its modernity in Joyce results from the commonness of the objects 'epiphanized'.

7 Dominic Manganiello, *Joyce's Politics* (London: Routledge, 1980).

8 Mark Shechner, *Joyce in Nighttown* (London: University of California Press, 1974). Shechner gives a bibliography (262–4) of psychoanalytic approaches to Joyce of which the best, to my mind, remains that in

Frederick Hoffmann's *Freudianism and the Literary Mind* (Baton Rouge: Louisiana State University Press, 1957), 116–50. Margaret Solomon, *Eternal Geomater: The Sexual Universe of 'Finnegans Wake'* (Carbondale: Southern Illinois University Press, 1969). Articles touching on sexuality in *Finnegans Wake* include Fritz Senn, 'Some Conjectures about Homosexuality in *"Finnegans Wake"'*, *A Wake Newslitter (AWN)* 6 (Oct. 1969), 70–2 and 'Every Klitty of a Scoldery-maid: Sexual-Political Analogies', reprinted in Clive Hart and Fritz Senn (eds.), *A Wake Digest* (Sydney: Sydney University Press, 1968), 27–38; henceforth cited as *WD*. Much interesting annotative material has also been gathered by Ian MacArthur, 'Sexuality in *Finnegans Wake'*, *AWN* 15 (Feb. 1978), 1–15 and (Aug. 1978), 59.

9 Marilyn French, *The Book as World* (London: Harvard University Press, 1976), 48. The most interesting parts of the book from the point of view of sexual politics are the pages (44–53) where she draws together some of the thoughts on sexuality that run through the book and in her extended footnote (275–6) criticizing the anti-feminist attitudes of Darcy O'Brien, Hugh Kenner, Stanley Sultan and D.S. Savage. Since this work was completed another book has appeared, edited by Suzette A. Henke and Elaine Unkeles, entitled *Women in Joyce* (Carbondale: Southern Illinois University Press, 1982), which contains many useful essays on the theme.

10 A typical anti-Molly Bloom critic is J.Mitchell Morse, who in his essay 'Molly Bloom Revisited', in *A James Joyce Miscellany: 2nd series*, ed. Marvin Magalaner (Carbondale: Southern Illinois University Press, 1959), 139–49, argued that Molly 'is the very centre of paralysis' (102) and, rather absurdly, that the only positively portrayed women in *Ulysses* are 'the midwife, her companion, and Mrs Purefoy, pure faith, whose achievement in giving birth is the basis of the only joyful episode in the book' (103).

Over the years, especially since the famous examination of the plausibility of the list of Molly's 25 supposed lovers in the 'Ithaca' episode of *Ulysses* in Robert Martin Adams's *Surface and Symbol* (New York: OUP, 1972, 35–43), the tendency has been to veer away from critical commentary into examining textual 'facts'. This tendency can be seen in essays by David Hayman, 'The Empirical Molly' in *Approaches to 'Ulysses'*, ed. Thomas Staley and Bernard Benstock (University of Pittsburgh Press, 1970), 103–35; and by Phillip Herring, 'The Bedsteadfastness of Molly Bloom', *Modern Fiction Studies* 15 (Spring 1969), 49–61 and 'Towards an Historical Molly Bloom', *English Literary History (ELH)* 45 (Autumn 1978), 501–21.

11 Clive Hart, 'The Sexual Perversions of Leopold Bloom', in *'Ulysses': 50 ans après*, ed. Louis Bonnerot (Paris: Didier, 1974), 131.

12 Michel Foucault, *Histoire de la sexualité*, vol.I, *La Volonté de savoir* (Paris: Gallimard 1976), trans. Robert Hurley as *The History of Sexuality: An Introduction* (London: Allen Lane, 1979).

13 James Joyce, *The Critical Writings of James Joyce*, ed. Ellsworth Mason and Richard Ellmann (London: Faber, 1959). Hereafter cited as *CW*.

14 C.P. Curran, *James Joyce Remembered* (London: OUP, 1968), 9. John J. Slocum and Herbert Cahoon, *A Bibliography of James Joyce, 1882–1941* (London: Hart-Davies, 1953), 176–8.

15 Richard Ellmann, *The Consciousness of Joyce* (London: Faber, 1977), 45–72. Books acquired in 1919–20 which seem related to his composition of these chapters include a prose anthology by H.A. Treble and *The Study of Sociology* by Herbert Spencer, who is parodied in 'The Oxen of the Sun' (Ellmann, *Consciousness*, 131 and 128 respectively). Joyce requested 'a bundle of other novelettes and any penny hymnbook' from his aunt at this time which, though they apparently went astray (*L* I 134 and 137), were of most obvious use for the 'Nausicaa' episode (*L* I 135).

16 The book bills and inventory are held in the Joyce collection at Cornell University and discussed in my 'Addenda and Corrigenda to Ellmann's *The Consciousness of Joyce*', *James Joyce Quarterly* (*JJQ*) 17 (Spring 1980), 313–17. Many of my suggestions have been incorporated in later editions of Ellmann's book.

17 The library was first described in the catalogue of the Paris exhibition of 1949: *James Joyce: sa vie, son oeuvre, son rayonnement* (Paris: La Hune, 1949). The fuller descriptive listing is Thomas E. Connolly's *The Personal Library of James Joyce*, University of Buffalo Studies 22 (April 1955).

18 *L* III 76.

19 Arthur Power, *Conversations with James Joyce* (London: Millington 1974), 42.

20 Clive Hart, in an introduction to Arthur Power's book, offers a relevant representative view of Joyce's reading: 'Except for his sporadic and highly specialised research into works of reference and comparatively rare books (much of it in any case carried out for him by willing amanuenses), Joyce was not often a great reader ...' (Power, *Conversations*, 5).

21 *Tauchnitz Edition Centenary Catalogue 1837–1937* (Leipzig: Tauchnitz, 1937), 5.

22 Marvin Magalaner, *Time of Apprenticeship: The Fiction of Young James Joyce* (London: Abelard-Schuman, 1959), 33.

23 Ellmann, *Consciousness*, 7–8. *Uric Acid*, for instance, has nothing to say about urination. It is about vegetarianism and the harmful effects of meat to the body's chemical balance.

24 Weldon Thornton, *Allusions in 'Ulysses'* (Chapel Hill: University of North Carolina Press, 1968).

25 Don Gifford and Robert J. Seidman, *Notes for Joyce* (New York: Dutton, 1974). Another volume with the same title first published in 1967 and expanded and revised in 1982 annotates *Dubliners* and *A Portrait*.

26 Ulrich Schneider, *Die Funktion der Zitate im 'Ulysses' von James Joyce* (Bonn: Bouvier, 1970).

27 James S. Atherton, *The Books at the Wake* (New York: Viking, 1960).

28 Edmund Wilson, *Axel's Castle* (London: Fontana, 1961), 93.

29 Ivor Winters, 'The Anatomy of Nonsense', reprinted in *In Defense of Reason* (London: Routledge, 1960), 480.

30 Harold Bloom, *The Anxiety of Influence* (Oxford: OUP, 1973); *A Map of Misreading* (Oxford: OUP, 1975) and *Agon: Towards a Theory of Revisionism* (Oxford: OUP, 1982). Roland Barthes, *Image/Music/Text* (London: Fontana, 1977), 146–8. See also Jonathan Culler, *On Deconstruction* (London: Routledge, 1980), 32–3.

31 Gérard Genette, *Palimpsestes* (Paris: Editions du Seuil, 1982).

32 Hugh Kenner, *Ulysses* (London: Allen & Unwin, 1980), 35. One book among those which have treated allusiveness in the novel is Michael Wheeler's *The Art of Allusion in Victorian Fiction* (London: Macmillan, 1979).

33 T.S. Eliot, 'Milton I' and 'Milton II' in *On Poetry and Poets* (London: Faber, 1957).

34 Foucault, *Histoire de la sexualité*, vol.I, 20.

35 Roy K. Gottfried, *The Art of Joyce's Syntax in 'Ulysses'* (London: Macmillan, 1981), 117–18.

1 Love and marriage

1 Charles Dickens, *Hard Times* (London: Bradbury & Evans, 1854).

2 Raymond Williams, *Culture and Society 1780–1950* (London: Chatto & Windus, 1967), 92–7.

3 The account of Marie Stopes's legal conflict with Dr Halliday Sutherland is in Ruth Hall, *Marie Stopes* (London: Deutsch, 1977), 213–41.

4 Historical information of this kind is available from two uncomplicated outlines of the changes in the law: William Latey, *The Tide of Divorce* (London: Longman, 1970) and David Morris, *The End of Marriage* (London: Cassell, 1971).

5 This attention to guilt marks an obvious advance from *Stephen Hero* (at least in its surviving portions) to *A Portrait*.

6 *L* II 147–8 and 150.

7 Robert Hand in *Exiles* (hereafter cited as *E*) sends a message to Bertha which reads '*There is one word I have never dared to say to you*' (*E* 38). This suggests, Robert's furtiveness, to which Richard so objects, but it also echoes the more fully articulated objection to the word 'love' that Joyce makes in his letter to Nora (*L* II 55).

8 *L* II 89.

9 *L* II 99.

10 *L* II 73 n6, 97 and n2, 107 and n1, and 108.

11 James Joyce, *Chamber Music* (London: Cape, 1927), 25. Hereafter *CM*. The title is mentioned in *L* II 92 and the term occurs in *Finnegans Wake* (hereafter *FW*) 192.28. The word 'companion' has a further sinful connotation in *Stephen Hero* (hereafter *SH*) where Maurice, on a Church retreat, is forbidden to walk with any 'companion' (*SH* 62).

12 *L* II 68.

13 The relationships are with Amalia Popper (his Trieste pupil), Marthe

Fleischmann (whom he saw in Zurich) and, as the new edition of
Ellmann's biography reveals, Gertrude Kaempffer, a lady doctor in
Zurich (Ellmann, *James Joyce*, 342–6, 418 and 448–53).

14 *L* II 95–6.
15 *L* II 107–8, 119 and 129. Joyce reused the phrase about paternity in
    'Scylla and Charybdis' (*Ulysses* 266). Hereafter cited as *U*.
16 *L* I 53.
17 *L* I 98.
18 *L* II 48.
19 *L* II 48.
20 *L* II 50.
21 Stanislaus Joyce, *The Complete Dublin Diary of Stanislaus Joyce*
    (London: Cornell University Press, 1971), 51.
22 Ian Watt, *The Rise of the Novel* (Harmondsworth: Penguin, 1972),
    ch.5: 'Love and the Novel', 152ff.
23 Tony Tanner, *Adultery in the Novel* (London: Johns Hopkins Univer-
    sity Press, 1974), 11.
24 Ford Madox Ford, *The Good Soldier* (London: John Lane, 1915) and
    Joseph Conrad, *Victory* (London: Methuen, 1915).
25 Robert Hand, at the start of Act 2 of *Exiles*, is playing Wolfram's song
    from Act 3 of Wagner's opera *Tannhäuser* – a romantic song appro-
    priate to the troubadour he is – 'O du mein holder Abendstern' ('O star
    of evening'). The use of operatic analogy to suggest adulterous
    intrigue, of course, foreshadows the more famous use of the seduc-
    tion duet from *Don Giovanni* in *Ulysses*. Wolfram is a suggestive
    analogy for Robert for he loves a woman (Elizabeth) who prefers
    another man (Tannhäuser). Tannhäuser himself is an interesting
    analogy for Richard: his sexual rebellion (love of Venus) bringing
    him into conflict with the Pope, just as Richard's relationship with
    Bertha brings him the opposition of Dublin opinion. The operatic
    analogy, besides exposing Robert's stereotypical seductive manners,
    also serves to define Richard as the central figure of the play and
    Robert as his disappointed rival.
26 Gustave Flaubert, *Madame Bovary*, trans. Gerard Hopkins (Oxford:
    OUP, 1981), 332.
27 Flaubert, *Madame Bovary*, 339 and 332 respectively.
28 Such events are noted in chronological order in John Henry Raleigh,
    The Chronicle of Leopold and Molly Bloom (Berkeley: University of
    California Press, 1977).
29 *U* 134, 146, 552–3, 653, 778, 792, 795, 921 etc.
30 *U* 196, 231, 863, 893 etc.
31 *U* 196–7, 863, 881 etc.
32 *U* 75–6, 196, 345, 863 etc.
33 The Lenehan incident is described by Molly (*U* 887) and by Lenehan
    (*U* 300–1). Other memories of the dinner occur at *U* 196, 348, 483,
    887, 920 etc. It is noticeable that ALP has a sexual 'past' too; she had
    'a flewmen of her owen' (*FW* 202.5–6), we are told, including her
    'Curraghman' (*FW* 202.29), 'two lads in scoutsch breeches' (*FW*
    204.5) and a 'hound' called 'Chirripa-Chirruta' (*FW* 204.12).

34 This adulterous climax is again foreshadowed in *Exiles* when Richard, realizing that Robert has arranged for him to be at the university just when he has planned his rendezvous with Bertha, comments 'Curious, isn't it? The same hour' (*E* 70). Simultaneity evidently fascinated Joyce.

35 Adams, *Surface and Symbol*, 35–43.

36 Ezra Pound, 'Joyce et Pécuchet', *Mercure de France*, 156 (1922), 315. A full-length study of the two authors can be found in Richard K. Cross, *Flaubert and Joyce* (Princeton: Princeton University Press, 1971) and see also Haskell M. Block, 'Theory of Language in Flaubert and Joyce', *Revue de Littérature Comparée*, (1961).

37 Ellmann, *James Joyce*, 75.

38 *L* II 107.

39 Connolly, *Personal Library*, 40.

40 Ellmann, *Consciousness*, 130. The title is included on the basis of its appearance on the 1920 shelf inventory.

41 Ellmann, *Consciousness*, 130. The information depends upon Joyce's use of the 'J.J.' stamp that Ellmann describes on p.97.

42 Honoré de Balzac, *Mémoires de deux jeunes mariées* (Paris: Calmann-Lévy, n.d.). Ellmann *Consciousness*, 100. I have used *La Comédie humaine*, trans. Scott, ed. G. Saintsbury (London: Dent, 1897), vol. XII.

43 Honoré de Balzac, *Pysiologie du mariage* (Paris: Calmann-Lévy, n.d.). Ellmann, *Consciousness*, 100. I have used *La Comédie humaine*, trans. G.B. Ives and others: *Physiology of Marriage*, 2 vols., including *Petty Worries* (London: Caxton, 1899).

44 Honoré de Balzac, *La Femme de trente ans* (Paris: Calmann-Lévy, n.d.), and *A Woman of Thirty*, trans. Ellen Marriage (London, 1910). Ellmann, *Consciousness*, 100. The name of Balzac's translator seems to be incorporated into *Finnegans Wake* in the name 'Llewelyn Mmarriage' (*FW* 210.12).

45 Ellmann, *Consciousness*, 120.

46 Marco Praga, *La Porta Chiusa* (Milan: Treves, 1914). Ellmann, *Consciousness*, 124. My ed. trans. A.S. Macdonald (London: Brentano's, 1924), 78. Michael Mason's article 'Why is Leopold Bloom a Cuckold?' *ELH*, 44 (1977) further discusses Joyce's relation to the Italian drama.

47 Oscar Wilde, *An Ideal Husband* (Leipzig: Tauchnitz, 1907). Ellmann, *Consciousness*, 133.

48 *E* 175. Ellmann, *Consciousness*, 120. The use of the subtitle suggests that Joyce had in mind the preface to Charles Paul de Kock's *Le Cocu* (Ghent: Vandenhaege Maya, 1839), where the propriety of both de Kock's own and Molière's titles is discussed.

49 *SH* 34–5, *E* 163. See also James A. Joyce *et al.*, *The Workshop of Daedalus*, ed. Robert Scholes and Richard M. Kain (Evanston: Northwestern University Press, 1965), 62, where its 'coarse expressions' are at issue. (Henceforth cited as *WD*.)

50 *L* I 146–7.

51 Richard Ellmann, *'Ulysses' on the Liffey* (New York: OUP, 1972), appendix gives both Linati and Gorman-Gilbert plans for *Ulysses*.

52 Frank Hopewell, *The Oddity* (Dublin: James Carson, 1741). Connolly, *Personal Library*, 19. Joyce apparently uses its repetitive short
lines and persistent rhyme on '-ation' in a passage in 'Ithaca' (*U* 867)
and, perhaps, in the famous repeated '-ation' of *Our Exagmination*
and the appearance of the twelve jurors in *Finnegans Wake*.

53 *WD* 72, S. Joyce, *Dublin Diary*, 83 and *SH* 196.

54 'Leo M. Taxil' (Gabriel Jogand-Pagès), *La Vie de Jésus* (Paris:
Librairie Anti-Cléricale, 1884), 15. Taxil is described in Marvin
Magalaner's *Time of Apprenticeship*, 49–71. The quotation is repeated
in the 'Oxen of the Sun' episode (*U* 511).

55 Adrian Beverland, *The Law Concerning Draped Virginity*, trans. F. D.
Byrne (Paris: Carrington, 1905), 466.

56 Herbert Spencer, *The Study of Sociology* (London: Kegan Paul,
Trench, 1888). Ellmann, *Consciousness*, 128. My reference is to a 1908
edition of the same, 136. Balzac, *Physiology*, vol.II, 338.

57 Ellmann, *Consciousness*, 116. *U* 78, 591 etc. One point in the novel
that may have especially interested Joyce was the names of the
characters. Belan, who in the first part of the novel is a rather
mercenary bachelor, has a name that sounds a little like that of Boylan;
and Blemont, a married man to whose happiness the possibility of
adultery poses a threat, a little resembles Bloom.

58 James Joyce, Buffalo Notebook VI.A in Michael Groden *et al.*, *The
James Joyce Archive* (New York: Garland Publishing, 1979), hence-
forth cited as *Archive*. Vol. 28; transcr. and ed. by Thomas E.
Connolly as *Scribbledehobble: The Ur-Workbook for 'Finnegans Wake'*
(Evanston: Northwestern University Press, 1961), henceforth cited
as *Scribbledehobble*.

59 Edward A. Westermarck, *The History of Human Marriage* (London:
Macmillan, 1891).

60 J. J. Bachofen, *Das Mutterrecht* (Stuttgart: Krais & Hoffmann, 1861).
J. F. McLennan, *Primitive Marriage* (Edinburgh, 1865) reprinted in
Studies in Ancient History (London: Quaritch, 1876). Sir John
Lubbock, *The Origin of Civilisation* (London: Longman, 1870). L. H.
Morgan, *Ancient Society* (New York: Henry Holt, 1877).

61 Friedrich Engels, *The Origin of the Family* (London: Lawrence &
Wishart, 1972).

62 Bertrand Russell, *Marriage and Morals* (London: Allen & Unwin,
1929), 20–4.

63 *Scribbledehobble*, 162, 173 (*FW* 546.13) and 120 respectively.

64 Engels, *Origin*, 82.

65 *Scribbledehobble*, 173.

66 *Voyages in China* is unidentified by Gifford and Seidman, who
identify William Ellis's *Three Trips to Madagascar* (London: Murray,
1858) and cite it as the source of Dixon and Lenehan's 'rite of
wedlock'. In fact there is no account of marital mores in Ellis's book
on Madagascar though, as James Atherton pointed out in his essay on
'Oxen of the Sun' in Hart and Hayman's *'Ulysses': a Collection of
Critical Essays* (Berkeley: University of California Press, 1974),
321–2, the idea most likely comes from Ernest Crawley's well-known

anthropological work, *The Mystic Rose* (London: Macmillan, 1902), where such practices were identified, if not in Madagascar, then in other places. Havelock Ellis in his *Studies in the Psychology of Sex*, 7 vols. (Philadelphia: Davies, 1905–28), vol. VI, 149, refers to the outrage about the 'pollutions' of the Tahitan islanders in William Ellis's *Polynesian Researches* (London: 1829).

67 Beverland, *Draped Virginity*, ch. 11, 'The Sacrifice of a Virgin', 352–71. Connolly, *Personal Library*, 9. Joyce, though, need have looked no further than Mozart's *Marriage of Figaro* for an interest in such marital customs.

68 G. B. Shaw, *Prefaces by Bernard Shaw* (London: Constable, 1934), 16. Joyce had *Getting Married* and *The Shewing-Up of Blanco Posnet* (Leipzig: Tauchnitz, 1914). Ellmann, *Consciousness*, 127.

69 Joyce is known to have owned two copies of the *Arabian Nights*: *Arabian Nights* (*Le Mille e una Notte*) trans. into Italian by Armando Dominicis (Florence: Adriana Salani, 1915). Ellmann, *Consciousness*, 99. Sir Richard F. Burton, *The Book of a Thousand Nights and a Night* ... 17 vols. (London: The Burton Club, n.d.). Connolly, *Personal Library*, 10. My references are to an edition also in 17 vols. (London: Kamashastra Society, 1884).

70 Charles Albert, *L'Amour libre* (Paris: Stock, 1910). Ellmann, *Consciousness*, 98. My references throughout are to the fourth edition (Paris: Stock, 1902).

71 Charles Grant Blairfindie Allen, *The Woman Who Did* (Leipzig: Tauchnitz, 1895), Ellmann, *Consciousness*, 98.

72 Alfred de Musset, *La Confession d'un enfant du siècle* (Paris: Bibliothèque Larousse, n.d.). Ellmann, *Consciousness*, 121, trans. G.F. Monkshood, *A Modern Man's Confession* (London: Greening, 1908).

73 Pierre Loti, *The Marriage of Loti*, trans. G. F. Monkshood (London: Siegle Hill, 1908), Ellmann, *Consciousness*, 117. Arthur Power mentions Loti in his *Conversations with James Joyce*, 87. The quotation is from Loti, 13.

74 Henry Havelock Ellis, *The New Spirit* (London: Walter Scott, pref. d. 1892), 79. Ellmann, *Consciousness*, 107.

75 *L II* 78.

76 *L II* 93.

77 W. E. H. Lecky, *The History of European Morals*, 2 vols. (London: Longman, 1869), vol. II, 299–300.

78 A fact confirmed by the publication date (1910) of Albert's book and by the date (1913) of Joyce's purchase of Lecky.

79 Evident in the utopian aspirations of Fourier, Saint-Simon, Godwin, Owen and Shelley.

80 See above, note 7.

81 *L II* 192.

82 'All the descriptions of fierce love and hatred which he had met in books had seemed to him therefore unreal' (*P* 84). In *Stephen Hero*, Stephen describes the popular myth of the Byronic profligacy of the poetic life as a cowardly 'burgher notion' (*SH* 37).

83 Frank Budgen, *James Joyce and the Making of 'Ulysses' and Other Writings* (London: OUP, 1972), 349.

84 Budgen, *The Making of 'Ulysses'*, 349.

85 Havelock Ellis, *The New Spirit*, 141.

86 It is tempting to speculate on Joyce's choice of names here. Though there was a Pleasants Street (*U* 73 and Raleigh, *Chronicle*, 102–3) in the Jewish quarter of Dublin, the Blooms' happily remembered early married days could hardly have a more appropriately named location. We might note that Bleibtreustrasse – the address on the planter's company advertisement that Bloom picks up from the butcher's counter in 'Calypso' and another idyll in his imagination – translates from the German as 'remain-true-street'. (There was a Karl Bleibtreu whose Shakespeare theory occurs in 'Scylla and Charybdis', but he seems less relevant here.) Eccles Street may be suggestive too.

   We may find ample reason for Joyce's choice of residence for his hero in the fact that his schoolfriend Curran lived in Eccles Street and in that it is given as the setting for Stephen's first 'epiphany' in *Stephen Hero* (*SH* 216). Eccles Street, however, reads remarkably like an abbreviation for Ecclesiastes, and several books in Joyce's library use reference to Ecclesiastes as a kind of shorthand for a resigned philosophy appropriate to the sexual uncertainties of modern life. Thus in the introduction to Havelock Ellis's *The New Spirit* we are told, as a warning of the sexually advanced ideas that are to come: 'You might spare yourself some unhappiness if, beforehand, you slip the book of *Ecclesiastes* beneath your own' (*The New Spirit*, 33). Octave, in de Musset's *A Modern Man's Confession*, after discovering a trunk of books that 'were so many catechisms of debauchery', reads Ecclesiastes and (though it is hard to imagine what so upsets him) recoils. '"So," I said to it,' he says '"you also doubt, book of hope"' (51–2).

   Perhaps Joyce, placing Leopold and Molly in Eccles Street, wished to suggest the sexual uncertainty of modern life in relation to which Bloom remembers a 'Pleasants Street' in the past and dreams of a 'Remain-true-street' in the future.

87 Oscar Wilde, *The Soul of Man Under Socialism* (London: privately printed, 1904), 77. Ellmann, *Consciousness*, 133.

88 Russell, *Marriage and Morals*, 249.

89 J. S. Mill, *On Liberty* (London: Walter Scott, n.d.), 104. Ellmann, *Consciousness*, 119.

90 Ellmann, *James Joyce*, 142. *SL* 23 and 23n.

91 Ellmann, *Consciousness*, 121.

92 See above notes 74 and 68; and for Joyce's reading of Brandes, Ellmann, *Consciousness*, 103 and *L* II 83, where Joyce plans to send Brandes his novel when it is finished.

93 The writings of both Spencer and Huxley appear in Joyce's library (Ellmann, *Consciousness*, 113 and 128 respectively) and, besides his use of Spencer for the parodies in 'Oxen of the Sun' (*U* 547ff), Joyce may well have been struck by two examples of 'unscientific' thought that Spencer discusses in *The Study of Sociology*. They include a 'labourer' who 'over his pipe in the village ale house' 'says very

positively what Parliament should do about the "foot and mouth disease"' (p.1), just like Joyce's Mr Deasy, who asserts 'There can be no two opinions on the matter' to Stephen (*U* 40). Even more strikingly, Spencer discusses our ignorance of the process behind the water in the tap, 'tracing it back from the reservoir through the stream and the brook and the rill, the separate raindrops which fell wide apart . . .' (p.16), surely anticipating the famous description of the passage of water from reservoir to tap in 'Ithaca' (*U* 782–5).

94 In 1904 Joyce poked fun at Renan (*L* II 72) but his admiration for him grew; see *SH* 194 and *L* II 82 (where his *Life of Jesus* is held up as a 'model' of good writing), *L* I 305 on Renan's conversion *'vers l'héllenisme préchrétien'* and Ellmann, *James Joyce*, 567, where Joyce visits Renan's birthplace. Joyce also asked Stanislaus to send him Strauss's *Das Leben Jesu*, of which the English translation, appearing in 1846, was, of course, the work of George Eliot (*L* II 76, 78 and 82). Further interest in rationalist and related approaches to the Bible can be seen in the reference to the scurrilous version by Leo Taxil mentioned in 'Proteus' (see *U* 51 and 511 and note 54 above). Bloom has the title *'The Hidden Life of Christ'* on his bookshelf in 'Ithaca' (*U* 833) and joins the rationalist historians in his memory of the incident at Georgina Simpson's, where he declared Christ to be 'a carpenter' and the 'first socialist' (*U* 878).

95 Wilde, *Soul of Man*, 7.

96 *Soul of Man*, 87.

97 Epictetus, *The Teachings*, trans. T. W. Rolleston (London: Walter Scott, n.d.), 60. Ellmann, *Consciousness*, 108.

98 Marcus Aurelius Antoninus, *The Thoughts*, trans. John Jackson (Oxford: OUP, 1906). Ellmann, *Consciousness*, 99. Marcus Aurelius appears at *FW* 306, left margin.

99 In Rolleston's translation the remarks read, 'For a man loses only what he had . . . *I have a pain in my head*. Have you any pain in your horns?' (Epictetus, *Teachings*, 80).

100 *Nouveau scandale de Londres: l'Affaire Crawford* (Paris: Librairie Illustrée, 1886). Ellmann, *Consciousness*, 121. There is a copy in the Bibliothèque Nationale in Paris.

101 A recent attempt to redefine Joyce's understanding of Parnell in political terms may be found in Colin MacCabe's *James Joyce and the Revolution of the Word* (London: Macmillan, 1978), 34, though Parnell's adultery gets no comment there.

102 Kitty O'Shea writes: 'Parnell's moral standard was a high one, if it is once conceded that as regards the marriage bond his honest conviction was that there is none where intense mutual attraction – commonly called love – does not exist, *or where it ceases to exist*,' Katherine O'Shea (Mrs Parnell), *Charles Stuart Parnell*, 2 vols. (London: Cassell, 1914), vol. II, 247. Ellmann, *Consciousness*, 122.

103 R. Barry O'Brien, *The Life of Charles Stuart Parnell* (London & Edinburgh: Nelson, 1910). Ellmann, *Consciousness*, 121.

104 *L* I 241. It was, of course, St John Ervine, of whose books Joyce had two in Trieste (Ellmann, *Consciousness*, 108), who wrote *Parnell* (London: Benn, 1926).

105 O'Brien, *Parnell*, 511: 'he looked like a hunted hind' and 481, title of ch.22: 'At Bay' (this is borrowed by O'Shea, ch.13). Ellmann, *James Joyce*, 32–3 and 320.

106 O'Brien, *Parnell*, 508–11. (*U* 754, 761 and 779–80). O'Shea borrows the scene, adding the adjective 'Homeric' (vol. II, 180), which perhaps gave Joyce a clue.

107 Shaw (*Prefaces*, 4) observes that 'we find the austere Shelley denounced as a fiend in human form, whilst Nelson, who openly left his wife and formed a *ménage à trois* with Sir William and Lady Hamilton, was idolised'.

108 As Don Gifford and Robert J. Seidman note in *Notes for Joyce*, 2 vols. (New York: Dutton, 1967 and 1974).

109 *FW* 547.28–9 and 548.9–10. *Bryllup* is Danish for wedding, *weib* German for wife and *hochzeit* German for wedding. See below for a full list of marital terms in the passage.

110 Ellmann, *James Joyce*, 638 and *FW* 243.8.

111 *U* 258. Emmanuel Swedenborg, *The Delights of Wisdom Relating to Conjugal Love after which follow the Pleasures of Insanity Relating to Scortatory Love* (London: Swedenborg Society, 1891). I am grateful to Dr Ulrich Schneider for drawing my attention to this book.

112 *The Book of Common Prayer and the Administration of the Sacraments* ... (Glasgow: Collins, n.d.) and *Le Livre des prières publiques* ... (London: *La Société pour la Propagation des Connaissances Chrétiennes*, 1839). Connolly, *Personal Library*, 9 and 24–5.

113 Connolly, *Personal Library*, 25.

114 *FW* 167.30–1; see also *FW* 20.16–17, 438.26, 547.28, 626.31–2, *Scribbledehobble*, 114, notes in Atherton, *Books at the Wake*, etc. The following terms related to marriage appear in the passage *FW* 545.24 – 548.05; 545.27, 'morgenattics' (morganatic); 546.13, 'group marriage'; 547.4, 'goods waif' (good wife); 547.5, 'iddle woman' (little woman); 547.6, 'tillstead' (till death ...); 547.15 'beyashmakt' (yashmak), 547.16, 'snood' (see also *Chamber Music* X); 547.27, 'my baresark bride' (barefoot bride); 547.27–8, 'knew her fleshly' (carnal knowledge); 547.28, 'all my bawdy did' (with my body I thee worship); 547.28–9, 'bryllupswibe' (Danish: wedding and German: wife); 547.29, 'Heaven, he hallthundered' (in Viconian theory it was divine thunder that scared men into marriage); 548.2, 'herbrides' music'; 548.5, 'wedlock'; 548.9, 'hochsized' (German: wedding); 548.11, 'expoused' (espoused).

115 Ellmann, *James Joyce*, 638. *Scribbledehobble*, 109–10 and 161; and *FW* 577.18 and 243.10–11. Connolly (*Scribbledehobble*, 161) has evidently mistranscribed 'jactitation' as 'factifation': see Buffalo Notebook VI.A, 641, ll. 12–13 (*Archive* 144 and 267). In this passage of the notebook, headed 'Cyclops', Joyce included a number of legal terms relating to offspring: 'heirs of tailzie: in fee: coparceners: heir of line: by patent: in abeyance: heirs male of body of grantee: sole heir general'. Some are reused in *FW* Book 1 Chapter 4 (96), apparently as synonyms for children. Joyce evidently enjoyed the sexual suggestiveness of the courtroom, for the following entry records a legal joke (which he did not include in the final text): 'witness won't swear no

faith judge asks "no faith in your husband?"'

116 *L* I 302. Maud Isabel Crofts, *Women Under English Law* (London: National Council of Women, 1925 repr. Butterworth, 1928). Other books Joyce may have used for this information include *Every Man's Own Lawyer* by A Barrister at Law (London: Crosby Lockwood, 1919). Ellmann, *Consciousness*, 108. Marriage law is covered on pp. 356–98.

117 *L* III 208.

118 Ellmann, *James Joyce*, 637–9.

119 Ellmann, *James Joyce*, 724, where Paul Leon refers to legal consultations. In letters to me of 25 July and 14 September 1979, David Monro of Monro, Pennefather & Co. reports that no records of any such consultations remain.

120 *L* III 221.

121 Hélène Cixous, *The Exile of James Joyce*, trans. Sally Purcell (London: John Calder, 1976), 51.

122 *L* III 222.

123 *L* II 189 and 194. The case itself is described in Ellmann, *James Joyce*, 230.

124 Power, *Conversations*, 61.

125 Connolly, *Personal Library*, 25; and see Mason, 'Why is Leopold Bloom a Cuckold?', where the book is discussed (pp. 171–88).

126 *FW* 571.28 – 576.9. The use of Matharan is noted by both Adaline Glasheen (*A Census of Finnegans Wake* (London: Faber, 1956), 129 and Atherton (*Books at the Wake*, 266–7). There are the other casus-like passages starting *FW* 161.15 ('Burrus and Caseous') and *FW* 166.30 ('Margareena and Caseous'). For the dating of the composition of these passages see A. Walton Litz, *The Art of James Joyce* (London: OUP, 1961), 147.

127 André de Nerciat, *Felicia* (Paris; Cazin, 1976).

128 *FW* 573.4 and Glasheen, *Census*, 193.

129 The fables, whose narrative coherence made them ideal candidates for early publication (as *Two Tales Told of Shem and Shaun*, London: Faber, 1932), derive, in the case of the 'Ondt and the Gracehoper' (*FW* 414.16–419.10) from La Fontaine and the 'Mookse and the Gripes' (*FW* 152.15–156.34) from Aesop. For Joyce's father's story about Buckley see Ellmann, *James Joyce*, 398.

130 Samuel Beckett, 'Dante ... Bruno. Vico ... Joyce', in *Our Exagmination Round his Factification for Incamination of Work in Progress* (Paris: Shakespeare & Co., 1929, repr. London: Faber, 1972).

131 *The New Science of Giambattista Vico*, abridged and trans. T. G. Bergin and M. H. Fisch (London: Cornell University Press, 1970), 127–34.

2 Emissio seminis inter vas naturale

1 William Acton, *Functions and Disorders of the Reproductive System* (London: Churchill, 1857). This quotation comes from the 6th edition of 1875, p.i. Acton is the 'typical Victorian' attacked by modern writers like Steven Marcus in *The Other Victorians* (London:

Weidenfeld, 1966) and Alex Comfort in *The Anxiety Makers* (London: Nelson, 1967).

2 Sigmund Freud, *Three Essays on the Theory of Sexuality* in *The Standard Edition of the Complete Psychological Works of Sigmund Freud*, ed. James Strachey (London: Hogarth Press, 1953), vol. VII, 138–9.

3 Freud, 'Civilized Sexual Morality', *Standard Ed.* vol. IX. My quotation is taken from another edition, 'Modern Sexual Morality and Modern Nervousness', trans. W.J. Robinson (New York: Eugenics Publishing, 1931), intro. p.vi and pp. 16–17, where the passage is italicized and where Robinson stresses the importance of the essay for modern sexual morality.

4 H.M. Ruitenbeek, *The New Sexuality* (New York: Franklin Watts, 1974), ch. 2, 16–29.

5 Baron Richard von Krafft-Ebing, *Psychopathia Sexualis* (Stuttgart: Ferdinand Enke, 1886), trans. from 7th German edition by C.G. Chaddock (London and Philadelphia: Davies, 1892), 34.

6 What is now the second volume of the studies was originally published as *Studies in the Psychology of Sex*, vol. 1, *Sexual Inversion* by H. Ellis and J.A. Symonds (London: Wilson & Macmillan, 1897).

7 Ellmann, *James Joyce*, 140.

8 Augustin Galopin, *Le Parfum de la femme* (Paris: Dentu, 1889), 195. Ellmann, *Consciousness*, 109.

9 *L* II 134.

10 Dr Paul Garnier, *Onanisme seul et à deux sous toutes ses formes et leurs consequences* (Paris: Librairie Garnier Frères, n.d.). Ellmann, *Consciousness*, 7 and 109. The full title begins *Hygiène de la génération* and the edition I use is dated 1885.

11 S. A. A. D. Tissot, *L'Onanisme* (Lausanne: Chapius, 1760), is specifically mentioned by Garnier on pp. 7 and 24. The work first appeared in Latin as part of Tissot's *Dissertatione febribus biliosis* (Lausanne: Bousquet, 1788). Edward Hare, 'Masturbatory Insanity: the History of an Idea', *Journal of Mental Science* 108 (1962), 3.

12 John Laws Milton, *On the Pathology and Treatment of Spermatorrhoea.* 12th edition (London: Renshaw, 1887).

13 Louis Bergeret, *Des Fraudes dans l'accomplissement des fonctions génératrices* (Paris: Baillière, 1868), trans. P. de Marmon, *The Preventative Obstacle or Conjugal Onanism* (New York: Turner & Mingard, 1870).

14 M. M. Matharan, *Casus de Matrimonio fere quingenti* (Paris: Retaux, 1893), 400 and 393, 398 and 405.

15 There is a problem of date in concluding that Joyce took this note directly from Garnier, since Ellmann says that Garnier's book was purchased in Switzerland (*Consciousness*, 109) whilst the *Exiles* notes are usually thought to have been completed before Joyce left Trieste. The similarity is nevertheless striking.

16 S. Joyce, *Dublin Diary*, 67–8 and 42 respectively.

17 S. Joyce, *Dublin Diary*, 96 and 58 respectively.

18 *L* II 72.

19 *Scribbledehobble*, 88.

20 Hart and Hayman, *Critical Essays*, 278.

21 Ellmann, '*Ulysses*', 133.
22 This is the 'technic' of the episode as noted in the Gorman-Gilbert Plan; see Ellmann, '*Ulysses*' between pp. 188 and 189.
23 Paul Robinson, *The Modernisation of Sex* (London: Elek, 1976), 13 and 142–5.
24 This notion of the sensual irritation of women's clothing is echoed in *Finnegans Wake* (109.25). In 'Circe' Kitty Ricketts 'sits perched on the edge of the table swinging her leg' (*U* 621).
25 David Hayman's article ('Stephen on the Rocks', *JJQ*, 15, 1, Autumn 1977, 5–17) recently commended in Hugh Kenner's *Ulysses*, does a fine job of identifying the extravagant assumption (made by Tindall, Blamires and others) that Stephen urinates into Cock Lake in 'Proteus'. Hayman's tracing of associations in the passage is also impressive, yet his suggestion that Stephen actually masturbates is only a little less extravagant than the assumption it purports to displace.
26 Ellmann, *James Joyce*, 377.
27 Rev. Thomas Robert Malthus, *An Essay on the Principle of Population* (London: Johnson, 1798). Malthus's idea was that population increased in a geometrical ratio whilst the means of subsistence only grew in an arithmetical ratio. To restore the balance nature stepped in with 'misery and vice', reducing population to its limits of growth. It was only in the later volume, *A Summary View of the Principle of Population* (London: Murray, 1830), 42, that the formula changed to 'moral restraint, vice and misery', seeming to offer some hope for the ameliorative designs of family planning.
28 Writers like Charles Bradlaugh and Annie Besant were active figures in Malthusianism. As J. A. and O. Banks pointed out in their well-known study, *Feminism and Family Planning in Victorian England* (Liverpool University Press, 1964), it was the publicity attracted by the prosecution following the publication of a pamphlet by Charles Knowlton, entitled *The Fruits of Philosophy* (which Bradlaugh and Besant reprinted in 1877), which spread the Malthusian message and led to a visible decline in the birth-rate rather than any general acceptance of feminist ideas. Two helpful studies of the history of the contraceptive movement are Norman E. Himes, *The Medical History of Contraception* (London: Allen & Unwin, 1936) and Peter Fryer, *The Birth Controllers* (London: Secker & Warburg, 1965).
29 Marie Stopes is the most influential representative of modern contraception. Her books *Married Love* (London: Fifield, 1918) and *Wise Parenthood* (London: Fifield, 1918) represent one of the clearest statements of accepted modern morality.
30 Russell, *Marriage and Morals*, 133.
31 Jane Lidderdale and Mary Nicholson, *Dear Miss Weaver* (London: Faber, 1970), 48.
32 Shaw, *Prefaces*, 15.
33 Sidney Webb, *The Decline in the Birthrate* (London: Fabian Society, 1907), 8, 19 and 16. The tract is no. 131 in *Fabian Tracts* nos. 1–173

(bound together) (London: Fabian Society, 1884–1913). Ellmann, *Consciousness*, 108.

34 Leo Tolstoy, 'Afterword to the Kreutzer Sonata', in *Essays and Letters*, trans. Aylmer Maude (London: Frowde, 1904), 38.

35 Comte de Mirabeau (the attribution is questionable, see Fryer's *Birth Controllers*, 38), *The Curtain Drawn Up* (false imprint, London, Putitin, Rogers & Co., Nineinch Street, 1818) (trans. from *Le Rideau levé*). 1920 inventory. Ellmann, *Consciousness*, 120. See in G. Apollinaire, F. Fleuret and L. Perceau, *L'Enfer de la Bibliothèque Nationale* (Paris: Mercure de France, 1913), 86 and 114–15.

36 *SL* 158.

37 In 1908 there were advertisements in *Photo Bits* for *The Wife's Handbook*, a well-known book by Henry Arthur Allbutt; and 'To the Married', Place's pamphlet that is one of the earliest-known Malthusian pamphlets. The works are described in Fryer, *Birth Controllers*, 43–5. Similar advertisements are common throughout the run of *Photo Bits* and *Bits of Fun* which continued from 1899 to 1918. This one ran throughout 1907.

38 Harry Levin, *James Joyce: A Critical Introduction* (London: Faber, 1971, reprint of 2nd edn, 1960), 110.

39 Staley and Benstock, *Approaches to 'Ulysses'*, 115 and 104–5 respectively. His parenthetical page references are to the 1961 Random House edition and correspond to pages 919 and 89 in the 1960 Bodley Head edition.

40 Molly's vaginal douche leaves her in the worst of all possible contraceptive worlds. Matharan (*Casus de Matrimonio*) would condemn her contraceptive intentions whereas Marie Stopes (*Married Love*, 50–6) condemns douching (whilst recognizing it as 'the method most widely practised by women') as 'aesthetically' and 'physiologically' unsatisfactory and so unreliable as to be 'quite futile'.

41 Bernard Benstock, *Joyce-Again's Wake*, (London: University of Washington Press, 1965), 9, 64 and 277. Glasheen, *Census*, lxvii–lxviii.

42 *L* I 137.

43 In 1911 Georges Braque composed two Cubist, still-life etchings entitled 'Still-life with Bottles of Wine and Bass on a Table' and 'Glass and Bottle of Bass on a Table (Pale Ale)', whose centre (no doubt in part because of the musical pun) is the trade name Bass. In Paris in 1912 Picasso produced a pastel, charcoal and stencil work with the same feature. All three are reproduced in Douglas Cooper and Gary Tinterow's *The Essential Cubism* (London: Tate Gallery Publications, 1983).

44 Budgen, *The Making of 'Ulysses'*, 220.

45 Homer, *The Odyssey*, trans. William Cowper (London: Dent, 1913). Ellmann, *Consciousness*, 112. This is the second volume of the Everyman Homer, whose first volume (which Joyce also had) is the translation of *The Iliad* by the Earl of Derby.

46 *L* I 138–9.

47 For the idea that the fraud is the 'fraud of the Malthusians' see Gilbert, *'Ulysses'*, 259.

48 Ellmann, *'Ulysses'*, 188–9.

49 Ellmann, *'Ulysses'*, 133–40.

50 C. Peake, *James Joyce: The Citizen and the Artist* (London: Edward Arnold, 1977), 255.

51 French, *The Book as World*, 170.

52 It is briefly mentioned by Atherton in his chapter on 'Oxen' in Hart and Hayman's *Critical Essays*, 324.

53 Stopes, *Married Love* (London: Hogarth Press, 1918), p. 101.

54 Rhythm-method contraception arises in Bloom's contemplation of Martha's letter: 'Near her monthlies. Wonder if it's bad to go with them then. Safe in one way' (*U* 481).

55 *U* 539. Details of the fratricide perpetrated by Samuel Childs in 1899 are given in Gifford and Seidman's *Notes*. Its punning relevance is clear.

56 Annie Besant, *Une introduction à la théosophie* (Paris: Publications Théosophiques, 1907), *The Path of Discipleship* (London: Theosophical Publishing Society, 1904). Ellmann, *Consciousness*, 101.

57 Details of the contraceptive work of Besant, Sanger and Stopes are to be found in Fryer *Birth Controllers* and Himes, *Contraception*.

58 Gilbert, *'Ulysses'*, 255.

59 Oliver St John Gogarty, 'They Think They Know Joyce', *Saturday Review of Literature*, 18 March 1950.

60 Nicholas Culpeper, *A Directory for Midwives* (London: Cole, 1651).

61 Johann Friedrich Blumenbach (1752–1840), *An Essay on Generation*, trans. from the German by Sir Alexander Crichton (London: Cadell, 1792). Lazarro Spallanzani (1729–99), *Tracts on the Natural History of Animals and Vegetables*, trans. J.G. Dalyell (Edinburgh: Creech, 1803). Oscar Hertwig, *The Biological Problem of Today: Preformation or Epigenesis?* trans. P. C. Mitchell (London: Heinemann, 1896) and *The Text-Book of the Embryology of Man and Mammals*, trans. E. L. Mark (London: Swan Sonnenschein, 1892). William Thomson Lusk, *The Science and Art of Midwifery* (London: Lewis, 1885). Guilio Valenti, *Compendio di Anatomia dell'uomo* (Milan: P. Vallardi, 1909).

62 Phillip Herring, *The 'Ulysses' Notesheets in the British Museum.* (Charlottesville: University of Virginia Press, 1972). The *Notesheets* (193 and 252 respectively) contain, for example, notes on 'Weissman' and 'Epigenesis (Wolff) modern', which relate to the preformation vs. epigenesis debate. Notes on Culpepper (sic), Blumenbach and Lusk appear on *Notesheets*, 249, 257 and 190 respectively. See also *Notesheets*, 36: the Italian textbook to which Herring refers may well be that of Valenti.

63 *U* 890. The high significance of Rabelais for Joyce's work has long been recognized and it is no surprise to see his works in the Trieste library list, Ellmann, *Consciousness*, 124.

64 *Aristotle's Masterpiece* (of which the British Library lists some 34 separate editions between 1690 and the start of this century) is one of the most familiar books of folkloric sex and midwifery information.

Bloom turns over a copy in 'Wandering Rocks' (*U* 302), Molly remembers the illustrations of babies 'tucked up in bed' and of 'children with two heads and no legs' (*U* 918–19); and the 'chromo-lithographic illustrations' of 'monstrous births' come up in 'Oxen of the Sun' too (*U* 537).

65 Tanner, *Adultery in the Novel*, 52–3.
66 MacCabe, *Revolution of the Word*, 28, 32–7, 66–7, and 111–29.
67 See note 6 above.
68 *Three Essays on the Theory of Sexuality*, *Standard Ed.* vol. VII, 135–6.
69 Marilyn French discusses Stephen and Mulligan (*The Book as World*, 49, and her note). Ellmann (*James Joyce*, 121) describes Stephen and Cranly in these terms.
70 Glasheen, *Census*, 42.
71 Fritz Senn, 'Some Conjectures about Homosexuality in *Finnegans Wake*', *AWN* 6 (Oct. 1969), 70–2.
72 Joris-Karl Huysmans, *A Rebours* (Paris: Charpentier, 1884), mentioned in *L* II 150. No copy of the book survives, though there is a copy of *Là-Bas* in the Croessmann collection at Illinois which belonged to Joyce. André Gide, *L'Immoraliste* (Paris: Mercure de France, 1914). Ellmann, *Consciousness*, 109.
73 Burton, *Thousand Nights*, vol. X, 204.
74 *L* II 150.
75 R. H. Sherard, *Life of Oscar Wilde* (London: Werner Laurie, 1906), 338 *et passim*. This 'unexpurgated' edition (as it came to be known) was followed by a slimmer popular volume of reminiscences, *Oscar Wilde: The Story of an Unhappy Friendship* (London: Greening, 1908), which remains in Joyce's Trieste library (Ellmann, *Consciousness*, 128), though it has less in common with Joyce's review. The Paris collection contains the book by Comtesse Anna de Brémont, *Oscar Wilde and his Mother* (London: Everett, 1911).
76 Sherard, *Oscar Wilde*, 338.
77 Atherton, *Books at the Wake*, 95 and *CW* 203–4.
78 *FW* 290.28. Atherton says (*Books at the Wake*, 260), 'Joyce was given a copy of this book in Zurich and afterwards lost it'. Gifford and Seidman (*Notes*) use the *Psychopathia Sexualis* extensively to gloss 'Circe'.
79 Sigmund Freud, *Eine Kindheitserinnerung des Leonardo da Vinci* (Leipzig and Vienna, 1910). Sigmund Freud, *Zür Psychopathologie des Alltaglebens* (Berlin, 1917). Ellmann, *Consciousness*, 109.
80 Ernest Jones, *Das Problema des Hamlet und des Ödipus-Komplex*, trans. Paul Tausig (Leipzig and Vienna, 1911). Ellmann, *Consciousness*, 114.
81 Freud, *Standard Ed.* vol. VI, 106–7, also discussed in *The Interpretation of Dreams*, *Standard Ed.* vol. V, 246. For Freud Odysseus is the exhibitionist; for Joyce it is Gerty (or Nausicaa).
82 Havelock Ellis, *Studies*, vol. III, 111–12 and *U* 565.
83 *Studies*, vol. III, 152 and *U* 392.
84 *Studies*, vol. IV, 28 and *P* 203.
85 *Studies*, vol. II, 88.

86 *Studies*, vol. V, 105.

87 *Studies*, vol. III, 59–62. *U* 825.

88 *Studies*, vol. IV for description of bathing and vol. VII for the term.

89 F. H. C. de la Motte Fouqué, *Undine* (London: Lumley, n.d.). Ellmann, *Consciousness*, 116.

90 Havelock Ellis, *Studies*, vol. IV, 188.

91 *U* 224–5 (with a mention of Pygmalion and Galatea), 234, 257, 279, 334, 368, 834 etc.

92 Ellmann, *James Joyce*, 785–7.

93 The 1920 shelf inventory is item 1400 in Robert Scholes's catalogue of the Cornell Joyce Collection. Titles of collections of Sacher-Masoch tales are difficult to trace, particularly in translation. For those listed by Joyce the following extant editions seem likely originals. For 'Catherine II': *Katherina II: Russiche Hofgeschichten* (Berlin: Schreiter, [1891?]); for 'Liebesgeschichten': *Liebesgeschichten aus verschiedenen Jahrhunderten*, 3 vols. (Leipzig: Ernest Julius Günther, 1874–6). For 'Grausame Frauen (4 vols.)': *Grausame Frauen* [one volume only] (Leipzig: Leipziger Verlag, 1905). And for 'Scene del Ghetto' (no doubt the origin of the title '*Tales of the Ghetto*' that Bloom notices in 'Wandering Rocks': *U* 302): *Scene del Ghetto, prima traduzione Italiana di Cino Liviah* (Milan: Società Ed. Milanese (E. Zerboni), 1909).

94 James Lovebirch, *Les Cinq Fessés de Suzette* (Paris: Roberts & Dardaillon, 1910) and *The Flagellations of Suzette* (Paris: Librairie Artistique, 1915) are listed in the catalogue of the Bibliothèque Nationale.

95 That Budgen sent copies of this magazine to Joyce is shown in *L* I 144 and 148.

96 H. G. Wells, *The History of Mr Polly* (London: Nelson, 1910).

97 Jacques Desroix, *La Gynécocratie ou la domination de la femme* (Paris: Carrington, 1902). Connolly, *Personal Library*, 13.

98 Phrases like 'Petticoat government' (*U* 642) and 'a thing under the yoke' (*U* 647) are reminiscent of Desroix (whose fourteenth chapter is headed 'Sous le Joug d'Elise'), though not unfamiliar elsewhere. In the *Gynécocratie* story the protagonist Vicomte Julian Robinson is made, throughout his 'education', to wear female clothing. Just as Bloom becomes female (*U* 647), Julian becomes Julia; and as Julia is forced to entertain a suitor called Lord Alfred Ridlington who later turns out to have been a woman (174ff), so is Bloom offered to Charles Alberta Marsh. Under the governess that Julia serves there are three girl pupils (Maud, Beatrice, Agnes), who alternately help or hinder her. Bella Cohen also has three assistants: Kitty, Florry and Zoe.

99 Desroix, *La Gynécocratie*, 72–8. Phillip Herring, '*Ulysses* Notebook VIII A.5. At Buffalo', *Studies in Bibliography* 22 (1969), 289–310.

100 Robert Burton, *The Anatomy of Melancholy* (London: Blake, 1836), 569.

101 *SL* 189.

102 *SL* 172, 5 and 6.

103 *L* I 148.

3 Women

1   Kate Millet, *Sexual Politics* (London: Virago, 1977), 285.
2   French, *The Book as World*, 274.
3   F. J. C. Skeffington and James A. Joyce, *Two Essays: 'A Forgotten Aspect of the University Question' and 'The Day of the Rabblement'* (Dublin: Gerard Bros., 1901 ed.; reprinted Minneapolis: McCosh's bookstore, 1957).
4   *L* II 327–9.
5   For a history see Lidderdale and Nicholson, *Dear Miss Weaver*.
6   An appendix in *Dear Miss Weaver* makes the extent of her support quite clear.
7   Ellmann does so, (*James Joyce*, 351–2), as does Stuart Gilbert in his introduction to the first volume of Joyce's letters, *L* I 23–5.
8   *L* II 326.
9   *The Little Review* (Chicago) 1 (March 1914), 2.
10 Woolf, 'Modern Novels', 189–90. Patrick Parrinder in 'The Strange Necessity: James Joyce's rejection in England (1914–1930)', in *James Joyce: New Perspectives*, ed. Colin MacCabe (Brighton: Harvester, 1982) charts the Bloomsbury attitude to Joyce. For Mansfield's comment in a letter to Ottoline Morrell see *The Letters of Katherine Mansfield*, ed. J. Middleton Murry, 2 vols. (London: Constable, 1928).
11 Sylvia Beach, *Shakespeare and Company* (London: Faber, 1960), 52–4.
12 Budgen, *The Making of 'Ulysses'*, 354–5.
13 Ellmann, *James Joyce*, 529.
14 Ellmann, *James Joyce*, 246–7, indentifies her as Kathleen, one of the Sheehy daughters, later to become the mother of Conor Cruise O'Brien.
15 Sympathetic narration is of the utmost importance in the stories, not just in the word 'literally' (that Kenner in *Joyces's Voices* (London: Faber, 1978, 15 showed to be Lilly's word not the narrator's), but especially in the second section of the story when we hear what an 'expert carver' Gabriel is (*D* 225).
16 The fullest study of Joyce's debt to Ibsen is B. J. Tysdahl, *Joyce and Ibsen* (Oslo: Norwegian Universities Press, 1968).
17 Gifford and Seidman's *Notes* mentions the Papal edict of Pius X, *Motu Proprio Inter Sollicitudines*, of 22 November 1903.
18 Cixous, *Exile*, 485.
19 Ellmann, *James Joyce*, 694.
20 Power, *Conversations*, 35.
21 *Fortnightly Review* 73 (1900), 573–90. *CW* 64.
22 Havelock Ellis, *The New Spirit*, 10 and 147. Ellmann, *Consciousness*, 107.
23 Havelock Ellis, *The New Spirit*, 162 and *E* 158.
24 Arthur Schopenhauer, *Essays*, trans. Mrs Rudolf Dircks (London: Walter Scott, 1897), 64–79. Ellmann, *Consciousness*, 126.
25 Simone de Beauvoir, *The Second Sex*, trans. H. M. Parshley (London: Cape, 1953), 16.

26 Charles Darwin, *The Descent of Man* (London: Murray, 1871), 316.
27 Freud, *New Introductory Lectures on Psychoanalysis*, 'Femininity', *Standard Ed.*, vol. XXII, 132.
28 Henry Havelock Ellis, *Man and Woman: A Study of Human Secondary Sexual Characteristics* (London: Walter Scott, 1894).
29 Rémy de Gourmont, *Physique de l'amour* (Paris: Mercure de France, 1903), trans. Ezra Pound as *The Natural Philosophy of Love* (London: Casanova Society, 1926).
30 De Gourmont, *Physique de l'amour*, 39.
31 De Gourmont, *Physique de l'amour*, ch. viii, 'Sexual dimorphism and feminism'.
32 *L* II 95.
33 Ellmann, *James Joyce*, 463–4, and *Scribbledehobble*, 10 and 168.
34 Ellmann, *James Joyce*, 463–4. Buffalo Notebook VI.D 4 and V.C 7 136–269. Budgen, *The Making of 'Ulysses'*, 53. Otto Weininger, *Sex and Character* (London: Heinemann, 1906).
35 *L* III 253.
36 Schopenhauer, *Essays*, 64.
37 Jules Michelet, *La Femme* (Paris: Hachette, 1860), *L'Amour*, trans. J. W. Palmer as *Love* (New York: Rudd & Carlton, 1860), and *Priests, Women and Families*, trans. C. Cocks (London: Longman, 1846). See Atherton, *Books at the Wake*, 267.
38 *L* I 170.
39 Acton, *Functions and Disorders* (1875), 212–13.
40 Freud's version is to be found in 'A Special Type of Choice of Object Made by Men', *Standard Ed.* vol. XI, 165ff, and 'On the Universal Tendency to Debasement in the Sphere of Love', *Standard Ed.* vol. XI, 179ff. Bernard Benstock, *The Undiscover'd Country* (Dublin: Gill & Macmillan, 1977), 9–16 and Hugh Kenner, *Dublin's Joyce* (Gloucester, Mass: Peter Smith, 1969), 129–31 give two examples of the charge as levelled against Joyce.
41 J. P. Jacobsen, *Siren Voices*, trans. E. F. L. Robertson (London: Heinemann, 1896), 198–9. Ellmann, *Consciousness*, 114.
42 Marcelle Tinayre, *The House of Sin*, trans. A. Smythe (London: Maclaren, 1903), 216. Ellmann, *Consciousness*, 107.
43 Edouard Dujardin, *L'Initiation au péché et à l'amour* (Paris: Mercure de France, 1912). Ellmann, *Consciousness*, 107.
44 *L* I 206.
45 Both de Gourmont and Havelock Ellis make this point.
46 *L* II 168, 193–4 and 198.
47 Samuel Butler, *The Authoress of 'The Odyssey'* (London: Fifield, pref. d. 1897), 129 and 118 respectively.
48 Epiphany 5. *WD* 15, *P* 70 and Ellmann, *James Joyce*, 84.
49 Schutte, *Joyce and Shakespeare*.
50 Allan Kardec, *La Genèse, les miracles et les prédictions selon le spiritualisme* (Paris: Librairie des Sciences Psychologiques, 1883), p. 269: '*La Femme formée d'une côte d'Adam est un allégorie, puérile en apparence, si on la prend à la lettre, mais profond par le sens. Elle a pour but de montrer que la femme est de la même nature que l'homme, son égale, par conséquent, devant Dieu, et non une créature à part faite pour être asservie et traitée en*

ilôte.' (The creation of woman from one of Adam's ribs is an allegory, childish if taken literally but profound in its true meaning. Its end is to show that woman's nature is the same as man's, she is his equal therefore before God and not set apart to be treated in isolation or enslaved.)

51 D. H. Lawrence, *Women in Love* (London: Martin Secker, 1921).

52 Joyce had a copy of the *Symposium* in Shelley's translation in *Five Dialogues* (London: Dent, 1913). Ellmann, *Consciousness*, 123. Aristophanes' speech is on pp. 35–9 of this edition. The story also appears in Book XI (lines 305–20) of *The Odyssey*. See *FW* 167.22, 493.24 and 128.35–6, where 'piles big pelium on little ossas like the pilluls of hirculeads; has an eatupus complex' seems to connect Mts Pelion and Ossa (which Otis and Ephialtes put one on top of the other to mount their rebellion) and Freud.

53 Herring, *Notesheets*, 252.

54 Manganiello, *Joyce's Politics*, especially pp. 46–59 and Susan Humphreys, 'Ferrero etc: James Joyce's debt to Guglielmo Ferrero', in *JJQ* 16 (Spring 1979), 239–51.

55 Cesare Lombroso, *La Donna delinquente*.

56 Guglielmo Ferrero, *L'Europa giovane* (Milan: Treves, 1897), 319–48. Ellmann, *Consciousness*, 108. 'Il Terzo Sesso' first appeared in *Revue des Revues* 1 January 1895. Ferrero's name appears in Buffalo Notebook VI.B, 18–168. His interest in the relations of the sexes led him to write a book on *The Women of the Caesars*, trans. Christian Gauss (New York: 1925) in which he argues that Greek women were subservient and secluded but Roman women more autonomous and influential. He cites the daughters of Agrippa, the sisters of Caligula and Nero's wife Livia (perhaps thereby inspiring Joyce to call his heroine for *Finnegans Wake* Livia).

57 Edward Carpenter, 'The Status of Women in Early Greek Times', *The New Freewoman* 4 (1 August 1913), 68–9; and see also E. B. Lloyd, 'Intermediate Sexual Types', *The New Freewoman* 8 (1 October 1913), 155–6.

58 Edward Carpenter, *The Intermediate Sex* (Manchester: Labour Press, 1896), 39–82, 'The Homogenic Attachment'.

59 Marilyn French suggests that the name implies virility and virulence (p. 204), but see also the virago who appears in 'Circe' (*U* 563 and 590).

60 Matthias and Mathilde Vaerting, *The Dominant Sex* (London: 1923), Buffalo Notebook VI.B 20–49, *Archive*, vol. 33, 349; and see Peter Spielberg's *James Joyce's Manuscripts and Letters at the University of Buffalo: A Catalogue* (Buffalo: University of Buffalo Press, 1962), 111 n51.

61 Jill Perkins (ed.), *Joyce and Hauptmann: Before Sunrise* (California, Huntingdon Library, 1978), 113.

62 Perkins, *Joyce and Hauptmann*, 93.

63 Stanislaus Joyce, *My Brother's Keeper* (New York: Viking, 1958), 125.

64 Ellmann, *James Joyce*, 77.

65 Ellmann, *James Joyce*, 418, 781, 419, 548–9.

66 *SL* 182.

67 *U* 576, 865, 93 and 114 respectively and see *U* 496.

68 Millet, *Sexual Politics*, 194–7.

69 Gilles Deleuze, *Sacher-Masoch: An Interpretation* (London: Faber, 1971), 42.

70 Bachofen, *Das Mutterrecht*. *FW* 14.25 'gynecure' and 389.9 'gyne-college'. Marilyn French notices the interest of the term (*The Book as World*, 275).

71 Desroix, *La Gynécocratie*, 155 and 272.

72 James Joyce, *Daniel Defoe*, ed. Joseph Prescott, *University of Buffalo Studies* 1 (December 1964), 20 and 23.

73 Albert, *L'Amour libre*, 251–306.

74 Albert, *L'Amour libre*, 259.

75 Germaine Greer, *The Female Eunuch* (London: Paladin, 1971), 106–7.

76 Albert, *L'Amour libre*, 300.

77 *Fabian Tracts*, nos. 1–173 (bound together) (London: Fabian Society, 1884–1913). Tract no. 129, 14 and see tract no. 157. Ellmann, *Consciousness*, 108.

78 Acton, *Functions and Disorders*, 6th ed., 212–13.

79 Suzette A. Henke, 'Joyce and Krafft-Ebing', *JJQ* 17 (Autumn 1979), 84–6.

80 S. Joyce, *Dublin Diary*, 15.

81 Beverland, *Draped Virginity*, 2–22.

82 *L* II 192.

83 *Married Love*, 26. Stopes quotes Windscheid's *Centralblatt für Gynäkologie*, where it is argued that 'In the normal woman, especially of the higher social classes, the sexual instinct is acquired not inborn; when it is inborn or awakens by itself, there is *abnormality*.'

84 Stephen Heath, *The Sexual Fix* (London: Macmillan, 1982), 137–46, is only one among a number of recent discussions of Freud's puzzlement over the problems of female desire.

85 Perkins, *Joyce and Hauptmann*, 102 and see the note on pp. 155–6. Joyce's partial mistranslation of the line seems to add to the suggestion of cynical sexual dealings.

86 *Scribbledehobble*, 60. *Archive*, vol. 28, 67.

87 Lecky, *History of European Morals*, vol. II, 298–394. Ellmann, *Consciousness*, 116.

88 *WD* 43, *Archive*, vol. 7, 61–2.

89 *WD* 72, Buffalo Notebook II.A–21, *Archive*, vol. 7, 91 and see *SH* 146.

90 Ellmann, *James Joyce*, 367–9. See also S. Joyce, *Dublin Diary*, 26–7 and Gogarty's novel *Tumbling in the Hay* (London: Constable, 1939) which recounts some similar night-time incidents.

91 *U* 242, 275, 278 and 565 respectively.

92 Danis Rose, *The Index Manuscript* (Colchester: A Wake Newslitter Press, 1980), 121–4.

93 Albert, *L'Amour libre*, 118.

94 Tolstoy, *Essays and Letters*, 136–7.

95 August Bebel, *Woman in the Past, Present and Future*, trans. H. B.

Adams Walther (London: Modern Press, 1885), 91. Bebel's name appears in 'Soferim Bebel' (*FW* 118.18).
96 Bebel, *Woman in the Past*, 92–3.
97 Perkins, *Joyce and Hauptmann*, 78. *U* 692 and 731.
98 *U* 566. It becomes 'Dublin's burning' later in the episode (*U* 694).
99 W. B. Yeats, *The Tables of the Law* and *The Adoration of the Magi* in *Mythologies* (London: Macmillan, 1959), 310.

4 Sexual reality

1 Mary Reynolds, *Joyce and Dante* (Princeton: Princeton University Press, 1982), 79–118.
2 *L* II 191. Joyce's criticism of the sexual views of *Sinn Fein* is reinforced in *Ulysses* where Gerty's flirtatious, sentimental desire is to have a real man 'for herself alone' (*U* 466). *L* II 170–1.
3 *L* II 191.
4 Burton A. Waisbren and Florence L. Walzl, 'Paresis and the Priest: James Joyce's Symbolic Use of Syphilis in "The Sisters"', *Annals of Internal Medicine* 80 (June 1974), 756–62.
5 Joyce explained this aspect of the story in a letter to Stanislaus (*L* II 186): 'I have also added in the story *The Clay* the name of Maria's laundry *Dublin by Lamplight Laundry*: it is such a gentle way of putting it'. Since the 'gentle way of putting it' was apparently too gentle for Stanislaus, Joyce wrote in explanation (*L* II 192): 'The meaning of *Dublin by Lamplight Laundry*? That is the name of the laundry at Ballsbridge, of which the story treats. It is run by a society of Protestant spinsters, widows and childless women – I expect – as a Magdalen's home. The phrase *Dublin by Lamplight* means that Dublin by lamplight is a wicked place full of wicked and lost women whom a kindly committee gathers together for the good work of washing my dirty shirts. I like the phrase because "it is a gentle way of putting it".' In Joyce's sociology Maria's celibacy was the *cause* of prostitution. The irony of her association with the reform of prostitutes is clear.
6 *WD* 71. Buffalo Notebook II. A 20. *Archive*, vol. 7, 90.
7 D. F. Strauss, *The Life of Jesus*, trans. George Eliot (London: Swan Sonnenschein, 1892). Joyce wrote to Stanislaus in January 1905 requesting a cheap Scott library edition of the Strauss book (these editions cost 1s/6d, not the 18s/6d given in the published letters). However, Walter Scott do not appear to have published Strauss (though they had published Renan) at this time. Stanislaus's delay might be further attributable to the high cost (15/-) of the most easily available Swan Sonnenschein edition. *L* II 76, 78 and 82. Ernest Renan, *The Life of Jesus* (London: Watts, 1913). Ellmann, *Consciousness*, 125. *L* II 72.
8 Maria Monk, *The Awful Disclosures of Maria Monk* (New York: Howe & Bates, 1936). *U* 302 and 635. C. P. T. Chiniquy, *The Priest, the Woman and the Confessional* (London: Gibson, 1874) and *Why I left the Church of Rome* (London: Kensit, 1887). *U* 230 and 635–6.

9 W. T. Noon, *Joyce and Aquinas* (London: Yale University Press, 1963).

10 Ellmann, *James Joyce*, 354.

11 S. Joyce, *My Brother's Keeper*, 129–30.

12 Mirabeau, *The Curtain Drawn Up*. See Apollinaire *et al.*, *L'Enfer de la Bibliothèque Nationale*, 86 and 114–15. Ellmann, *Consciousness*, 120.

13 *L I* 171.

14 *Le Tutu* is listed in the Bibliothèque Nationale Catalogue; the other title is not. For Joyce's knowledge and use of *Photo Bits, Bits of Fun* and related titles see Budgen, *The Making of 'Ulysses'*, 246–7 and p. 66 and 86 above. Titles included *Fun, New Fun, Photo Fun* and *New Photo Fun* as well as a group of publications based on the comic character Ally Sloper, whose huge nose and accomplice Iky Mo (Isaac Moses etc.) appear in *Ulysses* (*U* 68, 257 and 623) and *Finnegans Wake* (*FW* 178.6, 248.10, 288 n4, 291.26 and 319.18).

15 The reader is William Empson who, in a BBC radio talk (reprinted as 'The Theme of *Ulysses*', *Kenyon Review* 18 (Winter 1956), 26–52), and more recently in the *London Review of Books* 4, nos. 15 and 16 (August and September 1982), argues that *Ulysses* conceals a love triangle between Bloom, Molly and Stephen that is to be consummated on 17 June 1904.

16 Grant Allen, *A Splendid Sin* (London: White, 1896); Henry Johnson, *The World of Sin* (London: Aldine, 1913); Hume Nisbet, *A Sweet Sinner* (London, White, 1897). Mary Power, 'The Discovery of *Ruby*', *JJQ* 18 (Winter 1981), 115–21, identifies the main debt of Joyce's title to *Ruby* by Amye Reade (London: Author's Co-operative Publishing Company, 1889).

17 *L II* 201.

18 *L II* 199–200.

19 *L II* 173.

20 Raymond Williams, *Drama from Ibsen to Brecht* (London: Chatto & Windus, 1968), 25.

21 *CW* 48n explains that Joyce, in his Ibsen review, borrowed a phrase from Shaw.

22 Havelock Ellis, *The New Spirit*, xiii, xvi, 8, 62–3, 69, 79–80, 114 and 123 respectively.

23 S. Joyce, *My Brother's Keeper*, 242, *U* 19.

24 Havelock Ellis, *The New Spirit*, 206.

25 Georg Brandes, *Det Moderne Gjennembruds Maend* (Copenhagen: Guldendal, 1883), *Moderne Geister* (Frankfurt: Rütten & Loening, 1882). 'I think that by the time my novel is finished', wrote Joyce, 'I shall be a good German and Danish scholar and, if Brandes is alive, I shall send it to him' (*L II* 83). Joyce had earlier associated the plan to write a play called *A Brilliant Career* with Ibsen's strongest English supporter William Archer (S. Joyce, *My Brother's Keeper*, 116–17).

26 Tysdahl, *Joyce and Ibsen*.

27 Kenner, *Dublin's Joyce*, 69.

28 Power, *Conversations*, 33–5, 51, 53, 57 and 54 respectively.

29 Janko Lavrin, *Aspects of Modernism from Wilde to Pirandello* (London:

Nott, 1935), 9–10, 15 and 102–3 respectively. Connolly, *Personal Library*, 24.

30 Ellmann, *James Joyce*, 661.

31 *L* III 509–10. The poem was published in *The Little Review* 4 (September 1917), 8–16.

32 *Little Review* 4, 16.

33 Ezra Pound, 'Rémy de Gourmont: a distinction', *Selected Essays* (London: Faber, 1960), 341.

34 *CW* 271–3 and Ellmann, *James Joyce*, 670–1.

35 *CW* 201–5 and Ellmann, *James Joyce*, 274.

36 *CW* 205. The phrase, as Mason and Ellmann note, is a direct reminiscence of Owen Aherne's Faustian understanding in Yeats's story 'The Tables of the Law' in *Mythologies*, 305.

37 *FW* 355.21 – 358.16. Oscar Wilde's *Salomé* was first published in Paris (Librairie de L'Art Indépendant, 1893); it first appeared in English with Beardsley's illustrations in the following year (London: Elkin Matthews, 1894). Aubrey Beardsley's *Under the Hill*, left in manuscript at his death, was printed in extracts in *Under the Hill and Other Essays* (London: Lane, 1904). A full edition was privately printed in London by Leonard Smithers in 1907.

38 Iris Murdoch, 'Against Dryness', *Encounter* 16 (January 1961), 16–20.

39 T. S. Eliot, '*Ulysses*, Order and Myth', *Dial* 75 (November 1923), 480–3, reprinted in Deming, 268–71.

40 For an account of these 'lost pages' see Michael Mason's essay 'Why is Leopold Bloom a Cuckold?', 171–88.

41 Budgen, *The Making of 'Ulysses'*, 350.

42 Ellmann, *James Joyce*, 144–7; S. Joyce, *Dublin Diary*, 11 and 19; *WD* 66.

43 *L* I 163.

44 Ellmann, *James Joyce*, 264.

45 *L* I 64.

46 Lecky, *History of European Morals*, 153.

47 The phrases 'Farrington said he wouldn't mind having the far one' and 'changed the position of her legs often' (MS Yale 2. 4–20, *Archive*, vol.4, 85) do not appear in any published version (*D* 105).

48 *L* II 324–5 and 291–3 respectively.

49 *L* II 211–12. The text of Sheehan's article is given in *SL* 147.

50 Richard Findlater, *Banned* (London: MacGibbon & Kee, 1967), 85 and 84 respectively.

51 Frank Wedekind, *Die Büchse der Pandora* (Berlin: Bruno Cassirer, n.d.) and *Die Zensur* (Berlin, 1908). Ellmann, *Consciousness*, 132.

52 Arthur Schnitzler, *Lieutenant Gustl* (Berlin: Fischer, 1906). Ellmann, *Consciousness*, 126.

53 *WD* 28. Buffalo Notebook I.A 30, *Archive*, vol. 7, 23. There was a book of this title by a Margaret Mary Moult: *The Escaped Nun* (London: Cassell, 1909). See my note in *James Joyce Broadsheet* 2 (May 1980), 3.

54 *WD* 62 and *SH* 34–5.

55 *L* I 138 and *FW* 537.27–8.

56 Harry Levin (*James Joyce*, 61–2) sees the importance of Daedalus as artificer but not of Pasiphaë. King Minos, like Bloom, is a cuckold.

57 *U* 522–5. The story of the bull and its explanation in terms of Nicholas Brakespear (Pope Hadrian VI who gave Ireland to Henry II), of Henry VIII (who declared the sovereignty of king over church) and of imperialist John Bull, is given by Stuart Gilbert ('*Ulysses*', 262) and repeated by many commentators (Blamires, *The Bloomsday Book*, London: Methuen, 1966, 157–81; Atherton in Hart and Hayman, *Critical Essays*, 326 etc.). It might be added that the 'Oxen' passage parodies the styles of Defoe and Swift and that Joyce, in his Trieste lecture, argued that *Robinson Crusoe* constituted a prophecy of English imperialism. The connection between this bull story and Ovid's has not, to my knowledge, previously been suggested. It might be noted that in *A Portrait* the climactic sexual encounter is set at Dublin's 'Bull Wall'. The anti-imperialist element of the story seems also to connect with *Finnegans Wake*. The colourful phrase, 'a portlier bull, says he, never shat on a shamrock' (*U* 523), whose origins Atherton traces, may be related to the story of Buckley and the Russian General (*FW* 99.32–3, 366.20–1 and Ellmann, *James Joyce*, 398–9), in which the invader similarly desecrates the Irish sward.

58 *U* 538. Glossed by William York Tindall, *A Reader's Guide to James Joyce*, (New York: Noonday Press, 1959), 202, but not developed in any way.

59 Wilson, *Axel's Castle*, 163–8. Other parts of Wilson's chapter remain among the best passages of Joycean criticism. Some recent impatience with the subsequent excesses of 'symbolist' interpretations of Joyce can be felt in Charles Peake, *James Joyce: The Citizen and the Artist*, 11–13.

60 *WD* 60–8. Buffalo Notebook II.A 1–18, *Archive*, vol. 7, 71–88.

61 Viktor Shklovsky, 'Art as Technique', in L. T. Lemon and M. J. Reis (eds.), *Russian Formalist Criticism* (London: Nebraska University Press, 1965), 18–21.

62 *SH* 65 and S. Joyce, *My Brother's Keeper*, 164.

63 T. S. Eliot, 'Tradition and the Individual Talent', in *Selected Essays* (London: Faber, 1951), 14.

64 *WD* 64. Buffalo Notebook II.A 7, *Archive*, vol. 7, 77.

65 Hugh Miller, *The Testimony of the Rocks* (Edinburgh: Constable, 1857), 261. See Gifford and Seidman, *Notes*, 219.

66 Michael Riffaterre, *The Semiotics of Poetry* (Bloomington: Indiana University Press, 1978).

67 Yeats, *Mythologies*, 302–3.

68 Bloom, *The Anxiety of Influence, A Map of Misreading* and most recently *Agon: Towards a Theory of Revisionism*.

69 *FW* 182.2, 183.24 and 188.16. 'Pelagiarist pen' at 192.1 remembers the Pelagian heresy.

70 *CW* 216 and *P* 246 and 250. An article by T. Webb in *James Joyce and Modern Literature*, ed. W. J. McCormack and A. Stead (London: Routledge, 1982), 49–50 also notices the relevance of these heresies.

71 M. H. Abrams in *The Mirror and the Lamp* (New York: Norton, 1951), 251 gives the history of this reading of Milton with Satan as hero from its origin with Dryden in 1697 to its burgeoning among the Romantic critics. Abrams formulates Blake's crucial contribution to 'that radical mode of Romantic polysemism in which the latent personal significance of a narrative poem is found not merely to underlie, but to contradict and cancel the surface intention'.

72 Levin, *James Joyce*, 30 and *CW* 214.

73 *SH* 116–17 and 181–2.

74 Dante, *The Divine Comedy Paradiso* Book XII, ll.131–2.

75 Yeats, *Mythologies*, 307. It is perhaps inevitable and highly appropriate that Stephen's should be a partial mis-remembering of Yeats's more explicit lines: 'Why do you fly from our torches that were made out of the trees under which Christ wept in the Garden of Gethsemane?'

Bibliography

Section A

References in this section are to the editions used in this study.

Works by James Joyce

Chamber Music. London: Cape, 1927.

The Critical Writings of James Joyce. Ed. Ellsworth Mason and Richard Ellmann. London: Faber, 1959.

Daniel Defoe. Ed. Joseph Prescott. *University of Buffalo Studies* 1 (1964).

Dubliners. Ed. Robert Scholes. London: Cape, 1967.

Exiles. London: Cape, 1952.

Finnegans Wake. London: Faber, 1939.

Giacomo Joyce. Ed. Richard Ellmann. London: Faber, 1968.

The Letters of James Joyce. Vol. I Ed. Stuart Gilbert. London: Faber, 1957.

The Letters of James Joyce. Vols. II and III. Ed. Richard Ellmann. London: Faber, 1966.

Selected Letters of James Joyce. Ed. Richard Ellmann. London: Faber, 1975.

A Portrait of the Artist as a Young Man. Ed. Chester Anderson. London: Cape, 1968.

Stephen Hero. Ed. Theodore Spencer. London: Cape, 1956. Reprinted London: Panther, 1969.

Ulysses. London: Bodley Head, 1960.

Berrone, Louis, ed. *James Joyce in Padua*. New York: Random House, 1977.

Joyce, James, *et. al. The Workshop of Daedalus*. Ed. Robert Scholes and Richard M. Kain. Evanston: Northwestern University Press, 1965.

Perkins, Jill, ed. *Joyce and Hauptmann: Before Sunrise*. California: Huntingdon Library, 1978.

Skeffington, Frances J. C. and Joyce, James A. *Two Essays: A Forgotten Aspect of the University Question and The Day of the Rabblement* Dublin: Gerard Bros, 1901.

The James Joyce Archive. Ed. Michael Groden, Hans Walter Gabler, A. Walter Litz, David Hayman and Denis Rose. In 63 volumes with an index volume. New York: Garland Publishing, 1979.

Joyce, James. Buffalo Notebook VI. A, *The James Joyce Archive*, vol. 28, transcr. and ed. by Thomas E. Connolly as *Scribbledehobble: The Ur-Workbook for Finnegans Wake*. Evanston: Northwestern Univ. Press, 1961.

Manuscript works not in Archive

1920 shelf inventory. Scholes catalogue item no. 1400.

1913–14 Schimpff bill. Scholes item 1401.

Book bills. Scholes items 1402 and 1403.

Letter to Stanislaus Joyce. Scholes item 358.

Letter from Jane Heap. Scholes item 582.

Letter from Robert Ross. Scholes item 1189.

Secondary Works concerning James Joyce

Abrams, M. H. *Natural Supernaturalism*. New York: Norton, 1973.

Adams, Robert Martin. *Surface and Symbol*. New York: OUP, 1972.

Almeida, Hermoine de. *Byron and Joyce through Homer*. London: Macmillan, 1982.

'Aramis'. 'The Scandal of *Ulysses*.' *Sporting Times* 34 (1 April 1922), 4.

Atherton, James S. *The Books at the Wake*. New York: Viking, 1960.

Aubert, Jacques. *Introduction à l'esthétique de James Joyce*. Paris: Didier, 1973.

Beach, Sylvia. *Shakespeare and Company*. London: Faber, 1960.

   Ulysses in Paris. New York: Harcourt, Brace, 1956.

Beckett, Samuel. 'Dante ... Bruno. Vico ... Joyce.' In *Our Exagmination Round His Factification for Incamination of Work in Progress*. London: Faber, 1972. 1–22.

Beja, Morris. *Epiphany in the Modern Novel*. London: Owen, 1971.

Benstock, Bernard. *Joyce-Again's Wake*. London: University of Washington Press, 1965.

   The Undiscover'd Country. Dublin: Gill & Macmillan, 1977.

Blamires, Harry. *The Bloomsday Book*. London: Methuen, 1966.

Block, Haskell M. 'Theory of Language in Flaubert and Joyce.' *Revue de Littérature Comparée* 35, 1961.

Booth, Wayne C. *The Rhetoric of Fiction*. Chicago: Chicago University Press, 1961.

Boyd, John D. and Ruth A. 'The Love-Triangle in Joyce's "The Dead".' *University of Toronto Quarterly* 42 (Spring 1973), 202–17.

Boyle, Robert. *James Joyce's Pauline Vision: A Catholic Exposition*. London: Feffer and Simons, 1978.

Brivic, Sheldon. *Joyce between Freud and Jung*. Port Washington: Kennikat Press, 1980.

Brown, Richard. 'Addenda and Corrigenda to Ellmann's *The Consciousness of Joyce*.' *James Joyce Quarterly* 17 (Spring 1980), 313–17.

   'The Escaped Nun.' *James Joyce Broadsheet* 2 (May 1980), 3.

Budgen, Frank. *James Joyce and the Making of 'Ulysses' and Other Writings*. London: OUP, 1972.

Cixous, Hélène. *The Exile of James Joyce*. Trans. Sally Purcell. London: Calder, 1976.

Cohn, Alan M. and Peterson, Richard F. 'Mysterious Coppinger.' *JJQ* 16 (Summer 1979), 425–31.

Connolly, Thomas E. *The Personal Library of James Joyce. University of Buffalo Studies* 22 (April 1955).

Cross, Richard K. *Flaubert and Joyce*. Princeton: Princeton University Press, 1971.

Culler, Jonathan. *On Deconstruction*. London: Routledge, 1980.

Curran, C. P. *James Joyce Remembered*. London: OUP, 1968.

Davis, Stan Gebler. *James Joyce: A Portrait of the Artist*. London: Davis-Poynter, 1975.

Deming, Robert H. ed. *James Joyce: The Critical Heritage*. 2 vols. London: Routledge, 1970.

Dombrowski, Theo Q. 'Joyce's *Exiles*: The Problem of Love.' *JJQ* 15 (Winter 1978), 118–27.

Eliot, Thomas Stearns. '*Ulysses*, Order and Myth'. *Dial* 75 (November 1923). Reprinted in *James Joyce: The Critical Heritage*. Ed. R.H. Deming, vol. I, 268–71.

On Poetry and Poets. London: Faber, 1957.

Ellmann, Richard. *James Joyce*. London: OUP, 1959, revised 1982.

The Consciousness of Joyce. London: Faber, 1977.

'*Ulysses*' *on the Liffey*. New York: OUP, 1972.

Empson, William. 'The Theme of "Ulysses".' *Kenyon Review* 18 (Winter 1956), 26–52.

London Review of Books 4, nos. 15 and 16 (August and September 1982).

Ernst, Morris L. *United States Circuit Court of Appeals for the Second Circuit, USA vs. 'Ulysses' by James Joyce. Brief for Claimant Appellee*. New York: Bakou Press, 1934.

French, Marilyn. *The Book as World*. London: Harvard University Press, 1976.

Genette, Gérard. *Palimpsestes*. Paris: Editions du Seuil, 1982.

Gifford, Don and Seidman, Robert J. *Notes for Joyce*. 2 vols. New York: Dutton, 1967 and 1974.

Gilbert, Stuart. *James Joyce's 'Ulysses': A Study*. London: Faber, 1930, rev. 1952.

Glasheen, Adaline. *A Census of 'Finnegans 'Wake'*. London: Faber, 1956.

Third Census of 'Finnegans Wake'. Berkeley: University of California Press, 1977.

Gogarty, Oliver St John. 'They Think They Know Joyce'. *Saturday Review of Literature* (18 March 1950).

Gorman, Herbert. *James Joyce: His First Forty Years*. London: Bles, 1924.

James Joyce: A Definitive Biography. London: Faber, 1941.

Gottfried, Roy K. *The Art of Joyce's Syntax in 'Ulysses'*. London: Macmillan, 1981.

Hart, Clive. 'The Sexual Perversions of Leopold Bloom.' In *Ulysses': 50 ans après*. Ed. Louis Bonnerot. Paris: Didier, 1974, 131–6.

'James Joyce's Sentimentality.' *Philological Quarterly* 46 (October 1967), 516–26.

Hart, Clive and Hayman, David. *Ulysses': a Collection of Critical Essays*. Berkeley: University of California Press, 1974.

Hart, Clive and Senn, Fritz. eds. *A Wake Digest*. Sydney: Sydney University Press, 1968.

Hayman, David. 'The Empirical Molly.' In *Approaches to 'Ulysses'*. Ed.

Thomas Staley and Bernard Benstock. University of Pittsburgh Press, 1970.

'Stephen on the Rocks.' *JJQ* 15, 1 (Autumn 1977).

Henke, Suzette. 'Joyce's moraculous sindbook: a study of *Ulysses*.' Diss: Stanford, 1972. Published as *Moraculous Sindbook*. Columbus: Ohio State University Press, 1978.

'Joyce and Krafft-Ebing.' *JJQ* 17 (Autumn 1979), 84–6.

Henke, Suzette A. and Unkeles, Elaine. *Women in Joyce*. Carbondale: Southern Illinois University Press, 1982.

Herring, Phillip. 'The Bedsteadfastness of Molly Bloom.' *Modern Fiction Studies* 15 (Spring 1969).

'Towards an Historical Molly Bloom.' *ELH* 45 (Autumn 1978), 501–21.

'*Ulysses* Notebook VIII. A 5. At Buffalo.' *Studies in Bibliography* 22 (1969), 289–310.

'Molly Bloom and Lady Hamilton.' *JJQ* 15 (Spring 1978), 262–4.

The 'Ulysses' Notesheets in the British Museum. Charlottesville: University of Virginia Press, 1972.

Humphreys, Susan L. 'Ferrero etc.: James Joyce's Debt to Guglielmo Ferrero.' *JJQ* 16 (Spring 1979), 239–51.

Hutchings, William. 'Ontogenesis/Phylogenesis. The Pattern of Historical Development in Chapter IV of *A Portrait*.' *JJQ* 15 (Summer 1978), 339–45.

James Joyce: sa vie, son oeuvre, son rayonnement. [Exhibition catalogue.] Paris: La Hune, 1949.

Jenkins, Ralph. 'Theosophy in "Scylla and Charybdis".' *Modern Fiction Studies* 9 (1969), 65–8.

Joyce, Stanislaus. *My Brother's Keeper*. New York: Viking, 1958.

The Complete Dublin Diary of Stanislaus Joyce. London: Cornell University Press, 1971.

Kenner, Hugh. *Dublin's Joyce*. Gloucester, Mass.: Peter Smith, 1969.

Joyce's Voices. London: Faber, 1978.

Ulysses. London: Allen & Unwin, 1980.

Klein, A. M. 'The Oxen of the Sun.' *Here and Now* 1, 28 (1949), 29–31.

Leavis, F. R. 'Joyce and "The Revolution of the Word".' *Scrutiny* 2, no. 2 (1933), 193–201.

Levin, Harry. *James Joyce: A Critical Introduction*. London: Faber, 1971.

Lidderdale, Jane and Nicholson, Mary. *Dear Miss Weaver*. London: Faber, 1970.

Litz, A. Walton. *The Art of James Joyce*. London: OUP, 1961.

Lyons, J. B. *James Joyce and Medicine*. Dublin: Dolmen Press, 1973.

MacArthur, Ian. 'Sexuality in *Finnegans Wake*?' *AWN* 15 (February 1978), 1–15 and (August 1978), 59.

MacCabe, Colin. *James Joyce and the Revolution of the Word*. London: Macmillan, 1978.

Ed. *James Joyce: New Perspectives*. Brighton: Harvester Press, 1982.

McCormack, W. J. and Stead. A. *James Joyce and Modern Literature*. London: Routledge, 1982.

Magalaner, Marvin. *Time of Apprenticeship: The Fiction of Young James Joyce*. London: Abelard-Schuman, 1959.

Manganiello, Dominic. *Joyce's Politics*. London: Routledge, 1980.

Mansfield, Katherine. *The Letters of Katherine Mansfield*. Ed. J. Middleton Murry. 2 vols. London: Constable.

Mason, Michael. 'Why is Leopold Bloom a Cuckold?' *ELH* 44 (1977), 171–88.

Monro, David. Letters to the author 25 July and 14 September 1979.

Morse, J. Mitchell. 'Molly Bloom Revisited.' In *A James Joyce Miscellany: 2nd series*. Ed. Marvin Magalaner. Carbondale: Southern Illinois University Press, 1959.

   The Sympathetic Alien: Joyce and Catholicism. London: Vision Press, 1959.

Noon, William T. *Joyce and Aquinas*. London: Yale University Press, 1963.

O'Brien, Darcy. Review of Richard Ellmann's *The Consciousness of Joyce*. *JJQ* 15 (Summer 1978), 395–6.

   'Joyce and Sexuality.' *Twentieth Century Studies* 2 (November 1969), 32–8. [A special issue on 'the treatment of sexual themes in the modern novel'.]

Owen, Rodney. Paper delivered at the 6th International Joyce Symposium, 13 June 1977.

Peake, Charles. *James Joyce: The Citizen and the Artist*. London: Edward Arnold, 1977.

Pound, Ezra. 'Joyce et Pécuchet.' *Mercure de France* 156, 1922.

Pound/Joyce: The Letters of Ezra Pound to James Joyce. London: Faber, 1968.

Power, Arthur. *Conversations with James Joyce*. London: Millington, 1974.

Power, Mary. 'The Discovery of *Ruby*.' *JJQ* 18 (Winter 1981).

Raleigh, John Henry. *The Chronicle of Leopold and Molly Bloom*. Berkeley: University of California Press, 1977.

Reynolds, Mary. *Joyce and Dante*. Princeton: Princeton University Press, 1982.

Rose, Danis. *The Index Manuscript*. Colchester: A Wake Newslitter Press, 1980.

Schneider, Ulrich. *Die Funktion der Zitate im 'Ulysses' von James Joyce*. Bonn: Bouvier, 1970.

Scholes, Robert. *The Cornell Joyce Collection: A Catalogue*. Ithaca: Cornell University Press, 1961.

Schutte, William M. *Joyce and Shakespeare*. New Haven: Yale University Press, 1957.

Senn, Fritz. 'Some Conjectures about Homosexuality in "*Finnegans Wake*".' *AWN* 6 (October 1969), 70–2.

   'Every Klitty of a Scolderymaid: Sexual-Political Analogies.' Reprinted in *A Wake Digest*. Ed. Hart and Senn, 27–38.

Shechner, Mark. *Joyce in Nighttown*. London: University of California Press, 1974.

Slocum, John J. and Cahoon, Herbert. *A Bibliography of James Joyce, 1882–1941*. London: Hart-Davies, 1953.

Solomon, Margaret. *Eternal Geomater: The Sexual Universe of 'Finnegans Wake'*. Carbondale: Southern Illinois University Press, 1969.

Spielberg, Peter. *James Joyce's Manuscripts and Letters at the University of Buffalo : A Catalogue*. Buffalo: University of Buffalo Press, 1962.

Sullivan, Kevin. *Joyce Among the Jesuits*. New York: Columbia University Press, 1958.

Sultan, Stanley. *The Argument of 'Ulysses'*. Columbus: Ohio State University Press, 1964.

Thornton, Weldon. *Allusions in 'Ulysses'*. Chapel Hill: University of North Carolina Press, 1968.

Tindall, William York. *A Reader's Guide to James Joyce*. New York: Noonday Press, 1959.

Tysdahl, B. J. *Joyce and Ibsen*. Oslo: Norwegian Universities Press, 1968.

Waisbren, Burton A. and Walzl, Florence L. 'Paresis and the Priest: James Joyce's Symbolic Use of Syphilis in "The Sisters".' *Annals of Internal Medicine* 80 (June 1974), 756–62.

Wheeler, Michael. *The Art of Allusion in Victorian Fiction*. London: Macmillan, 1979.

Wilson, Edmund. *Axel's Castle*. London: Fontana, 1961.

Winters, Ivor. *In Defense of Reason*. London: Routledge, 1960.

Woolf, Virginia. 'Modern Novels'. Unsigned review in *The Times Literary Supplement* (10 April 1919), 189–90.

Section B

This section contains those works that Joyce read and that are discussed in this study; references are to the edition that Joyce himself knew. Where the edition cited is not certainly known to have been the one read by Joyce an asterisk is used to note the fact. If a different edition from that which Joyce knew has been used in this study, the details of that edition are placed second. The sources of our knowledge of Joyce's reading, unless otherwise stated are Thomas E. Connolly, *The Personal Library of James Joyce*; and Richard Ellmann, *The Consciousness of Joyce*.

Adam of Cobsam. *The Wright's Chaste Wife*. London: Early English Text Society, 1865.

Albert, Charles. *L'Amour libre*. Paris: Stock, 1910. The edition I used (Paris: Stock, 1902) is the only one listed in the Bibliothèque Nationale catalogue.

Allen, Charles Grant Blairfindie. *The Woman Who Did*. Leipzig: Tauchnitz, 1895.

Anderson, Margaret. *My Thirty Years' War*. New York: Covici, Friede, 1930. London: Knopf, 1930.

Arabian Nights (*Le Mille e una notte*). Trans. into Italian by Armando Dominicis. Florence: Adriana Salani, 1915.

'Aristotle'. Aristotle's Masterpiece. In *The Works of Aristotle*. London: Clifton, Chambers, *Clear-Type edition* [1905]. *U* 302, 537 and 918.

Arnold, Matthew. *Culture and Anarchy*. London: Nelson, n.d. [1909].

Aurelius Antoninus, Marcus. *The Thoughts*. Trans. John Jackson. Oxford: OUP, 'The World's Classics', 1906.

Author, Playwright and Composer, The. London. Vol. XLIV, nos. 3 and 4 (Spring and Summer, 1934), vol. XLV, nos. 1, 2 and 4 (Autumn and Christmas 1934 and Summer 1935), and vol. XLVII, no. 4 (Summer 1937).

Bakunin, Michael. *God and the State*. London: Freedom Press, 1910.

Balzac, Honoré de. *La Femme de trente ans*. Paris: Calmann-Lévy, n.d. Trans. Ellen Marriage as *A Woman of Thirty*. London, 1910.

Mémoires de deux jeunes mariées. Paris: Calmann-Lévy, n.d. Trans. Scott. Ed. G. Saintsbury. London: 1897.

Physiologie du mariage. Paris: Calmann-Lévy, n.d. I have used *La Comédie humaine*, trans. G. B. Ives and others: *Physiology of Marriage*, 2 vols. (including *Petty Worries of Conjugal Life*), London: Caxton, 1899.

Barrister at Law, A. *Every Man's Own Lawyer*. London: Crosby Lockwood, 1919.

*Beardsley, Aubrey. *Under the Hill and Other Essays*. London: Lane, 1904.

Besant, Annie. *The Path of Discipleship*. London: Theosophical Publishing Society, 1904.

Une Introduction à la théosophie. Paris: Publications Théosophiques, 1907.

Beverland, Adrian [Hadriani Beverlandi]. *The Law Concerning Draped Virginity: An Academical Study*. Trans. F. D. Byrne. Paris: Charles Carrington, 1905.

Bits of Fun. London. 1917–1920. U 655–61 and 894. L I 144 and 8.

Blake, William. *Poems*. Ed. W. B. Yeats. London: Routledge [1905].

Poems. London: Walter Scott, n.d.

The Poetical Works. Ed. W. M. Rossetti. London: Bell, 1911.

*Blumenbach, Johann Friedrich. *An Essay on Generation*. Trans. Sir A. Crichton. London: T. Cadell, 1792. U 547.

*Boine, Giovanni. *Il Peccato ed altere cose*. Florence: Libraria Della Voce, 1913. 1920 inventory.

Bontempelli, Massimo. *Eva Ultima*. Milan: Mondadori, 1924.

Book of Common Prayer and the Administration of the Sacraments, The. Glasgow: Collins, Clear-Type Press, n.d. London: Eyre & Spottiswoode, n.d.

Brandes, George. *Shakespeare: A Critical Introduction*. London: Heinemann, 1911. Same imprint 1917.

Brémont, Comtesse Anna de. *Oscar Wilde and his Mother*. London: Everett, 1911.

Brillat-Savarin, *Physiologie du goût ou méditations du gastronomie transcendante*. Paris: Garnier, n.d.

*Browne, W. J. *Botany for Schools and Science Classes*. Belfast: Mullan, 1875. Atherton, *The Books at the Wake*, 238.

Burton, Sir Richard F. *The Book of a Thousand Nights and a Night* ... 17 vols. London: The Burton Club, n.d. London: Kamashastra Society, 1884.

Burton, Robert. *The Anatomy of Melancholy*. London: Blake, 1836.

Butler, Samuel. *The Authoress of 'The Odyssey'*. London: Fifield, pref. d. 1897. London: Longmans, Green, 1897.

Byron, George Gordon Lord. *Poems*. London: Routledge, n.d. [1880]. *Poetical Works*. Ed. Page. London: OUP, 1970.

*Chiniquy, C. P. T. *The Priest, the Woman and the Confessional*. London: Gibson, 1874. *U* 636.

 **Why I left the Church of Rome*. London: Kensit [1887]. *U* 230 and 635–6. Gifford and Seidman, *Notes*.

Cicero, Marcus Tullius. *Tuscalanarum Disputationem*. Ed. C. F. W. Muller. Leipzig: Taubner, 1888.

*Cleland, John. *Fanny Hill*. 2 vols. London: Fenton, 1749. In requesting an 'unexpurgated' edition (*L* I 171) Joyce may be referring to either of the editions printed in Paris by Isidore Lisieux in 1888 or 1890.

Crofts, Maud Isabel. *Women Under English Law*. London: National Council of Women, 1925. Or more likely on grounds of availability, London: Butterworth, 1928. *L* I 302.

Crommelynck, Fernand. *Le Cocu magnifique*. Paris: Editions de la Sirène, 1931. Budgen, 350.

*Culpeper, Nicholas. *The English Physician*. London: Peter Cole, 1652. *U* 547.

 **A Directory for Midwives*. London: Peter Cole, 1651. *U* 547.

*D'Annunzio, Gabriele. *Il Fuoco*. Milan: Treves, 1900. Trans. Kassandra Vivaria. London: Heinemann, 1900. *L* III 392.

 Notturno. Milan: Treves, 1912.

 Giovanni Episcopo. Florence: Editore Quattrini, 1917.

 **La Città Morta*. Milan: Treves, 1898. Trans. Arthur Symons, *The Dead City*. London: Heinemann, 1900. Ellmann, *James Joyce*, 77, 415n and *L* III 392.

Desroix, Jacques. *La Gynécocratie ou la domination de la femme* ... Paris: Charles Carrington, 1902.

D'Ivray, Jehan. *Mémoires de l'eunuque Béchir-Aga*. Paris: Albin Michel, n.d. Copy in Bibliothèque de l'Arsenal.

Dodge, Janet. *Twelve Elizabethan Songs*. London: Bullen, 1902.

Dujardin Edouard. *L'Initiation au péché et à l'amour*. Paris: Mercure de France, 1912. Same imprint, 1898.

Egoist, The. London. 1914–1919.

Ellis, Henry Havelock. *The New Spirit*. London: Walter Scott, pref. d. 1892.

 **Studies in the Psychology of Sex*. 7 vols. Philadelphia: Davies, 1905–28. All except vol. 7 published in 1910. See text above, and n6, p. 177.

Ellis, William. *Three Trips to Madagascar*. London: Murray, 1858. *U* 832. Gifford and Seidman, *Notes*.

Eltzbacher, Paul. *Anarchism*. Trans. Steven T. Byington. New York: Tucker, and London: Fifield, 1908.

Epictetus. *The Teachings*. Trans. T. W. Rolleston. London: Walter Scott, n.d.

Ervine, St John. *Parnell*. London: Benn, 1926. *L* I 241.

Fabian Tracts. Nos. 1–173 (Bound together). London: Fabian Society, 1884–1913.

*Ferrero, Guglielmo. *L'Europa giovane*. Milan: Treves, 1897. 1920 inventory and *L* II 133 and 190.

  *The Women of the Caesars. Trans. Christian Gauss. New York, 1925.

Ffrench, Canon J. *Prehistoric Faith and Worship*. London: Nutt, 1912.

Flaubert, Gustave. *Madame Bovary*. Trans. Henry Blanchamp. London: Greening [1910].

  *Madame Bovary. Paris: Charpentier, 1873. *E* 165 and *L* III 295.

  Salammbô. Paris: Bibliothèque Charpentier, 1914.

  La Tentation de Saint Antoine. Schimpff bill.

*Fletcher, Phineas. 'The Purple Island.' Probably in Giles and Phineas Fletcher, *Poetical Works*. Ed. F. S. Boas. Cambridge: Cambridge English Classics, 1908. Atherton, *The Books at the Wake*, 249, Budgen, 13–14 etc. and Lyons, *James Joyce and Medicine*, 156–62.

Fogazzaro, Antonio. *Piccolo mondo antico*. Milan: Baldini, Castoldie, 1900.

  Piccolo mondo moderno. Milan: Hoepli, 1902.

Freewoman, The. London. 1911–13. And *The New Freewoman*. 1913.

Freud, Sigmund. *Eine Kindheitserinnerung des Leonardo da Vinci*. Leipzig and Vienna, 1910.

  The Standard Edition of the Complete Psychological Works of Sigmund Freud. Ed. James Strachey. London: Hogarth Press, 1953– . Vol. XI, 57–137.

  Zür Psychopathologie des Alltaglebens. Berlin, 1917. *Standard Ed*. vol. VI.

Galopin, Augustin. *Le Parfum de la femme*. Paris: Dentu, 1889.

Garnier, Paul. *Onanisme seul et à deux sous toutes ses formes et leurs conséquences*. Paris: Librairie Garnier, n.d. Paris: Garnier, 1885.

Gide, André. *L'Immoraliste*. Paris: Mercure de France, 1914.

*Gissing, George. *Demos: A Story of English Socialism*. London: Smith Elder, 1886. *L* II 186.

  *Crown of Life. London: Methuen, 1899. *L* II 186.

Godwin, William. *Caleb Williams*. London: Routledge, 1903.

Haig, Alexander. *Uric Acid: An Epitome of the Subject*. London: Churchill, 1904.

Hall, H. S. and Stevens, F. H. *A Text-Book of Euclid's Elements*. London: Macmillan, 1900.

Hardy, Thomas. *Tess of the D'Urbervilles*. 2 vols. Leipzig: Tauchnitz, 1892. London: Macmillan, 1965.

*Hargrave, Francis. *A Collection of Tracts Relative to the Law of England*. Dublin: n.p., 1787. *L* III 222.

Hauptmann, Gerhart. *Michael Kramer*. Berlin: Fischer, 1920.

  *Vor Sonnenaufgang. See Perkins ed. *Joyce and Hauptmann* above.

*Hertwig, O. *The Biological Problem of Today: Preformation or Epigenesis?* Trans. P.C. Mitchell. London: Heinemann, 1896. *U* 547.

  *The Text-Book of the Embryology of Man and Mammals. Trans. E. L. Mark. London: Swan Sonnenschein, 1892. *U* 547.

Homer. *The Iliad*. Trans. Earl of Derby. London: Dent, Everyman, 1913 (Everyman Homer, vol. I).

The Odyssey. Trans. William Cowper. London: Dent, Everyman, 1913 (Everyman Homer, vol. II).

Hopewell, Frank. *The Oddity*. Dublin: James Carson, 1741.

Huxley, T.H. *Twelve Lectures and Essays*. London: Watts, 1908.

*Huysmans, Joris-Karl. *A Rebours*. Paris: Charpentier, 1884. *L* II 150.

Là-Bas. Paris: Stock, 1901.

Ibsen, Henrik. *A Doll's House*. Trans. William Archer. London: Heinemann, 1912. *Collected Works*, vol. VII.

A Doll's House and Two Other Plays. London: Dent, Everyman, 1932.

[*An Enemy of the People*.] *Ein Volksfiend*. Trans. Wilhelm Lange. Leipzig: Universal Bibliothek, n.d.

Love's Comedy. Trans. various hands. London: Heinemann, 1910.

Jacobsen, J. P. *Siren Voices*. Trans. E. F. L. Robertson. London: Heinemann, 1896.

*Johnson, Henry T. *The Pride of the Ring*. London: Aldine, 1902. *U* 77 et.seq.

Jones, Ernest. *Das Problema des Hamlet und des Ödipus-Komplex*. Trans. Paul Tausig. Leipzig and Vienna, 1911. In Ernest Jones, *Essays in Applied Psychoanalysis*. London and Vienna: International Psychoanalytical Press, 1923, 1–98.

Jung, C. G. *Die Bedeutung des Vaters für das Schiksal des Einzelnen*. Leipzig and Vienna, 1909. *Collected Works*. London: Routledge, 1953– , vol. IV, 292–323.

Kardec, Allan. *La Genèse, les miracles et les prédictions selon le spiritualisme*. Paris: Librairie des Sciences Psychologiques, 1883.

Karr, Alphonse. *Voyage autour de mon jardin*. Paris: Lévy, 1892. Trans. J. G. Wood. *A Tour Round my Garden*. London, 1885.

*Kipling, Rudyard. *Plain Tales from the Hills*. Calcutta: Thacker, Spink, 1888.

Kock, Charles Paul de. *Le Cocu*. Ghent: Vandenhaege Maya, 1839.

*Krafft-Ebing, Baron Richard Von. *Psychopathia Sexualis*. Stuttgart: Ferdinand Enke, 1886. Trans. from 7th German ed. C. G. Chaddock. London and Philadelphia: Davies, 1892. *FW* 290.28.

Le Psicopatie sessuali. Trans. Enrico Sterz and Luigi Waldart. Turin: Bocca, 1889.

*Kropotkin, Pieter. *La Grande Rivoluzione 1789–93*. Geneva: Edizione del Gruppo del Risveglio, 1911. 1920 inventory.

Fields, Factories and Workshops. London: Nelson, n.d. [1912 or 1919].

The Commune of Paris. London: Freedom Office, 1909.

La Conquista del Pane. 3rd ed. Milan, n.d.

Lavrin, Janko. *Aspects of Modernism from Wilde to Pirandello*. London: Nott, 1935.

*Lecky, W. E. H. *The History of European Morals*. 2 vols. London: Longmans, Green, 1869. Schimpff bill.

Lévy-Bruhl, Lucien. *L'Ame primitif*. Paris: Félix Alcan, 1927.

L'Expérience mystique et les symboles chez les primitifs. Paris: Felix Alcan, 1938.

Little Review, The. Chicago. 1914– .

Livre des prières publiques, Le. London: La Société pour la Propagation des Connaissances Chrétiennes, 1839.

*Lockhart, John Gibson. *The History of Napoleon Buonaparte*. 2 vols. London: Murray, 1829. *U* 833.

Loti, Pierre. *The Marriage of Loti*. Trans. G. F. Monkshood. London: Siegle Hill, 1908.

*Lusk, William Thomson. *The Science and Art of Midwifery*. London: Lewis, 1885. *U* 547.

Mackirdy, A. and Willis, W. N. *The White Slave Market*. London, 1912. Rose, *Index Manuscript*, 131–41.

Maeterlinck, Maurice. *Vie des Abeilles*. Paris: Fasquelle, 1901. Ellmann, *James Joyce*, 141.

Maher, Michael. *Psychology*. New York: Benziger, n.d.

Marinetti, F. T. *et. al*. *Enquête Internationale sur le vers libre*. Milan: Editions de 'Poesie', 1909.

Matharan, M. M. *Casus de Matrimonio fere quingenti*. Paris: Retaux, 1893.

*Maurier, George du. *Trilby*. London: Osgood, McIlvane, 1894. *SH* 77.

*Michelet, Jules. *Priests, Women and Families*. Trans. C. Cocks. London: Longman, 1846. *U* 51.

La Femme. Paris: Hachette, 1860. *U* 51.

L'Amour. Trans. J. W. Palmer as *Love*. New York: Rudd & Carlton, 1860. *U* 51.

Mill, J. S. *On Liberty*. London: Walter Scott, n.d.

Miller, Hugh. *The Testimony of the Rocks*, Edinburgh: Constable, 1857.

*Mirabeau, Comte de. *The Curtain Drawn Up*. 1920 inventory. False imprint on my edition, London: Putitin, Rogers & Co., 1818.

Modern Society. London. 4 December 1880. *U* 849.

*Monk, Maria. *The Awful Disclosures of Maria Monk*. New York: Howe & Bates, 1936. *U* 302 and 635.

Moore, George, *Lewis Seymour and Some Women*. Paris: Conard, 1917. London: Heinemann, 1917.

Moorhouse, Esther Hallam. *The Story of Lady Hamilton*. London & Edinburgh: Foulis, 1911.

*Morrison, Arthur. *Tales of Mean Streets*. London: Methuen, 1894. *L* II 205.

Motte Fouqué, F. H. C. de la. *Undine*. London: Lumley, n.d.

*Moult, Margaret Mary. *The Escaped Nun*. London: Cassell, 1909.

Musset, Alfred de. *La Confession d'un enfant du siècle*. Paris: Bibliothèque Larousse, n.d. Trans. G. F. Monkshood. London: Greening, 1908.

*Nietzsche, Friedrich. *The Antichrist*. Trans. A. M. Ludovici. *The Complete Works of Friedrich Nietzsche*. Ed. Oscar Levy. Edinburgh & London: Foulis, 1911. Vol. XVI. *U* 27.

The Birth of Tragedy. Trans. W. A. Haussmann. Edinburgh & London: Foulis, 1909.

The Case of Wagner. Trans. A. M. Ludovici. Edinburgh & London: Foulis, 1911.

The Joyful Wisdom. Trans. Thomas Common. London: Foulis, 1910.

Nouveau Scandale de Londres: l'affaire Crawford. Paris: Librairie Illustrée, 1886. 1920 inventory.

O'Brien, R. Barry. *The Life of Charles Stuart Parnell*. London & Edinburgh: Nelson, 1910 [?].

O'Shea, Katherine (Mrs Parnell). *Charles Stuart Parnell*. 2 vols. London: Cassell, 1914.

*Otway, Thomas. *Venice Preserved*. Ed. Malcolm Kelsall. London: Edward Arnold, 1969. (Philip Herring's article on *Ulysses*, Buffalo Notebook VIII. A 5., cited above, argues that Joyce used a 1732 two-volume edition.)

*Palazzeschi, Aldo. *Il Codice di Perelà: Romanza futurista*. Milan: Polografia Italian, 1911. 1920 inventory.

Pardies, F. Ignatius Gaston. *Short, but yet Plain Elements of Geometry*. Trans. John Harris. London: printed for R. Knaplock, 1711. (This edition is cited in the *National Union Catalogue*.) *U* 833. Gifford and Seidman, *Notes*.

Photo Bits. London. 1899–1916. *U* 655–61 and 894. *L* I 144 and 148. Budgen, 246–7.

Pisacane, Carlo. *Saggi sulla rivoluzione*. Milan: Sonzogno, n.d.

*Place, Francis. 'To the Married.' See Fryer (cited below), 43, 5 etc. *U* 656.

Plato. *Five Dialogues*. London: Dent, Everyman, 1913.

Plato and Xenophon. *Socratic Discourses*. London: Dent, Everyman, 1913.

Poppy's Paper. Vol. XII, no. 287 (3 August 1929) and vol. XII, no. 288 (10 August 1929).

Praga, Marco. *La Porta Chiusa*. Milan: Treves, 1914. Trans. A. S. Macdonald. London: Brentano's, 1924.

Proudhon, P. J. *Qu'est-ce que la propriété*. Paris: Lacroix, 1873.

Psychologie et la vie, La. Vol. II, no. 10 (October 1928).

Reade, Amye. *Ruby*. London: Author's Co-operative Publishing Company, 1889. Above, 188 n16.

Renan, Ernest. *The Life of Jesus*. London: Watts, 1913.

Souvenirs d'enfance et de jeunesse. Paris: Calmann-Lévy, 1883.

Sacher-Masoch, Leopold von. *Liebesgeschichten aus verschiedenen Jahrhunderten*. 3 vols. Leipzig: Ernest Julius Günther, 1874–6. 1920 inventory.

Grausame Frauen. Leipzig: Leiziger Verlag, 1905. (1920 inventory. Ellmann, 126.)

Scene del Ghetto. Trans. Cino Liviah. Milan: Società Ed. Milanese (E. Zerboni), 1909. 1920 inventory.

Katharina II: russiche Hofgeschichten. Berlin: Schreiter [1891?]. 1920 inventory.

Venus in Furs. London: Luxor Press, 1965.

Sarrat, Lieutenant. *Life of Buonaparte*. London: Tegg & Castleman, n.d.

*Schiller, F. C. S. *Humanism: Philosophical Essays*. London: Macmillan, 1903. *CW* 135–6.

Schnitzler, Arthur. *Lieutenant Gustl*. Berlin: Fischer, 1906.

*Liebelei; Lieutenant Gustl; Die Letzen Masken. Ed. with an intro. by J. P. Stern. Cambridge: CUP, 1966.

Schoolgirl's Own, The. Vol. XVII, no. 442 (27 July 1929).

Schopenhauer, Arthur. Essays. Trans. Mrs Rudolf Dircks. London: Walter Scott, 1897.

Shaw, G. B. Getting Married and The Shewing-Up of Blanco Posnet. Leipzig: Tauchnitz, 1914. Prefaces by Bernard Shaw. London: Constable, 1934.

The Philanderer. London: Constable, 1910.

*The Quintessence of Ibsenism. London: Walter Scott, 1891. CW 48 and 48n.

The Three Unpleasant Plays. Leipzig: Tauchnitz, 1914.

*Sherard, Robert Harborough. Life of Oscar Wilde. London: T. Werner Laurie, 1906. Above, 80–3 and n75.

Oscar Wilde: The Story of an Unhappy Friendship. London: Greening, 1908.

*Spallanzani, Lazarro. Tracts on the Natural History of Animals and Vegetables. Trans. J. G. Dalyell. Edinburgh: Creech, 1803. U 547.

Spencer, Herbert. The Study of Sociology. London: Kegan Paul, Trench, 1888. Same imprint, 1908.

Stern, Ernesta (Maria Star). Sémiramis. Paris: Editions de la Revue Mondiale, 1924.

*Strauss, D. F. The Life of Jesus. Trans. George Eliot. London: Swan Sonnenschein, 1892. L II 76.

Swedenborg, Emmanuel. The Delights of Wisdom Relating to Conjugal Love after which follow the Pleasures of Insanity Relating to Scortatory Love. London: Swedenborg Society, 1891.

Swinburne, Algernon Charles. Atalanta in Calydon and Lyrical Poems. Leipzig: Tauchnitz, 1901.

*Swinburne, Algernon Charles et. al. The Whippingham Papers. London, 1888. FW 19.15.

Symons, Arthur. Cities of Italy. London: Dent, 1907.

Confessions: A Study in Pathology. New York: Fountain Press, 1930.

*The Symbolist Movement in Literature. London: Heinemann, 1899. L II 173n.

*'Taxil, Leo M.' (Gabriel Jogand-Pagès). La Vie de Jésus. Paris: Librairie Anti-Cléricale, 1884. U 51 and 511.

Thompson, Frederick D. In the Track of the Sun: Diary of a Globetrotter. London: 1893. U 833 and 868.

Tinayre, Marcelle. The House of Sin. Trans. A. Smythe. London: Maclaren, 1903.

Titbits. London. 1881–1984.

Tolstoy, Leo. Essays and Letters. Trans. Aylmer Maude. London: Frowde, 1904. Connolly, 36–40. London: Grant Richards, 1903.

*Der Roman der Ehe. 1920 inventory.

La Sonata a Kreutzer. n.p.: n.d.

War and Peace. New York: Modern Library, n.d.

Tucker, Benjamin R. Instead of a Book by a Man Too Busy to Write One … New York: Benjamin R. Tucker, 1897.

Tutu, Le. Paris. 1901–3. *U* 52.

Vaerting, Matthias and Mathilde. *The Dominant Sex.* London: 1923.

*Valenti, Giulio. *Compendio di Anatomia dell'uomo.* Milan: P. Vallardi, 1909. *U* 547.

Valéry, Paul. *Le Serpent.* Paris: Editions de la Nouvelle Revue Française, 1922.

Verlaine, Paul. *Les Poètes Maudits.* Paris, 1900. Curran, *James Joyce Remembered*, 9.

*Vico, Giambattista, *The New Science of Giambattista Vico.* Abridged and trans. T. G. Bergin and M. H. Fisch. London: Cornell University Press, 1970.

Vie Parisienne, La. Paris. 1863–1915.

Wedekind, Frank. *Die Büchse der Pandora.* Berlin: Cassirer, n.d. Ellmann, 132. In *Tragedies of Sex.* Trans. Samuel A. Eliot, Jr. London: Frank Henderson, 1923, 216–304.

Die Zensur. Berlin, 1908.

Whitman, W. H. *Leaves of Grass.* New York & London: Appleton, 1912. *Democratic Vistas.* London: Routledge, n.d.

Wilde, Oscar. *An Ideal Husband.* Leipzig: Tauchnitz, 1907.
The Picture of Dorian Gray. Leipzig: Tauchnitz, 1908. *L* II 150.
The Soul of Man Under Socialism. London: privately printed, 1904.
*The Importance of Being Ernest. London: privately printed, 1894.
*Salomé. Illustrated by Aubrey Beardsley. London: Elkin Matthews, 1894.

Woman. Vol. XI, no. 4 (July 1929).

Woman's Friend. No. 286 (17 August 1929).

Wood, Rev. J. G. *The Common Objects of the Sea Shore.* London: Routledge, 1912.

*Yeats, W. B. *The Tables of the Law* and *The Adoration of the Magi* in *Mythologies.* London: Macmillan, 1959.

Zimmer, Heinrich. *Maya der Indische Mythos.* Berlin: Deutsche Verlags-Anstalt, 1936.

Zola, Emile. *Nana.* 3 vols. Paris: Editions Parisiennes, n.d.

Section C

Relevant contemporary works which Joyce need not necessarily have known at first hand, or works discussed as background to Joyce's reading.

Acton, William. *Functions and Disorders of the Reproductive System.* London: Churchill, 1875. 6th edition.

Allbutt, Henry Arthur. *The Wife's Handbook.* 2nd edition. London: Ramsey, 1886.

Allen, Grant. *A Splendid Sin.* London: White, 1896.
The British Barbarians. London: Lane, 1895.

Apollinaire, G., F. Fleuret and L. Perceau. *L'Enfer de la Bibliothèque Nationale.* Paris: Mercure de France, 1913.

Bachofen, J. J. *Das Mutterrecht*. Stuttgart: Krais & Hoffmann, 1861.

Barnes, H. G. and J. E. G. Montmerency. *The Divorce Commission*. London: King, 1912.

Bebel, August. *Women in the Past, Present and Future*. Trans. H. B. Adams Walther. London: Modern Press, 1885.

Bergeret, Louis. *Des Fraudes dans l'accomplissement des fonctions génératrices* Paris: Baillière, 1868. Trans. P. de Marmon. *The Preventative Obstacle or Conjugal Onanism*. New York: Turner & Mingard, 1870.

Besant, Annie. *The Law of Population*. London: Freethought, 1877.

Blakeney, Rev. R. P. *Awful Disclosure of the Iniquitous Principles ...* London: Groombridge, 1846.

Blum, Léon. *Du Mariage*. Paris: Albin Michel, 1907. Trans. Warren Bradley Wells. London: Jarrolds, 1937.

Bonner, H. B. and John M. Robertson. *Charles Bradlaugh*. 2 vols. London: Fisher Unwin, 1894.

Brandes, Georg. *Det Moderne Gjennembruds Maend*. Copenhagen: Guldendal, 1883.

 Moderne Geister. Frankfurt: Rütten & Loening, 1882.

Burton, Richard (trans.). *The Perfumed Garden of Sheik Nefzawi*. Benares: Kamashastra Society, 1886.

Carpenter, Edward. *The Intermediate Sex*. Manchester: Labour Press, 1896.

 Love's Coming of Age. Manchester: Labour Press, 1896.

 Woman and her Place in a Free Society. Manchester: Labour Press, 1894.

 'The Status of Women in Early Greek Times.' *The New Freewoman* 4 (1 August 1913), 68–9.

Conrad, Joseph. *Victory*. London: Methuen, 1915.

Crawley, Alfred Ernest. *The Mystic Rose*. London: Macmillan, 1902.

Darwin, Charles. *The Descent of Man*. 2 vols. London: Murray, 1871.

Day, Henry C. *The New Morality*. London: Heath Cranton, 1924.

Dickens, Charles. *Hard Times*. London: Bradbury & Evans, 1854.

Dinesen, T. 'The End of Sexual Morals.' *Proceedings of the Second World League for Sexual Reform Congress*. Copenhagen: Levin & Munksgaard, 1929.

Drysdale, George. *The Elements of Social Science*. 4th edition. London: Truelove, 1861.

Eliot, George. *Middlemarch*. Harmondsworth: Penguin, 1965.

Eliot, T.S. 'Tradition and the Individual Talent', in *Selected Essays*. London: Faber, 1951.

Ellis, Henry Havelock. *Man and Woman: A Study of Human Secondary Sexual Characteristics*. London: Walter Scott, 1894.

Ellis, William. *Polynesian Researches*. London, 1829.

Engels, Friedrich. *The Origin of the Family*. London: Lawrence & Wishart, 1972.

Ford, Ford Madox. *The Good Soldier*. London: Lane, 1915.

Freud, Sigmund. 'A Special Type of Choice of Object Made by Men.' *Standard Ed*. vol. XI, 165ff.

 'On the Universal Tendency to Debasement in the Sphere of Love.' *Standard Ed*. vol. XI, 179ff.

New Introductory Lectures on Psychoanalysis. 'Femininity'. *Standard Ed.*
  vol. XXII, 112–35.
Jokes and their Relation to the Unconscious. Standard Ed. vol. VIII.
The Interpretation of Dreams. Standard Ed. vols. IV and V.
Three Essays on the Theory of Sexuality. Standard Ed. vol. VII.
'The Economic Problem of Masochism.' *Standard Ed.* vol. XIX,
  157–70.
Civilisation and its Discontents. Standard Ed. vol. XXI.
'Modern Sexual Morality and Modern Nervousness.' Trans. W. J.
  Robinson. New York: Eugenics Publishing, 1931.
Gogarty, Oliver St John, *Tumbling in the Hay.* London: Constable, 1939.
Gourmont, Rémy de. *Physique de l'amour.* Paris: Mercure de France,
  1903. Trans. Ezra Pound. *The Natural Philosophy of Love.* London:
  Casanova Society, 1926.
Guyon, Réné. *La Légitimité des Acts Sexuelles.* Saint-Denis: Dardaillon,
  1929. Trans. J. C. and I. Flugel. *Sex Life and Ethics.* London: Lane,
  1933.
Hall, Radclyffe. *The Well of Loneliness.* London: Cape, 1928.
Hansard's Parliamentary Debates. London: Cornelius Buck, 1857- .
Huxley, T. H. *Evolution and Ethics.* London: Macmillan, 1893.
Ibsen, Henrik. *The Lady from the Sea. Collected Works.* London: Heine-
  mann, 1906–12. Vol. IX.
Jonhson, Henry T. *The World of Sin.* London: Aldine, 1913.
Jonson, Ben. *Three Comedies.* Harmondsworth: Penguin, 1966.
Knowlton, Charles. *The Fruits of Philosophy.* London: Watson, 1841.
Lawrence, D. H. *Women in Love.* London: Martin Secker, 1921.
  Lady Chatterley's Lover. London: Martin Secker, 1932.
Lloyd, E. B. 'Intermediate Sexual Types.' *The New Freewoman* 8 (1 Oct
  1913), 155–6.
Lombroso, Cesare. *L'Uomo di genio.* Torino: Bocca, 1888. Trans. H.
  Ellis. London: Walter Scott, 1891.
Lovebirch, James. *Les Cinq Fessés de Suzette.* Paris: Roberts & Dardaillon,
  1910. Trans. *The Flagellations of Suzette.* Paris: Librairie Artistique,
  1925.
Lubbock, Sir John. *The Origin of Civilisation.* London: Longmans, Green,
  1870.
McLennan, J. F. *Primitive Marriage.* Edinburgh, 1865. Reprinted as
  Studies in Ancient History. London: Quaritch, 1876.
Malthus, Rev. Thomas Robert. *An Essay on the Principle of Population.*
  London: Johnson, 1798.
  A Summary View of the Principle of Population. London: Murray, 1830.
Miller, G. Noyes, *The Strike of a Sex.* London: Reynolds, 1891.
Milton, John Laws. *On the Pathology and Treatment of Spermatorrhoea.*
  12th edition. London: Renshaw, 1887.
Morgan, L. H. *Ancient Society.* New York: Henry Holt, 1877.
Nerciat, André de. *Felicia.* London: 1775. (False imprint.)
Nietzsche, Friedrich. *Beyond Good and Evil.* Trans. Helen Zimmern.
  Edinburgh and London: Foulis, 1907.
Nisbet, Hume. *A Sweet Sinner.* London: White, 1897.

Owen, Robert Dale. *Moral Physiology*. New York: Wright & Owen, 1831.

Pearson, Karl. *The Ethic of Freethought*. London: Fisher Unwin, 1888.

Pound, Ezra. 'Rémy de Gourmont: a Distinction.' *Selected Essays*. London: Faber, 1960.

Russell, Bertrand. *Marriage and Morals*. London: Allen & Unwin, 1929.

Spencer, Herbert. *Principles of Ethics*. 2 vols. New York: Appleton, 1896.

Stockham, Alice. *Karezza: Ethics of Marriage*. Chicago: Alice B. Stockham, 1896.

Stopes, Marie. *Married Love*. London: Fifield, 1918.

   Wise Parenthood. London: Fifield, 1918.

'Taxil, Leo M.' (Gabriel Jogand-Pagès). *Les Livres secrets des confesseurs*. Paris: Author, 1883.

Tissot, S. A. A. D. *L'Onanisme*. Lausanne: Antoine Chapius, 1760.

Waugh, Evelyn. *Vile Bodies*. London: Chapman & Hall, 1930.

Weininger, Otto. *Geschlecht und Charakter*. Vienna and Leipzig, 1903. Trans. *Sex and Character*. London: Heinemann, 1906.

Wells, H. G. *The History of Mr Polly*. London: Nelson, 1910.

Westermarck, Edward A. *The History of Human Marriage*. London: Macmillan, 1891.

Williams, C. M. *A Review of the Systems of Ethics Founded on the Theory of Evolution*. London: Macmillan, 1893.

Wollstonecraft, Mary. *A Vindication of the Rights of Women*. London: Walter Scott, 1892.

Zola, Emile. *Le Roman expérimental*. Paris: Charpentier, 1880.

Section D

Other works. Editions are again those used in this study.

Abrams, M. H. *The Mirror and the Lamp*. New York: Norton, 1951.

Adam, Ruth. *A Woman's Place*. London: Chatto & Windus, 1975.

Adams, M. E. *Censorship. The Irish Experience*. Dublin: Scepter Books, 1968.

Banks, J. A. and O. *Feminism and Family Planning in Victorian England*. Liverpool: Liverpool University Press, 1964.

Barthes, Roland. *S/Z*. Trans. Richard Miller. London: Cape, 1975.

   Plaisir du Texte. Paris: Editions du Seuil, 1973. Trans. Richard Miller. London: Cape, 1976.

   Image/Music/Text. London: Fontana, 1977.

Beauvoir, Simone de. *The Second Sex*. Trans. H. M. Parshley. London: Cape, 1953.

Benjamin, Walter. *Illuminations*. London: Fontana, 1973.

Bloom, Harold. *The Anxiety of Influence*. Oxford: OUP, 1973.

   A Map of Misreading. Oxford: OUP, 1975.

   Agon: Towards a Theory of Revisionism. Oxford: OUP, 1982.

Brittain, Vera. *Lady into Woman*. London: Andrew Dakers, 1953.

Brome, Vincent. *Freud and his Early Circle*. London: Heinemann, 1967.

Comfort, Alex. *The Anxiety Makers*. London: Nelson, 1967.

Cooper, Douglas and Tinterow, Gary. *The Essential Cubism*. London: Tate Gallery Publications, 1983.

Craig, Alec. *The Banned Books of England*. London: Allen & Unwin, 1962.

Deleuze, Gilles. *Sacher-Masoch: An Interpretation*. London: Faber, 1971.

Derrida, Jacques. *Of Grammatology*. Trans. G. C. Spivak. London: Johns Hopkins University Press, 1976.

Dingwall, E. J. *Very Peculiar People*. London: Rider, 1949.

Ernst, M. L. and V. Seagle. *To the Pure*. London: Cape, 1929.

Eversley, D. C. *Social Theories of Fertility and the Malthusian Debate*. Oxford: Clarendon Press, 1959.

Faulkner, Peter. *Humanism in the English Novel*. London: Elek, 1975.

Findlater, Richard. *Banned*. London: MacGibbon & Kee, 1967.

Foucault, Michel. *The Archaeology of Knowledge*. Trans. A. M. Sheridan-Smith. London: Tavistock, 1972.
Histoire de la sexualité. Paris: Gallimard, 1976. Trans. Robert Hurley. *The History of Sexuality*. London: Allen Lane, 1979.

Fryer, Peter. *The Man of Pleasure's Companion*. London: Barker, 1968.
The Forbidden Books of the Victorians. London: Odyssey Press, 1970.
The Birth Controllers. London: Secker & Warburg, 1965.

Greer, Germaine. *The Female Eunuch*. London: Paladin, 1971.

Hall, Ruth. *Marie Stopes: A Biography*. London: Deutsch, 1977.

Hare, Edward. 'Masturbatory Insanity: the History of an Idea.' *Journal of Mental Science* 108, 1962.

Heath, Stephen. 'Difference.' *Screen* 9 (Autumn 1978).
The Sexual Fix. London: Macmillan, 1982.

Himes, Norman E. *The Medical History of Contraception*. London: Allen & Unwin, 1936.

Hoffmann, Frederick. *Freudianism and the Literary Mind*. Baton Rouge: Louisiana State University Press, 1957.

Houghton, Walter. *The Victorian Frame of Mind*. London: Yale University Press, 1957.

Hyde, Montgomery. *A History of Pornography*. New York: Farrar, Strauss & Giroux, 1964.

Johnson, Barbara. 'The Frame of Reference: Poe, Lacan, Derrida.' *Yale French Studies* 55/56 (1977).

Kahane, Jack. *Memoirs of a Booklegger*. London: Michael Joseph, 1939.

Kristeva, Julia. *Le Texte du roman*. Paris: Mouton, 1970.

Latey, William. *The Tide of Divorce*. London: Longman, 1970.

'Legman, G.' Introduction to *My Secret Life*. New York: Grove Press, 1966.

Macherey, Pierre. *A Theory of Literary Production*. Trans. Geoffrey Wall. London: Routledge, 1978.

Marcus, Steven. *The Other Victorians*. London: Weidenfeld & Nicolson, 1966.

Millett, Kate. *Sexual Politics*. London: Virago, 1977.

Morris, David. *The End of Marriage*. London: Cassell, 1971.

Murdock, Iris. 'Against Dryness.' *Encounter* 16 (January 1961).

Pankhurst, Sylvia. *The Suffragette Movement*. London: Longmans, Green, 1931. Reprinted London: Virago, 1977.

Praz, Mario. *The Romantic Agony*. Trans. Angus Davidson, 2nd edition. Oxford: OUP, 1951.

Rhys, Jean. *Wide Sargasso Sea*. Harmondsworth: Penguin, 1968.

Riffaterre, Michael. *The Semiotics of Poetry*. Bloomington: Indiana University Press, 1978.

Robinson, Paul. *The Modernisation of Sex*. London: Elek, 1976.

Ruitenbeek, H. M. *The New Sexuality*. New York: Franklin Watts, 1974.

Sartre, J. P. *What is Literature?* Trans. B. Frechtman. London: Methuen, 1967.

Saveson, John E. *Joseph Conrad: The Making of a Moralist*. Amsterdam: Rodopi, 1972.

Shklovsky, Viktor. 'Art as Technique'. In L. T. Lemon and M. J. Reis. eds. *Russian Formalist Criticism*. London: Nebraska University Press, 1965.

Tanner, Tony. *Adultery in the Novel*. London: Johns Hopkins University Press, 1974.

Tauchnitz Edition Centenary Catalogue (1837–1937). Leipzig: Tauchnitz, 1937.

Vittorini, Domenico. *The Modern Italian Novel*. Philadelphia: University of Pennsylvania Press, 1930.

Watt, Ian. *The Rise of the Novel*. Harmondsworth: Penguin, 1972.

West, Donald J. *Homosexuality Re-examined*. London: Duckworth, 1977.

Williams, Raymond. *Drama from Ibsen to Brecht*. London: Chatto & Windus, 1968.

Culture and Society 1780–1950. London: Chatto & Windus, 1967.

Index